Nietzsche's *Beyond Good and Evil*

Edinburgh Critical Guides to Nietzsche
Series editors: Keith Ansell-Pearson and Daniel Conway

Guides you through the writings of Friedrich Nietzsche (1844–1900), one of modernity's most independent, original and seminal minds

The Edinburgh Critical Guides to Nietzsche series brings Nietzsche's writings to life for students, teachers and scholars alike, with each text benefiting from its own dedicated book. Every guide features new research and reflects the most recent developments in Nietzsche scholarship. The authors unlock each work's intricate structure, explore its specific mode of presentation and explain its seminal importance. Whether you are working in contemporary philosophy, political theory, religious studies, psychology, psychoanalysis or literary theory, these guides will help you to fully appreciate Nietzsche's enduring significance for contemporary thought.

Books in the series
Nietzsche's *The Birth of Tragedy from the Spirit of Music*, Tracy B. Strong and Babette Babich
Nietzsche's *Philosophy in the Tragic Age of the Greeks*, Sean Kirkland
Nietzsche's *Unfashionable Observations*, Jeffrey Church
Nietzsche's *Human, All Too Human*, Ruth Abbey
Nietzsche's *Dawn*, Katrina Mitcheson
Nietzsche's *Gay Science*, Robert Miner
Nietzsche's *Thus Spoke Zarathustra*, Daniel Conway
Nietzsche's *Beyond Good and Evil*, Daniel Conway
Nietzsche's *On the Genealogy of Morality*, Robert Guay
Nietzsche's *The Case of Wagner and Nietzsche Contra Wagner*, Ryan Harvey and Aaron Ridley
Nietzsche's *Twilight of the Idols*, Vanessa Lemm
Nietzsche's *The Anti-Christ*, Paul Bishop
Nietzsche's *Ecce Homo*, Matthew Meyer
Nietzsche's *Late Notebooks*, Alan Schrift

Visit our website at edinburghuniversitypress.com/series-edinburgh-critical-guides-to-nietzsche to find out more

Nietzsche's *Beyond Good and Evil*

A Critical Introduction and Guide

Daniel Conway

EDINBURGH
University Press

Edinburgh University Press is one of the leading university presses in the UK. We publish academic books and journals in our selected subject areas across the humanities and social sciences, combining cutting-edge scholarship with high editorial and production values to produce academic works of lasting importance. For more information visit our website: edinburghuniversitypress.com

© Daniel Conway, 2024

Edinburgh University Press Ltd
The Tun – Holyrood Road
12(2f) Jackson's Entry
Edinburgh EH8 8PJ

Typeset in 11/13 Bembo by
IDSUK (DataConnection) Ltd

A CIP record for this book is available from the British Library

ISBN 978 1 4744 3545 1 (hardback)
ISBN 978 1 4744 3546 8 (paperback)
ISBN 978 1 4744 3547 5 (webready PDF)
ISBN 978 1 4744 3548 2 (epub)

The right of Daniel Conway to be identified as the author of this work has been asserted in accordance with the Copyright, Designs and Patents Act 1988, and the Copyright and Related Rights Regulations 2003 (SI No. 2498).

Contents

Acknowledgements	viii
Chronology	x
Primary Sources and Abbreviations	xiii
Introduction	1
The title and subtitle of *Beyond Good and Evil*	2
Nietzsche's aims in *Beyond Good and Evil*	5
Nietzsche's target readership	12
1. Nietzsche's Preface	19
2. Part One: On the Prejudices of Philosophers	33
Preview	33
Summary of sections	35
The will to truth	37
The will to truth and the prejudices of philosophers	41
Untruth as a condition of life	43
Introducing the will to power	44
Psychology: the once and future ruler of the sciences	49
Review	53
3. Part Two: The Free Spirit	55
Preview	55
Summary of sections	58
The self-overcoming of morality	61
Reintroducing the will to power	65
Turning to the future	68
Review	70

4. Part Three: The Religious Character 72
    Preview 72
    Summary of sections 74
    Dissolving the paradox of the saint 77
    The religious instinct 82
    The misanthropic atheism of modern philosophy 84
    The 'new' philosophers 91
    The calamity of European Christianity 94
    Review 95
5. Part Four: Epigrams and Interludes 97
    Preview 97
    Summary of sections 99
    Nietzsche's influences 99
    Recurring themes and persistent motifs 102
    Review 107
6. Part Five: On the Natural History of Morality 109
    Preview 109
    Summary of sections 111
    The imperative of nature 112
    The moral neurosis 117
    The 'new' philosophers: commanders and legislators 119
    Review 122
7. Part Six: We Scholars 124
    Preview 124
    Summary of sections 125
    Philosophers as legislators 131
    Scholarly virtues 137
    What a philosopher is (and does) 140
    Review 142
8. Part Seven: Our Virtues 143
    Preview 143
    Summary of sections 144
    Revisiting the virtues 145
    The many colours of virtue 148
    The many costumes of virtue 149
    'We immoralists!' 155
    A new task 159
    Review 168

CONTENTS

9. Part Eight: Peoples and Fatherlands   169
   Preview   169
   Summary of sections   171
   The German soul   173
   Creating a home for European Jewry   176
   How Europe might become one   185
   Review   187
10. Part Nine: What is Noble?   188
    Preview   188
    Summary of sections   190
    Exploiting a 'turning point in history'   196
    Nobility and self-respect   199
    Dionysus revealed   201
    Review   208
11. From Lofty Mountains: 'Aftersong'   210
    Preview   210
    Summary of stanzas 1–13   211
    Summary of stanzas 14–15   220
    Review   227

Glossary of Key Terms   229
Guide to Further Reading on *Beyond Good and Evil*   235
Bibliography   237
Index   244

Acknowledgements

I am pleased to acknowledge the support and encouragement provided by Carol Macdonald and her excellent team at Edinburgh University Press. I have very much enjoyed the opportunity to work with such dedicated, patient and generous professionals.

I am fortunate to count among my friends and colleagues some outstanding philosophical interlocutors. With respect to this book, I am especially indebted to Christa Davis Acampora, Keith Ansell-Pearson, Babette Babich, Rebecca Bamford, Paul Bishop, Jeffrey Church, Christian Emden, Robert Gooding-Williams, Peter Groff, Robert Guay, Lawrence Hatab, Kathleen Higgins, Anthony Jensen, Claire Katz, Paul Kirkland, Manuel Knoll, Duncan Large, Vanessa Lemm, Paul Loeb, Michael McNeal, Allison Merrick, Robert Miner, David Owen, Antoine Panaïoti, Graham Parkes, Paul Patton, Robert Pippin, Gary Shapiro, John Seery and Jon Stewart. I also wish to honour the memory of the inimitable Tracy Strong (1943–2022), whom I knew for forty years as a teacher, advocate and friend.

This book took shape against the backdrop of the COVID-19 pandemic. I was fortunate to be quarantined with the three best people I know in the world: Claire, Olivia and Evelyn.

Research support was provided by the College of Liberal Arts and the Melbern G. Glasscock Center for Humanities Research at Texas A&M University.

ACKNOWLEDGEMENTS

I am grateful for permission to publish revised material that appeared originally in the following essays and publications:

'Nietzsche's Europe', in *European/Supra-European: Cultural Encounters in Nietzsche's Philosophy*, ed. Marco Brusotti, Michael J. McNeal, Corinna Schubert and Herman Siemens. Berlin: Walter de Gruyter, 2020, pp. 87–106.

'Why (and When) Philosophy Must Yield to Music: The Case of Nietzsche's Nachgesang', in *Nietzsche and Music*, ed. Aysegul Durakoglu, Michael Steinmann and Yunus Tuncel. Cambridge: Cambridge Scholars Press, 2022, pp. 391–409.

'The Religious Neurosis', in *The Modern Experience of the Religious in its Many Forms*, ed. Nassim Bravo and Jon Stewart. Leiden: Brill, 2023, pp. 294–323.

'Nietzsche's Philosophical and Rhetorical Aims in *Beyond Good and Evil*', in *The Contributions of 19th-Century Continental Philosophy*, ed. Patricia Dip and Jon Stewart. Leiden: Brill, 2024, pp. 9–32.

I am also grateful to Stanford University Press for granting permission to cite from several volumes in *The Complete Works of Friedrich Nietzsche*, edited by Alan D. Schrift and Duncan Large.

Finally, I am indebted to Keith Ansell-Pearson not only for his friendship, but also for his extensive comments on an earlier draft of this manuscript.

College Station, Texas
September 2022

Chronology

1844　Friedrich Wilhelm Nietzsche is born on 15 October to Karl Ludwig and Franziska Nietzsche in Röcken, Saxony.
1849　Nietzsche's father, a Protestant minister, dies of 'softening of the brain'.
1850　Nietzsche's younger brother, Joseph, dies, and the family moves to Naumburg.
1858–64　He attends the elite boarding school Schulpforta on a full scholarship that he received as the orphan of a minister.
1864　Enrols at the University of Bonn to study theology, although he no longer plans to become a minister. He joins a fraternity, but resigns soon after.
1865　Follows the philologist Professor Albrecht Ritschl to the University of Leipzig. He buys a copy of Schopenhauer's *World as Will and Representation* in his landlord's shop.
1865　Refuses to take Communion during his Easter visit home to Naumburg.
1866　Publishes an essay on Theognis in a philological journal edited by Ritschl. Studies F. A. Lange's *History of Materialism*.
1867　Enlists in an artillery regiment after managing to pass a physical exam.

1868	Injures himself while riding. Reads Kuno Fischer's book on Kant. Meets Richard Wagner in a café in Leipzig, through the mediation of Mrs Ritschl. After his 24th birthday becomes emancipated from his guardian.
1869	Appointed Extraordinary Professor of Classical Philology in Basel on Ritschl's recommendation. Renounces Prussian citizenship. Begins frequent visits to Wagner in nearby Tribschen.
1870	Volunteers as a medical orderly in the Franco-Prussian War, but after two months becomes ill with dysentery and diphtheria.
1872	Publishes his first, controversial book, *The Birth of Tragedy out of the Spirit of Music*. Accompanies Wagner to Bayreuth for the laying of the foundation stone for the new opera house.
1873	Meets Paul Rée in Basel.
1873–75	Publishes *Unfashionable Observations*. Relationship with Wagner begins to sour.
1875	Studies Paul Rée's *Psychological Observations*.
1876	Begins working with Peter Gast, who takes dictation for an essay on Wagner. Visits the Bayreuth Festival and sees Wagner for the last time in Sorrento.
1878	Publishes the first part of *Human, All Too Human*.
1879	Publishes the two additions to *Human, All Too Human*. Resigns from Basel with a small pension. Begins a long period of wandering, mostly through Italy and Switzerland, staying in off-season boarding houses.
1881	Publishes *Daybreak*.
1882	His friendship with Paul Rée ends. Publishes the first edition of *The Gay Science*. In April travels to Rome, meets Lou Salomé, and proposes marriage to her. She declines and the relationship ends badly.
1883–84	Publishes *Thus Spoke Zarathustra*.
1884	Breaks with his sister Elisabeth over her fiancé's anti-Semitism.
1886	Publishes *Beyond Good and Evil*. Plans new editions of previous works, for which he writes five new prefaces, among other material.

1887	Writes *On the Genealogy of Morality* in July and August. It is published in November in an edition of 600 copies. He pays for the printing himself.
1888	Subject of sympathetic, well-attended lectures in Copenhagen by Georg Brandes. Publishes *The Case of Wagner*. Writes *The Anti-Christ, Ecce Homo, Nietzsche Contra Wagner* and *Twilight of the Idols*.
1889	Suffers a breakdown and collapses in Turin, after writing megalomaniacal postcards to many friends and celebrities. He is retrieved by his friend Franz Overbeck, who takes him to Basel. Nietzsche's mother then takes him to an asylum in Jena.
1890	Nietzsche is moved to his mother's apartment in Jena, and then to Naumburg. His sister Elisabeth returns to Germany from Paraguay. She later takes control of her brother's literary estate.
1894	Belated publication of *The Antichrist*, written in 1888. Elisabeth founds the Nietzsche Archive, which houses Nietzsche and his papers.
1895	Publication of first volume of Elisabeth's biography.
1896	Elisabeth moves Nietzsche and the Archive to Weimar.
1897	Death of Franziska Nietzsche. Publication of second volume of Elisabeth's biography. Relocates to Weimar under the care of his sister.
1900	Dies in Weimar on 25 August.

Primary Sources and Abbreviations

Nietzsche's texts in German

KSA   *Sämtliche Werke*, Nietzsche 1980
SB   *Sämtliche Briefe*, Nietzsche 1986b

Nietzsche's texts in English translation
   The following key explains the abbreviations I have used to identify citations from Nietzsche's writings. Lower-case instances of these abbreviations are meant to identify citations from Nietzsche's review of his books in *Ecce Homo* (citations from other chapters of *Ecce Homo* are designated by 'Wise', 'Clever', 'Books' and 'Destiny'). Citations from Prefaces and Epigraphs are designated by P and E, respectively. In all instances, numbers refer to sections rather than to pages.

A   *The Antichrist*, in Nietzsche 2021
AS   'Attempt at a Self-Criticism', which Nietzsche added as a retrospective Preface to the 1886 edition of *The Birth of Tragedy*
BGE   *Beyond Good and Evil*, in Nietzsche 2014b
BT   *The Birth of Tragedy*, Nietzsche 1967
CW   *The Case of Wagner*, in Nietzsche 2021
D   *Dawn*, Nietzsche 2014a
EH   *Ecce Homo*, in Nietzsche 2021

GM	*On the Genealogy of Morality*, in Nietzsche 2014b
GS	*The Gay Science*, Nietzsche 1974
HH	*Human, All Too Human*, Nietzsche 1986a
TI	*Twilight of the Idols*, in Nietzsche 2021
UO	*Unfashionable Observations*, Nietzsche 1995
Z	*Thus Spoke Zarathustra*, Nietzsche 1982

Introduction

Completed and published in 1886, *Beyond Good and Evil* (hereafter *BGE*) is widely regarded as one of the finest expressions of Nietzsche's post-Zarathustran approach to, and vision for, the practice of philosophy. After experimenting in his previous books with various writing styles, aesthetic forms, literary tropes and modes of address, Nietzsche reintroduces himself in *BGE* by adopting a dialogical-narrative voice, which affords him the authorial latitude to speak to and for the idealised 'we' whose education and training he is keen to undertake. In an effort to consecrate this 'we', and to prepare its prospective members to join him in a 'task' reserved just for them, he guides his readers on a dizzying diagnostic tour of late modern European culture.[1] His goal in doing so, as his subtitle confirms, is to initiate his readers into the rhythms, routines and practices that collectively constitute what he calls a 'prelude [*Vorspiel*] to a philosophy of the future'. Toward this end, he divides *BGE* into nine 'main parts' [*Hauptstücke*], which he introduces with a short Preface [*Vorrede*] and seals with a valedictory poem or 'Aftersong' [*Nachgesang*].[2]

---

[1] My attention to Nietzsche's efforts to prepare his readers for this 'task' is indebted to the interpretation advanced by Lampert 2001: 1–7.
[2] In his letter to C. Heymons (at Carl Duncker's Verlag) on 12 April 1886, Nietzsche writes that *BGE* 'contains ten parts or sections' (*SB* 7: 175). The envisioned fourth part was to be called '*Das Weib an sich*', and the envisioned ninth part was to be called '*Masken*'. The letter makes no mention of the 'epigrams and interludes' that make up Part Four of the book in its eventual published form.

The title and subtitle of *Beyond Good and Evil*

A year later, in the book he advertised as a 'clarification and supplement to . . . *BGE*', Nietzsche openly acknowledged that the title of *BGE* essays a 'dangerous slogan' (GM I: 17). Although this acknowledgement no doubt alludes to the perils incident to the 'task' he has reserved for his best readers, in whom he intends to cultivate an appetite for innovation and experimentation,[3] it also might be understood to confirm the risks involved in the rhetorical-dramatic case he builds in *BGE* itself. Inasmuch as the title of *BGE* delivers a 'slogan', after all, it is evidently meant to mislead (or manipulate) his readers to some extent, creating in them expectations that he will be obliged in due course to lower, prune or tame. This may explain why, on a separate occasion, he intimates that he has selected for *BGE* what he concedes is a 'malicious' title.[4]

Especially at risk are those readers whose interest has been piqued by his apparent invitation to join him in a daring excursion beyond the confines and jurisdiction of morality. As we learn soon enough, the excursion referenced in the title of *BGE* will be made available, if at all, only to the audiences of a distant posterity, who, owing in large part to the preliminary labours performed by Nietzsche and his 'we', might face the future free of the distractions, doubts and estrangements that were introduced and exacerbated by the morality of good and evil. Moreover, what Nietzsche *does* offer his contemporary and late modern readers – namely, the *experience* of having ventured beyond good and evil – actually obliges them to intensify their investments in the morality whose constraints they are understandably eager to escape. Indeed, the *feeling* that one resides beyond good and evil will be most consistently enjoyed by those among Nietzsche's readers who resolutely lean into the morality they have pledged to retire.[5] As we shall see, in fact, complaints of a bait-and-switch scheme are not altogether without merit.

---

[3] Gooding-Williams thus characterises *BGE* as 'a school for the modernist innovator', who 'attempts to realize what is possible by transforming what is actual' (Gooding-Williams 2001: 306–8).

[4] See Nietzsche's letter to Irene von Seydlitz on 7 May 1886 (*SB* 7: 189).

[5] I am indebted here to the 'fatalistic' interpretations developed by Leiter 2002: 81–8; Miyasaki 2016: 257–61, 270–1; Leiter 2019: 147–57; and Miyasaki 2022a: chs 1–2.

The grand expectations raised by the title of *BGE* are partially deflated by the book's comparatively sober subtitle. Nietzsche presents *BGE* as preliminary to the as-yet-provisional 'philosophy of the future', with which it should not be confused, even if Nietzsche himself occasionally promotes this very confusion. As the subtitle of *BGE* confirms, in fact, his readers should neither form nor retain any expectation of completing the emigration suggested by the book's title. The takeaway that awaits his best readers involves their positive (albeit limited) contribution to the timely demise of what we might call the 'philosophy of the present', viz., a philosophy hopelessly entangled in moral prejudices and popular convictions that cannot be reconciled with the most thrilling of the recent advances in the natural and social sciences. As parties to the designated 'prelude', Nietzsche's best readers will learn that the optimal experience of freedom and agency that is available to them actually presupposes their ongoing placement *within* a regime of morality that is predicated on the (increasingly untenable) polar opposition between the values of 'good' and 'evil'.[6] Persuading them to accept this placement, and to affirm it in due course, is perhaps his most daunting rhetorical challenge in *BGE*.

To be sure, however, the proffered 'prelude' is not intended as a merely academic or theoretical exercise, as if Nietzsche's best readers were simply interested in contemplating the merits of a description of (or blueprint for) a possible future. As an example (or model) of philosophical 'fore-play',[7] *BGE* is meant to initiate his best readers into the somatic rhythms and routines that will eventuate – though not for them – in the anticipated emigration beyond good and evil.[8] While it might be a stretch to characterise this attempt at 'fore-play' as likely to produce sexual arousal, Nietzsche is certainly intent on enrolling his best readers in a discipline of affective-somatic practices that he regards as productive of (and continuous with) a meaningful worldly existence beyond good and evil.

---

[6] I develop this feature of my interpretation in Conway 2008: 142–7; and Conway 2014a: 287–92.
[7] See Dellinger 2013: 167.
[8] Here I follow Pippin 2019b: 197–8.

The envisioned mode of existing in a world no longer diminished by the morality of good and evil thus assumes its initial, embryonic shape in the affective-somatic transformation of Nietzsche's best readers.[9] As they turn away from an abiding preoccupation with those otherworldly realms that are deemed to be repositories of surpassing meaning and value, resisting in the process the 'value-emotions' to which they are accustomed (BGE 4), they will inaugurate an experimental encounter with (and reappraisal of) their worldly existence, wherein, Nietzsche surmises, the philosophy of the future is likely to find its anchorage and sustenance. As we shall see, the discipline on offer in *BGE* is meant to produce in his best readers a transformation of mind *and* body, intellect *and* passion, reason *and* faith, knowing *and* feeling.

Although the specific characterisation of the 'philosophy of the future' remains to be determined, Nietzsche is confident that it will authorise and support a viable *way of life*, on the strength of which future human beings may know and feel their mortal existence to be justified on its own terms and by its own merits. According to Nietzsche, that is, the 'philosophy of the future' is likely to have no (or little) need for the metaphysical comforts and supernatural consolations that continue to this day to hamper the progress of philosophy and science. Simply put, his best readers are meant not only to understand the need for humankind to move beyond good and evil, but also to sample (albeit experimentally) the affective-somatic enhancements he has identified as conducive to the proposed emigration. He thus urges his best readers to join the idealised 'we' he addresses in *BGE* and to constitute themselves as a philosophical vanguard. Duly fortified by the education and training on offer in *BGE*, they will conduct the initial (and very much preliminary) round of experiments pertaining to the viability of an 'extramoral' existence that is devoid, or nearly so, of metaphysical and supernatural assurances. By the time they arrive at the

---

[9] My attention to the 'affective-somatic transformation' that Nietzsche intends for his best readers is influenced by, and indebted to, Strong's seminal interpretation of Nietzsche's efforts to precipitate (and perhaps even transact) a 'politics of transfiguration' (Strong 1975: 12–19, 53–9, 100–7, 260–8). See also Strong 2003: 555–60; and Pippin 2019b: 213–14.

end of the book, as we shall see, they should be prepared to join him in *singing* their hopes for the uncertain future that beckons.

A brief note on the prospect of discipleship: although Nietzsche and Zarathustra are known to express their impatience with disciples, their disdain is (usually) reserved for those acolytes who attach themselves to others in the hope of relaxing (or even ceasing) their own labours of outgrowth and development. In *BGE*, Nietzsche's best readers are meant to become disciples not in the familiar (and pejorative) sense that they mimic him and parrot his teachings, but in the sense of becoming apprenticed to (and, eventually, accomplished in) the particular approach to philosophy that he recommends to them. Nietzsche's *genuine* disciples, in other words, are those readers who accept and eventually outgrow the upbuilding discipline he recommends and models to them. As they come to appreciate their world under the progressively clarifying aspect of science, they will become increasingly comfortable (if not exactly settled) in their surroundings.

As we shall see, the discipline Nietzsche dispenses in *BGE* will prepare his best readers to heal their self-estrangements, to seek and maintain an optimal experience of freedom and power, to pursue an innovative agenda of experimental scholarly research, to immunise themselves against the twin temptations of disgust and pity, to resist the influence of 'modern ideas', to repurpose the virtues and powers available to them, to adjust their expectations to reflect the non-negotiable conditions of their historical situation, and, finally, to take up the 'task' that will connect their truth-telling efforts with the future they are uniquely positioned to produce.

Nietzsche's aims in *Beyond Good and Evil*

A useful (if predictably self-serving) account of Nietzsche's aims in *BGE* appears in his *Ecce Homo* (1888), where, in the context of introducing himself to his new and old readers, he immodestly touts the accomplishments of the many 'good books' he has written.

BGE is one such 'good book', the first of many to follow in the wake of his poetic-philosophical masterpiece, *Thus Spoke Zarathustra*, which he completed in four parts over the period 1883–85. *BGE* thus inaugurates the post-Zarathustran period

(1886–88) of Nietzsche's philosophical career, a period in which he was increasingly concerned to cultivate and mobilise an audience worthy of the speeches and teachings of Zarathustra. In the context of *BGE*, this aim involves him in an attempt to mould his best readers into a disciplined collective – an idealised 'we' – and to guide them towards an experience of themselves as liberated from the constraints associated with the morality of good and evil.[10] The experience in question is meant not only to prepare them for the 'task' that awaits them, but also to sustain their will for the future of humanity.

Such readers are needed, he explains, because *BGE* is the first instalment in the 'No-saying, "*No-doing*" half [of his task]', which he intended to include 'the revaluation of the former values themselves, the great war – the summoning up of a day of decision' (EH: bge 1). As this immodest disclosure suggests, Nietzsche understands the teachings of Zarathustra to have landed prematurely, as is often the case with prophets and visionaries of world-historical significance.[11] In order for Zarathustra's teachings to take hold, or so Nietzsche has come to believe, a good bit of remedial work will need to be completed. If a worthwhile audience for Zarathustra's teachings is to materialise, in fact, much that currently exists and holds sway in late modern European culture must be challenged, denied, destroyed and cleared from view. This 'No-Saying, "*No-Doing*"' period of Nietzsche's career thus obliges him to undertake 'the slow look round for relatives, for those who, out of strength, would lend [him] a hand *in destroying*' (EH: bge 1). As we shall see, the focus of these destructive efforts is the 'task' Nietzsche assigns to himself and his best readers, the performance of which involves a collective campaign to 'translate humanity back into nature' (BGE 230).

---

[10] Here I follow Miyasaki 2016: 257–61.

[11] In the supplementary notes to his translation of *BGE*, Del Caro cites from a preface Nietzsche prepared for a proposed second volume of *BGE*, which he did not complete: 'Just as certainly as [*BGE*] offers no commentary nor should it to the speeches of Zarathustra, so perhaps it nonetheless provides a type of provisional *glossarium* in which the most important conceptual- and value-innovations of [*Zarathustra*] – an event without model, example, and likeness in all of literature – appear somewhere and are called by name' (Nietzsche 2014b: 355).

Nietzsche furthermore explains that the post-Zarathustran placement of *BGE* ensures that the book must be 'essentially a *critique of modernity* ... alongside pointers to an opposite type, the least modern it is possible to be, a noble, Yes-saying type' (EH: bge 2). Here he means to assure his readers that the 'No-saying, "*No-Doing*"' campaign to which he recruits them will not be limited in its yield to a strictly negative or privative outcome. While the installation of a new ideal of human flourishing lies beyond their reach, the manner in which they will dismantle the future-deferring morality of good and evil – namely, by comporting themselves as paragons of honesty and scientific rigour – will be conducive to the return and resurgence of the 'noble, Yes-saying type' on which late modern European culture has effectively declared war. Although his best readers will not be in a position to commence a philosophy of the future, or create the new values it will enshrine, they might succeed in pointing others in the direction of a more promising future. In this respect, the destructive task to which Nietzsche invites his readers will also yield (or at least anticipate) a 'Yes-Saying' and 'Yes-Doing' that might pique the interest of the 'philosophers of the future'.

This promise of an affirmative yield is especially important to bear in mind as Nietzsche recounts the various calamities that he associates with the overall degeneration of humanity and the decline of late modern European culture in particular. Although he may appear at times in *BGE* to abandon all hope, or to push his readers to the brink of despair, his more precise concern is to measure accurately the disasters of the late modern period, precisely so that he might plot and affirm a realistic way forward. In this respect, his goal in *BGE* is twofold: 1) to offer an objective, unsentimental assessment of the condition of late modern European culture; and 2) to recommend the most promising course of action that is available to his best readers. In order to frame a credible view of a possible future, he and his best readers will need to understand the present day not as they wish it to be, for example, as an idealised evolutionary apex, but as the product of historical and social forces that have nearly extinguished the will for the future of humanity.

With respect to the 'pointers' he provides along the way, we are meant to appreciate that 'ultimately, [*BGE*] is a *school for the gentilhomme*' (EH: bge 2).[12] His modest aim here is to enrol his readers in a finishing discipline – viz. a targeted programme of specialised education and training – that will prepare them to undertake the course of action (and embrace the 'task') he assigns to them. This programme of education and training is designed not only to apprise his best readers of the (potentially dispiriting) truth of the late modern condition into which they were born, but also to induce in them the affective-somatic transformation they will need (and eventually want) to undergo. Much as a school for gentlemen aspires to educate (and finish) the *whole* person, cultivating the mind (or soul) *and* body while steering each into productive alignment with the other, so Nietzsche wishes to encourage his self-estranged, misaligned readers to see the world differently and, as a consequence, to feel *very* differently about their place in it (cf. D 103).[13]

In light of the occasionally effusive rhetoric employed by Nietzsche in *BGE*, it may be useful at this early juncture to emphasise the modesty of his expectations for the select readership he aims to cultivate. The readers he has in mind are defined by a historical context and range of agency that were determined long ago. As a result, he cannot pretend to *improve* them, and he is resolved in any event to distance himself from any hint of the humbug he associates with the 'improvement-morality' (TI 'Improvers' 1–2). What he *can* do, or so he believes, is to apply to them his signature finish and thereby prepare them to flourish in the lonely, nomadic existence that awaits them. By showing them how to reconfigure their affects and repurpose their virtues, he will induce in them the affective-somatic transformation that will best ensure their success in performing the 'task' he has reserved for them. As we shall see, the overarching goal of his finishing school is to optimise their

---

[12] In a letter to Reinhart von Seydlitz on 26 October 1886, Nietzsche describes *BGE* as 'a kind of commentary on my *Zarathustra*' and 'a book [only] for men of the most extensive culture (or breeding) [*Bildung*], e.g., Jacob Burckhardt and Henri Taine' (*SB* 7: 270–1). In his letter of 22 September 1886, Nietzsche personally implored Burckhardt to read *BGE*: 'Please read this book [*Jenseits*'] (even though it says the same things as my *Zarathustra*, but differently, very differently' (*SB* 7: 254–5/Middleton 1969: 255).

[13] A similar account of Nietzsche's aims, as they emerge in *On The Genealogy of Morality*, is rendered by Janaway 2007: 1–15.

relationship to the morality of good and evil, precisely so that they might retire the 'old' morality while immunising themselves against the latent nihilism of modern science.[14] If successful in this venture, he will safeguard their will for the future of humanity while turning them towards the open future he bids them to behold.

And just as a properly educated gentleman would be expected, if necessary, to draw his pistol or sword, so Nietzsche expects his best readers to apply themselves to their 'task' with a quasi-martial ferocity – *and* to enjoy themselves while doing so. He thus mentions in particular the need for his best readers to demonstrate a 'fire in [the] belly' and to display the condition, exemplified by Wagner's Siegfried, of never having 'learned fear' (EH: bge 2).[15] Finally, just as a finishing school for gentlemen is expected to provide a comprehensive education in matters of taste, politesse, customs, habits and manners, so *BGE* is meant to refine ever so slightly the 'semi-barbarian' tastes and sensibilities of its late modern readers (BGE 224). To be sure, those who matriculate through Nietzsche's finishing school will never be mistaken for those paragons of 'good taste' whom traditional aristocracies have routinely produced; nor will he. Still, they will be optimally positioned to leverage their persistently 'bad taste', as evidenced by their wobbly grasp of measure and control (BGE 224), to their full advantage.

The affective-somatic transformation he has in mind for his best readers is required, he advises, if they are to join him in *destroying* the 'old' morality. As we shall see, however, the designated context of their efforts to do so might be a matter of surprise and even consternation. Rather than attack morality from a perspective or stronghold established external to its familiar jurisdiction, as Nietzsche's readers may have understood from the title of *BGE*, they will avail themselves of the authority vested in the newly ascendant, science-friendly regime of morality – designated by Nietzsche as the disciplinary regime of 'Christian truthfulness' (GM III: 27) – which places a premium on the virtues that support

---

[14] I am indebted here to Babich 1994: 136–46.
[15] As Large indicates in the notes to his translation of *Ecce Homo*, Nietzsche apparently intended *BGE* to enable his best readers to approximate the fearless, heroic type exemplified by Siegfried (Nietzsche 2007: 113).

the related practices of truth-seeking and truth-telling. The case they will prosecute against the 'old' morality will thus rest on an undeniably moral claim – namely, that the compromised authority of the 'old' morality derives from a tangle of assumptions and suppositions that we now *know* to be mendacious. Indeed, those who complete the programme of education and training on offer in *BGE* will both know and feel themselves to stand in contradiction to everything in which the late modern world takes pride.

Nietzsche also identifies *BGE* as a faithful testament to the conditions of its genesis, which notably include his experience of near-death depletion after birthing his *Zarathustra* and the period of leisure granted him in the aftermath. He thus identifies *BGE* as the product of a period of 'recreation' [*Erholung*], over the course of which he returned to the world after sketching its transfiguration at the hands of Zarathustra. Comparing himself to the G-d of *Genesis*, and associating *BGE* with the leisure of the first Sabbath, he eagerly claims for himself the role of the serpent in the Garden: 'The devil is just God on that seventh day, having a rest' (EH: bge 2). As this quip is meant to confirm, a central goal of *BGE* is to soften (or, in some cases, to obliterate) formerly authoritative distinctions between supposed binary opposites. (Indeed, the devil is no more the opposite (or opponent) of God than 'good' is the opposite of 'evil'.)

Appearing as it does in the wake of his *Zarathustra*, *BGE* is notable for its dramatic shift in perspective and approach: 'The eye, indulged by a tremendous necessity to see *far* – Zarathustra is more far-sighted than the Tsar – is here forced to focus on what is nearest, our time, what is "around-us" [*das Um-uns*]' (EH: bge 2).[16] As we have noted, what Nietzsche here designates as what is 'around-us', viz., the immediate context of the historical situation of his likely readers, is especially difficult to consider in detail and at length, precisely because it is so close to us and so disappointing (in his estimation) to view with the recommended degree of objectivity. For this reason, he explains, he was obliged to exchange the hyperopic perspective of his *Zarathustra* for the stubbornly myopic perspective

---

[16] See Gooding-Williams 2001: 306–8.

that informs *BGE*. Of particular concern to him in this respect are the difficulties associated with turning one's critical gaze towards oneself and telling the truth (to oneself and others) about who (or what) one is and has become. To accomplish this shift in perspective, Nietzsche implements an updated approach to the study and practice of psychology, an approach he regards as significantly more scientific (and severe) than any developed to date. Rather than seek insight into the vagaries of human nature by consulting traditional sources of authority – for example, mythology, Scripture, priests and sages, folk tales, received wisdom, indigenous and chthonic knowledges, etc. – Nietzsche calls for a rigorous scientific investigation of the soul. As he says of *BGE*, 'Refinement in form, in intent, in the art of remaining *silent*, is in the foreground, psychology is handled with avowed hardness and cruelty – the book eschews every good-natured word' (EH: bge 2). Good-natured words we have in abundance. What we need now is an honest (i.e., properly scientific) account or model of human nature, as determined by the hypotheses that emerge from a brutally invasive examination of the soul.

According to Nietzsche, *BGE* is intended, like *Zarathustra*, for a select group of readers who might not yet exist and certainly do not yet embrace the destiny reserved for them. (Although Nietzsche famously advertised his *Zarathustra* as 'a book for all and none', he subsequently determined that none (or very few) of the intended and desired readers had yet emerged.) Likening himself in *BGE* to an expert 'angler' (or, like Jesus, as a 'fisher of men'), he cautions the readers of *Ecce Homo* that he cannot be blamed if the 'fish' in question are not yet available to be caught by him (BGE 1). Partly to account for poor sales and uninformed reviews (EH 'Good Books' 1),[17] Nietzsche recasts the target audience of *BGE* as comprising those future readers – parties to his idealised 'we' – who will contribute materially to the production of a philosophy of the future. In his correspondence from the period, he occasionally remarks (perhaps in jest?) that worthy readers of *BGE*

---

[17] For example, see Nietzsche's letter to Gast on 8 June, 1887 (*SB* 8: 86–7).

might not arrive until the year 2000.[18] As this remark confirms, the underwhelming reception of *BGE* convinced him that he had written a second book that had landed prematurely. No wonder he was so firmly committed to producing a future that would not resemble the past.

Nietzsche's target readership

The readers whom Nietzsche has in mind for his finishing school are in many ways like him: friendly to the advance of science; impatient with the lingering (and corrosive) authority of moralities grounded in religious dogma; keen to innovate and experiment; iconoclastic and hardened by periods of extended solitude; suspicious of modern ideas and the 'democratic movement' in particular; impressively knowledgeable (though often at the expense of the self-knowledge Nietzsche encourages them to acquire); and ever alert to signs that an unacknowledged order of rank might have survived the decadence of late modern European culture. In other words: novices need not apply.

Nietzsche's readers are also like him in that they continue to express a robust will for the future of humanity, on the strength of which they are prepared to make the sacrifices that are and will be required of them. Excited in particular by the technical innovations that the progress of modern science has prompted, they look forward to a future in which research and scholarship are fully liberated from the constraints of religion and morality. Eager to meet and surmount the challenges that are most likely to elicit the best versions of themselves, they are predisposed to grant Nietzsche a fair hearing as he rolls out the programme of education and training he has devised for them. As we shall see, of course, a chief objective of this programme is to prepare them to attach their will for the future of humanity to the indeterminate, open future that he envisions in *BGE*. Aware that their

---

[18] In his letter of 24 September 1886 to Malwida von Meysenbug, Nietzsche informs her that he has sent her a copy of *BGE*, which he urges her neither to read nor to 'express to [him] [her] feelings about it. Let us assume that people will be *allowed* to read it in about the year 2000' (*SB* 7: 256–8/Middleton 1969: 256).

recommended contributions to the production of *this* future may surprise and even disappoint them, he is careful throughout *BGE* to support his best readers while simultaneously encouraging the pretenders among his readers to discontinue their enrolment in his programme of education and training.

In other respects, of course, Nietzsche's readers are *not* like him, as is confirmed by his elevated standing – *primus inter pares* – in the presumptive 'we'. They have not yet travelled the path along which he has offered to guide them, and they are as yet unaware of the precise sense in which they might expect to take their stand beyond good and evil. As we shall see, moreover, he regards his intended readers as dangerously 'unknown to themselves' (cf. GM P), especially with respect to their naïve enthusiasm for science and the tenacity of their unacknowledged investments in the morality of good and evil. As a result, they are largely ignorant of what they might accomplish and who (or what) they might yet become. If they wish to progress in their efforts to contribute to the production of a 'philosophy of the future', they will need to become 'knowers' with respect to themselves and to the world they as yet only lightly inhabit (cf. GM P1).

Although Nietzsche's best readers misunderstand themselves in myriad ways and on multiple levels, he is primarily concerned in *BGE* to address the self-misunderstandings that might be traced to the lingering influence on them of morality itself. Believing themselves to have outgrown the morality of good and evil, as evidenced by their enthusiasm for the 'dangerous slogan' embedded in the 'malicious' title of *BGE*, they are ignorant of the extent to which the morality of good and evil continues to shape the habits, routines and practices with which they are most familiar – including, we might note, those that inform their enthusiastic engagement with scientific research and scholarship.

As such, their lives are characterised by an unfortunate – but potentially corrigible – misalignment: their forward-leaning enthusiasm for science is constrained by their backward-leaning allegiance to religious belief and the morality it sponsors. Stranded somewhere between a moral-religious worldview they know to be bankrupt and a scientific worldview they believe to be preferable, they unwittingly hinder the progress of their own scholarly inquiries. They do so, as we shall learn, by continuing to rely on various presumptions and convictions – Nietzsche's preferred term is *prejudices* – that presuppose (and, so, reinforce) the ongoing validity of the moral-religious worldview they claim to have outgrown. As a result of this misalignment, his best readers enjoy neither the heady exhilaration that attends a daring scientific investigation unfettered by moral and religious concerns, nor the security that arises from the bedrock conviction that a better life awaits them in another realm or world.

Although Nietzsche does not distinguish explicitly in *BGE* between a *moral-religious* worldview and a *scientific* worldview, some such distinction may be a useful heuristic as we consider (and evaluate) his aims in *BGE*.[19] On the one hand, the *moral-religious* worldview may be understood to be the product of a culturally supported network of beliefs and values, which authorises (and subsequently reinforces) the familiar account of human nature as a contested site of conflict between opposing values (e.g., 'good' vs. 'evil'). Typically, those who are deemed 'good' are those who have prevailed in this contest by taking to heart the familiar prescriptions to police, disown and repudiate those thoughts, wishes, impulses, affects and desires that have been determined to be productive of 'evil'. According to Nietzsche, of course, those who are praised for their 'goodness' (and revel in the positive recognition they receive) have prevailed in this conflict at prohibitive expense to themselves and others. Their achievement of 'selflessness', which is hailed as a primary index of their 'goodness', has obliged them to abhor and sacrifice everything about themselves that might have served as a legitimate basis for self-respect. Like Pascal, they may have gone so far as to attempt – or even complete – a 'sacrifice of the intellect' (BGE 45, 229).

The preponderance of this worldview might be traced to the enduring value of morality and religion as instruments of 'breeding'

---

[19] I am indebted here to Young's account of the 'disjunction between . . . the traditional Christian morality of selfless love and . . . the reality of the world, as disclosed by modern, post-Darwinian scientific thinking' (Young 2010: 539-40). In his letter to Jacob Burckhardt of 22 September 1886, Nietzsche takes note of 'the contradiction between every moral concept and every scientific concept of *life* . . .' (*SB* 7: 254–5/Middleton 1969: 255).

(i.e., acculturation), which have aided (some) human beings in becoming invested with a memory of the past and a will for the future. Indeed, although the moral-religious worldview trades on (what Nietzsche exposes as) a massive 'falsification' of human nature, on the strength of which 'sinful' human beings are persuaded to find themselves guilty, it has consistently secured for humankind (or European civilisation as its proxy) the conditions of just-in-time selection and survival. Until very recently, Nietzsche allows, the moral-religious worldview served its adherents as a reliable guarantor of meaning, value, direction and purpose. By presenting earthly life as a trial of piety and perseverance, the moral-religious worldview has prepared its faithful adherents to cultivate those virtues (e.g., of selflessness) that enable them to endure the suffering, grief and loss that are incident to their mortal existence. As we shall see, however, confidence in the moral-religious worldview is now in decline, as is its value as a guarantor of meaning.

On the other hand, the more recently emergent *scientific* worldview has challenged the preponderance of the formerly regnant moral-religious worldview. Leveraging the superior explanatory power of modern science, especially as this power is displayed in the technical applications of scientific discoveries, the scientific worldview trades on a very different understanding of human nature. Rather than present human beings as sinful, weakling creatures, dependent for their meaning and value on the unearned mercy of an otherworldly deity, the scientific worldview celebrates the ingenuity and innovation of the human spirit and invites human beings to arrange for themselves the terms of their own (secular) salvation. Instead of urging its adherents to suffer selflessly as they await the adventitious grant of divine intervention (or grace), the scientific worldview encourages humanity to identify and solve the problems it confronts. The spirit of the scientific worldview is faithfully expressed by Kant's proposed motto for the project of European Enlightenment: *Sapere aude!* [Dare to know!]

Central to the appeal and success of the scientific worldview is the promise it extends of an existence 'beyond good and evil', viz., an existence no longer freighted with the unwanted metaphysical cargo of morality and religion. Like the moral-religious worldview, that is, the scientific worldview offers its adherents sufficient meaning – buoyed by a robust experience of freedom and power – to offset the suffering, grief and loss of their mortal, worldly existence. As Nietzsche remarks on various occasions in *BGE*, the scientific worldview affords its faithful adherents a welcome (albeit short-term) opportunity to take pride in the cumulative accomplishments of humanity and, so, to renew their will for the future.

My primary goal in drawing this distinction on Nietzsche's behalf, and in doing so with such broad strokes, is to characterise the unique situation of the readers whom he addresses in *BGE*, that is, those to whom he offers to apply his distinctive finish. That they are attracted to the scientific worldview is clear enough, for they have come to regard science as a reliable ally in their efforts to liberate themselves from the suffocating grip of morality and religion. That they nevertheless remain rooted in the moral-religious worldview, bound by the 'prejudices' exposed in Part One of *BGE*, is by no means clear to them, which is why their progress towards a full (or fuller) embrace of the scientific worldview has slowed or even stalled. In their present, unfinished condition, they may (and do) sample from both worldviews, drawing as needed from each, because both worldviews are currently productive of limited meaning. The resulting composite worldview is by no means coherent, much less sustainable over the long term, but it works tolerably well as Nietzsche's readers struggle to make sense of the 'turning point in history' at which they find themselves (BGE 262).

Although Nietzsche generally endorses the preference registered by his best readers for the scientific worldview, his pedagogical aims in *BGE* introduce an additional element of complexity. As he acquaints them with the full range of their heretofore unacknowledged investments in the moral-religious worldview, he also means to alert them to the dangers involved in a hasty, incautious embrace of the scientific worldview. Despite approving of their enthusiasm for science, he is concerned that they are as yet unaware of – and, so, vulnerable to – the nihilism that guides the practice of modern science. In light of this concern, he appreciates that their slow, halting progress thus far is not necessarily to their disadvantage, for they have not yet barged, unprepared, into the post-theistic, 'extramoral' future that awaits them. Had they done so, they might have placed themselves beyond the reach of the programme of education and training on offer in *BGE*.

The problem, as we shall see, is that modern science inherits from Platonism and Christianity the bedrock conviction that the mortal, worldly existence of human beings stands in need of otherworldly redemption. As a vehicle of the will to truth, modern science deputises humanity to seek the truth with a rigour, intensity and zeal that are intoxicating in the short term, but destructive (and even debilitating) over the longer term. No longer restricted by the ecclesiastical and cultural constraints that formerly served to guarantee the value of (some instances of) human endeavour, the will to truth now threatens to rage anarchically against anything it encounters (GS P). Nietzsche thus warns that a likely outcome of the rise of the scientific worldview is a breathlessly perilous exercise in misanthropy and self-contempt, culminating in the absurdly triumphant conclusion that human existence is (and presumably always has been) irremediably meaningless (GM III: 25). The cosmos, we are likely to discover, is complete without us.

The intervention Nietzsche stages in *BGE* is meant to guide his best readers towards (a version of) the scientific worldview, while steering them away from the nihilism he detects at the heart of modern science. Before they progress any further, he advises, they must take care to immunise themselves against the misanthropy that is encoded in the materialism of modern science. He thus aims to train the readers of *BGE* in the tactical deployment of the scientific worldview – primarily, as a weapon to be turned against the diminished authority of the morality of good and evil – while also alerting them to the dangers associated with modern science as a nihilistic expression of the will to truth.[20] The intended outcome of his programme of education and training in *BGE* is likely to put us in mind of the 'joyful science' he extols (BGE 293; cf. GS P 1–2), especially inasmuch as his best readers will employ their pursuits of science in the service of life itself.[21] The pride they are

---

[20] Hence the apt designation suggested by Emden: 'a cautious materialism' (2008: 53–64). See also Clark and Dudrick 2012: 68–72.
[21] See Babich 1994: 276–84.

urged to take in their performance of the 'task' assigned to them, which he identifies as their unique contribution to the production of a philosophy of the future, is meant to fortify them against the misanthropy of modern science.

Hence the irony of the evolved, hybrid position towards which Nietzsche aims to guide his best readers: owing in large part to their pro-science and anti-morality allegiances, they are neither sufficiently critical of modern science nor sufficiently appreciative of contemporary morality. So as to address these twin deficiencies, *BGE* offers Nietzsche's readers the education and training they will need in order to immunise themselves against the nihilism of modern science while optimising their relationship to the morality of good and evil. They will not emigrate cleanly beyond the morality of good and evil, but they may yet revel in the experience of accelerating its demise.

1
Nietzsche's Preface

As an exercise in 'fore-reading', Nietzsche's Preface is intended to accustom his readers to the frame of mind and intensity of affect that are appropriate to the investigation that will follow. As is often the case in Nietzsche's writings, he begins by raising a question that has not yet been answered because it has not yet been posed in a meaningful way to an audience that is prepared to grant it the consideration it deserves. In his own words, he means to isolate a 'problem' that has not yet been identified as such by other philosophers. His goal in doing so is to render the familiar unfamiliar, thereby alerting his readers to the uncanny character of the beliefs and values they (and others) have learned to take for granted.

1

Nietzsche begins his Preface by famously urging his readers to consider the supposition that 'truth is a woman'. This supposition is advanced as a thought experiment, but it is also meant to inaugurate a potentially transformative *life* experiment. The suspicion he wishes to raise with his readers is that dogmatic philosophers have been hapless swains of truth. In particular, he suggests, they have failed to consider the possible ways in which truth might withhold itself, mislead or tease its suitors, disguise its nature, or shed one medium or vessel or costume for another. In any event, or so his readers are meant to conclude, a *successful* pursuit of truth (as opposed to one that is merely earnest, mannered, familiar or disciplined) might require a new and different breed of philosopher. The education and production of just such a philosopher is the chief objective of *BGE*.

If truth *were* 'a woman', what would follow? For starters, we would need to withdraw a significant measure of the unverified confidence we have invested in philosophers as truth seekers, for they most certainly have not pursued truth as a determined suitor would pursue a 'woman'. Indeed, a key element of Nietzsche's opening 'supposition' is his as-yet-unstated assumption that the 'woman' in question is a fully functional agent in her own right, motivated by interests, beliefs and desires that might not be aligned with those of her pursuers. (In fact, Nietzsche later confirms that 'she' is likely to be bored by those swains who court her bearing positive evaluations of 'unegoistic' behaviour (BGE 220).) In a related exercise of creative gender assignment, Zarathustra records a similar (and similarly questionable) observation about those who would seek *wisdom*: 'Brave, unconcerned, mocking, violent – thus wisdom wants us: she is a woman and always loves only a warrior' (Z I: 7).

If truth were 'a woman', in other words, we might be obliged to consider the possibility that 'she' has simply outwitted the dogmatic philosophers among her pursuers. Indeed, his provocative 'supposition' is apparently intended to confirm the (urgent) need for an alternative to the pursuit of truth conducted by dogmatic philosophers. As we shall see, Nietzsche's recourse in *BGE* to a gendered personification of truth is meant to confirm that a new and daring approach to the pursuit of truth, wherein danger-loving philosophers engage in risky, innovative 'attempts' to disclose truths that are partial, kinetic, reclusive, perspective-dependent – *and* potentially lethal to creatures such as ourselves – has very recently become both possible and necessary.

In the event that Nietzsche's readers disagree with his unflattering characterisation of the philosophical dogmatists, they are nevertheless expected to acknowledge what is presented here as not merely suppositional, but 'certain' – namely, that truth 'has not allowed herself to be charmed' (BGE P). Even if his readers insist that truth is not a 'woman', in other words, they can no longer deny that truth has eluded the dogmatic philosophers who have been tasked with its capture. Briefly, his point is this: dogmatic philosophy, animated by a particular and venerable approach to the truth, has (nearly) run its course. Philosophical dogmatism is either 'gloomy and despondent', 'fallen' and lying 'on the ground', or 'in its last throes' (BGE P). Moreover, this bold claim about the failure and likely demise of dogmatic philosophy is supported by the palpable frustration of the dogmatists themselves: 'every kind of dogmatism stands there today with a gloomy and despondent look. *If* it stands at all anymore!' (BGE P; cf. TI 'True World' 5).

As this last point confirms, Nietzsche's intention here is not to claim a personal victory over dogmatism, but to draw attention to the crisis of confidence that afflicts the philosophical dogmatists to whom he refers. His critique of philosophical dogmatism is focused not on its ongoing failure to deliver the perspective-independent truths it has promised to disclose – for this, his biting satire will suffice – but on its recent failure to retain, much less warrant, the allegiance and loyalty of aspiring and committed philosophers. In this respect, he is content simply to document the plight of the dogmatists in question: they no longer believe that their pursuit of perspective-independent truth will vouchsafe for them a meaningful existence. Even if they continue as dogmatists, inured to its familiar routines and the camaraderie their pursuit of truth sponsors, they will do so half-heartedly and with diminished zeal. The formerly robust and vital enterprise of dogmatism has fallen, he observes, not because it has failed to 'win' the truth it claimed to pursue, but because it has run its course and exhausted (or nearly so) its authority as a guarantor of meaning and purpose.

In a word, dogmatism has been 'overcome' by its own efforts, which is a result that Nietzsche views both favourably in its own right and as productive of an opportunity that he intends to exploit. The time has come to do something new, something different, and to begin the process of building a philosophy neither of the past nor of the present day, but of the *future* – a future, moreover, that he and his best readers may help to shape. Indeed, Nietzsche spies amid the ruins of dogmatism a propitious opening: the collapse of dogmatic philosophy has rendered the morality of good and evil ripe for challenge and vulnerable to an assault launched by crafty merchants of untimely truths.

Who are these dogmatic philosophers whom Nietzsche is so keen to skewer? By *dogmatism*, he means any philosophical commitment that is maintained inflexibly, as a matter of prejudice or faith, even in the face of obvious and serial failure or invalidation. Deputised as (betrayed) agents of the will to truth, the dogmatic philosophers solemnly pursue the truth as if their lives depended on it – which, according to Nietzsche, it does. He thus introduces the dogmatists by referencing the 'ghastly earnest' and 'clumsy obtrusiveness' they display as they conduct their grim, joyless pursuit of truth (BGE P). If truth were a woman, he apparently means to suggest, 'she' would not be entertained, much less impressed, by the figure the dogmatists cut as they pay 'her' suit. Later on, moreover, Nietzsche reveals that 'the secret wish and background of all dogmatic endeavors' has been to capture 'a truth for everyone' (BGE 43). If truth were a 'woman', or so this disclosure is meant to suggest, 'she' would prefer those suitors who insist on a more exclusive and intimate relationship with 'her'.

But if dogmatic philosophers have not pursued truth as the 'woman' that 'she' is, what exactly have they been doing? Here Nietzsche's analysis acquires additional historical nuance: until very recently, philosophers have conducted a good faith search for the truth, but they have done so under the constraints imposed upon them by the norms, methods and traditions of the schools and disciplines in which they have studied and trained (TI 'True World' 1–4). The most important (and binding) of these constraints is the dominant characterisation of truth itself, upon which any search for the truth is (at least initially) dependent. In order to *be* a philosopher at all, and to enjoy the minimal, priesthood-adjacent cachet accorded to philosophers (D 42, GM III: 10), one has been obliged, until very recently, to follow and emulate the example of the dogmatists, who have been trained and dispatched to discover – or at least honour – a truth that is objective, permanent, unchanging and perspective-independent – in short, a 'truth for everyone' (BGE 43).

The dogmatists whom Nietzsche has in mind – he mentions Plato by name – have carried out this search by seeking truth not in the world in which they find themselves, viz., the *real* world of flux and becoming, but in an *ideal* world predicated on the permanence and perfection they have been trained to esteem. In order to gain access to this ideal world, they typically have subjected themselves (and others) to the ascetic disciplines that are prescribed within the order, school or tradition to which they belong. Inasmuch as these ascetic disciplines typically involve some combination of 'solitude, fasting, and sexual abstinence' (BGE 47), the dogmatic philosophers whom Nietzsche has in mind would be unlikely on their own to generate the supposition that 'truth is a woman'. If anything, they would be likely to regard 'woman' (and everything related to 'her') as antithetical to truth and the successful pursuit thereof.

In light of the discipline and training they have received, moreover, they would have every right to spurn Nietzsche's supposition. Everything they know, believe, feel and stand for militates against the possibility that 'truth is a woman'. Notwithstanding the obvious delight Nietzsche takes in ridiculing the philosophical dogmatists, he also succeeds in presenting them as sympathetic figures. They have done everything by the book, at least as far as their discipline and training would dictate. Yet here they stand (or lie), dispirited and discouraged, reluctant (or unable) any longer to invest the requisite intensity of belief in their accustomed pursuit of truth. Through no fault of their own, they find themselves at or near the exhausted conclusion of a grand cultural enterprise – that is, 'a promise spanning the millennia' – to which they have devoted their lives, and from which they have received very little in return (TI 'True World' 5). Although he does not say so explicitly, he implies here (and elsewhere) that these dogmatic philosophers were set up to fail: the truth they earnestly sought was not likely ever to be disclosed, and certainly not by an application of the methods and approaches in which they were trained (TI 'True World' 3–4). As we will learn, in fact, the discipline and training they have received served to spare them from a potentially disastrous brush with truth, which (or whom), as Nietzsche's impolitic 'supposition' implies, they would have encountered – much to their chagrin – as a *femme fatale*.

If 'truth is a woman', and if 'woman' is every bit as kinetic and mercurial as Nietzsche supposes, then those philosophers who have pursued truth on the model of an ideal, unchanging, strictly objective essence must be judged to be failures. They are like fishing enthusiasts who exhibit perfect form, perseverance, knowledge of the water and its native species and so on, but who never actually land a fish. Fishing itself, as opposed to catching fish, has become the unstated goal of their existence. If they lie (whether to themselves or others) about having caught a fish, usually a big one that 'got away', they will be obliged (and perhaps content) to spend the rest of their days in an effort to sustain and even embellish their subterfuge. (They might line their shelves with blurred, indistinct photos of 'their' fish, or with relics of their fateful encounter with the leviathan that barely escaped – or slashed – their nets.) If their disposable resources permit, they might recruit charismatic acolytes who will disseminate their fish tales with conviction and aplomb. An annual festival or holy day might be inaugurated to commemorate the event, which, over time, might be hailed as a miracle. And so on.

Like Nietzsche's supposition, this analogy is meant to be humorous. Empty-handed anglers are as ripe for ribbing as dispirited dogmatists, especially if they have been pompous and self-important in asserting their standing vis-à-vis their rivals. At the same time, however, this is not the story Nietzsche is most concerned to tell in *BGE*. Making sport of discouraged dogmatists is but a warm-up to the main event of his Preface.

2

Having had his fun, and having previewed the rough treatment in store for dogmatic philosophers more generally, Nietzsche resolves to speak 'seriously' to his readers (BGE P). He intimates that there are 'good reasons' to understand that philosophical dogmatism will very soon be understood to represent the childhood of a toddling species, which now finds itself poised on the threshold of an overdue maturation. In the event that humankind crosses this threshold and accedes to full (or fuller) maturity, future generations might look back on dogmatism as a necessary, if costly, stage in the overall development of humanity. Someday, they even might chuckle at the earnest naivety that was evident throughout the dogmatic arc of human evolution.

Having observed that 'perhaps the time is very near' to take the retrospective measure of dogmatism, Nietzsche confirms to his readers '*what* has actually sufficed to serve as the cornerstone of such sublime and unconditional philosophical edifices as the dogmatists have constructed to date' (BGE P). Relying on nothing more than a 'popular superstition', a 'play on words', a 'seduction on the part of grammar', or a 'daring generalization', dogmatists and their patrons have managed to build and maintain thriving cultures and civilisations. Despite delivering what his readers are likely to receive as a devastating critique of philosophical dogmatism, Nietzsche adopts the conciliatory tone of an objective critic. Rather than display anger or outrage at the massive swindle perpetrated by the dogmatists, he prepares his readers to join him in affirming what dogmatism has (unwittingly) wrought.

3

Now expressing his 'hope', which more generally informs the whole of *BGE*, Nietzsche explains what it would mean for his readers to regard dogmatism as 'a promise spanning the millennia', viz., as nothing more (and nothing less) than a transitional stage in a much longer process of contingent human development.

Citing the example of 'astrology', Nietzsche observes that 'more work, money, ingenuity, and patience were expended so far than for any real science' (BGE P). Noting that 'we owe the grand style of architecture in Asia and Egypt' to the preponderance of the '"superterrestrial" claims' asserted by court astrologers, he implies that a strictly scientific appraisal of astrology – which no doubt would yield a summary negative judgement – would fail to do justice to its complex legacy. Much, much more was going on there: the mobilisation of bodies and resources; progress in the arts, crafts and sciences; the consolidation of a will for the future; the liberation of the imagination; and the keening of the spirit. With respect to the 'promises spanning the millennia' that were extended, respectively, by 'Asian astrology' and Christian morality, Nietzsche later remarks that 'this tyranny, this arbitrariness, this strict and grandiose stupidity, has *trained* the spirit' (BGE 188). A similar evaluation someday might be advanced, or so he implies, of dogmatism, whose spiritual legacies are likely to eclipse its failed efforts to capture a truth that 'has not allowed herself to be charmed'.

Nietzsche's even-handed treatment of astrology in this paragraph models to his readers the critical approach he employs in *BGE*. While it is easy enough to ridicule or rue the staggering outlay of resources involved in supporting (what is now widely understood to be) a pseudo-scientific pursuit of the truth, the outlay in question *also* produced unintended and indirect results that merit our attention and, perhaps, warrant our affirmation. To wit: although astrology failed in its defining effort to find truth in the stars, it succeeded in raising and maintaining a vibrant culture, which presided over the breeding and development of those human beings who fell under its sway. Hence Nietzsche's claim that we 'owe' astrology a debt of gratitude that a strictly scientific appraisal of its efforts would not permit us to acknowledge. Simply put, the broken promise of astrology is redeemed by (and in) its positive contributions – even if unintended – to the advancement of culture and the elevation of humanity.

The signal benefit of this critical approach is that it positions Nietzsche (and his readers) to evaluate a 'promise spanning the millennia' on the basis of what the 'promise' in question actually delivers. Although astrology failed to disclose the truth it promised to find, it nevertheless succeeded in delivering (unintended) contributions to the enhancement of culture and the elevation of humanity. Similarly, although dogmatism failed to make good on its promise to deliver redemption-conferring, perspective-independent truths, what it actually has wrought merits a second look *and* something akin to gratitude.[1] Indeed, what remains vital and generative in the twilight of dogmatism is the disciplinary complex – of affects and passions, powers and possibilities, habits and practices, virtues and responsibilities, etc. – that was activated in 'civilised' human beings so that they might better serve the

---

[1] The importance of the theme of gratitude becomes clear when Nietzsche applauds 'the religiosity of the ancient Greeks' for 'the tremendous abundance of gratitude it exudes' (BGE 49).

dogmatic enterprise.[2] As we shall see, in fact, this disciplinary complex provides Nietzsche with the basis for the programme of education and training he conducts in *BGE*.

Although he makes no direct reference in his Preface to the morality of good and evil, his readers are apparently meant to regard it, too, from the (imagined) perspective of those who have survived its protracted period of disciplinary habituation. What is dead or dying in the morality of good and evil is the credibility of its claims to universal applicability and unchallenged moral authority. What remains viable (and ripe for redeployment) is the affective-somatic complex of virtues and powers that it has cultivated and reinforced in us. The morality of good and evil might be affirmed, in other words, by attending to its success – contrary to its stated aims and objections – in preparing (some) human beings to outgrow its dominion. On the one hand, then, Nietzsche consistently faults the morality of good and evil for its levelling assault on those 'higher' human beings whose exploits fund an affirmation of our mortal, worldly existence. On the other hand, he remains 'hopeful' that the morality of good and evil has prepared his best readers to accelerate – and perhaps survive – its demise.

Nietzsche concludes this portion of his Preface by revealing a more general truth about human history: '[A]ll great things, in order to inscribe themselves with eternal demands upon the heart of humanity, must first stalk the earth as colossal and fear-inducing masks' (BGE P). Plato's dogmatism is one such 'mask', as he confirms, but a mask of *what*? What is the 'great thing' that sought shelter within the recently vacated mantle of philosophical dogmatism? Perhaps for dramatic and/or rhetorical effect, Nietzsche does not say, though his postponement is mercifully brief. As the first four words of Section 1 confirm, *the will to truth* is the 'great thing' that, until very recently, lay hidden and coiled at the heart of philosophical dogmatism (BGE 1). Having frightened us and imposed upon us its 'eternal demands' – which, apparently, were conducive until very recently to the elevation of the human condition – the will to truth is now available for unprecedented philosophical scrutiny and evaluation.

---

[2] Here I follow Lampert 2001: 10–13; and Clark and Dudrick 2012: 24–5.

4

Buoyed by his hope for a post-dogmatic future, Nietzsche urges his readers to give dogmatism its due, including their (limited) gratitude for what it has accomplished. Before expressing his own (limited) gratitude, however, he confirms the gravity of the current situation. 'Plato's invention of the pure spirit and of good in itself' was not simply an error – and, therefore, the opposite of an expression of truth – but also 'the worst, longest lasting and most dangerous of all errors so far' (BGE P). This invention is particularly destructive, he continues, inasmuch as it has obliged Plato (and his epigones) to stand truth 'on its head' and deny 'the *perspectival*, [which is] the basic condition of all life' (BGE P).[3] So as to vouchsafe his own 'promise spanning the millennia', Plato recklessly defamed life itself, judging it to be inferior to a conjectured afterlife in a world or realm predicated on permanence and perfection. In order for this 'dangerous' error to be corrected and affirmed, something vital and life-enhancing must be wrought from the long (and now sputtering) career of dogmatism. Hence Nietzsche's overarching goal in *BGE*: Plato's error must be shown to have produced (unintended) positive consequences in excess of the extensive damage it has caused.

Liberated from the 'nightmare' of dogmatism, Europe now may enjoy a good night's sleep, even if Nietzsche and his 'we' are summoned anew to the '*task*' of '*wakefulness itself*' (BGE P). As the (rightful) 'heirs' to the 'strength' that was amassed and stored away over the course of a protracted campaign to expose Plato's 'error', Nietzsche and his 'we' are uniquely positioned to turn philosophy in a non- or extra-dogmatic direction.

5

As it turns out, Platonism has (unwittingly) provoked the 'struggle' that very recently has proved to be decisive. The good news here

---

[3] Nietzsche likely has in mind the twin sins of Plato when he later confirms that '[truth] is a woman: we should not do violence to her' (BGE 220). In his brief account of the 'History of an Error', he later confirms, parenthetically, that in the wake of Plato 'the idea [of the true world] . . . becomes more refined, trickier, more incomprehensible – it becomes woman, it becomes Christian. . .' (TI 'True World').

is that dogmatism, despite its influential sway over the development of European civilisation, has been an imperfect, contested fit from the very beginning. Although Europe has been formed and transformed under the impress of dogmatism, some Europeans – soon to be identified in their current incarnation as 'good Europeans' – have resisted this assault. Owing to the accumulated force of this resistance over time, or so Nietzsche assures his readers, 'the struggle against the Christian-ecclesiastical pressure of millennia . . . has created a magnificent tension of the spirit in Europe, such as never existed on earth' (BGE P).

What Nietzsche means to convey here is that the collapse of dogmatic philosophy is indicative of what he generally prefers to call the logic of *self-overcoming*, whereby a regnant structure of meaning and value inadvertently gives rise (and cedes authority) to emboldened forces of opposition and succession. Even as dogmatism imposed its brand upon European civilisation, it elicited a gradually rising swell of opposition to its continued preponderance. Here we learn, in fact, that the 'strength' that has been bred in the liberators of truth, to which Nietzsche and his 'we' are among the rightful 'heirs', is a 'strength' predicated on the *spirit*. As we shall see, in fact, the programme of education and training that Nietzsche conducts in *BGE* is meant to prepare his best readers to propagate the 'magnificent tension of the spirit' (BGE P), to escalate this tension if possible, and to safeguard the delivery of a fully flexed 'bow' to the 'philosophers of the future'.[4] Along the way, of course, they are authorised to expend tactical bursts of accumulated spirit in the furtherance of their appointed 'task'.

Thus we arrive at the anticipated moment of affirmation: notwithstanding the guiding aims of its leading practitioners, dogmatism 'has *trained* the spirit' (BGE 188). Although dogmatism has failed to deliver the perspective-independent truth that served as the animating pretext for its sway over European civilisation, the disciplinary complex it authorised has (inadvertently) produced creatures who have become moral and, *as a result*, are now poised to retire the morality of good and evil once and for all. (They will do so, as we shall see, in their 'immoral' efforts to inaugurate

---

[4] Here I follow Lampert 2001: 13–17, 224–31; and Clark and Dudrick 2012: 25–9, 257–63.

the 'extramoral' period in human history.) This is why we should 'not be ungrateful' to the dogmatists, notwithstanding the damage they have caused and the errors they have propagated. To borrow one of the most frequently sampled of Nietzsche's pithy aphorisms: having failed to kill us, dogmatism has made us stronger. Precisely *how* it has done so remains to be seen.

As newly anointed stewards of an untapped reservoir of disposable spirit, Nietzsche and his best readers are called to prepare for the formulation of a *new* 'promise spanning the millennia'. By way of alerting his readers to the opportunity now available to them, he advises, 'With such a tense bow we can now shoot for the most distant goals' (BGE P). As we shall see, in fact, *his* 'promise spanning the millennia' is every bit as grand and ambitious as those that launched the careers, respectively, of astrology and dogmatism, for it is intended to place the very project of human civilisation on a new and far more secure foundation.

Acknowledging that most Europeans experience this spiritual tension as indicative of a 'state of emergency', Nietzsche cautions against any reprise of those attempts – most notably, by 'Jesuitism' and the 'democratic Enlightenment', respectively – to reduce to a tolerable level the tension that thrums in the bow.[5] For Nietzsche and his best readers, there is only one path forward: to bend the bow nearly to its breaking point, so that those who follow – the 'new' philosophers (BGE 44) – might launch the arrows of European aspiration into a distant future, beyond the reach and jurisdiction of the morality of good and evil.[6]

It is for this reason that Nietzsche urges his readers to *persist* in the feelings of need and distress that accompany their own experience of spiritual tension. If nothing else, their raw, untreated experience of a 'state of emergency' will remind them of the opportunity available to them for growth and outgrowth. What

---

[5] In his letter to Overbeck on 3 February 1888, Nietzsche explains that 'in the state of a bow strung to the highest possible tension, any emotion is good for one, provided it is a violent emotion' (SB 8: 242/Middleton 1969: 282).

[6] Zarathustra's recourse to a similar set of images confirms that Nietzsche and his 'we' are tasked with preventing the emergence of the 'last man': 'Alas, the time is coming when man will no longer shoot the arrow of his longing beyond man, and the string of his bow will have forgotten how to whir!' (Z P5).

this means, of course, is that they will need (and need to want) to isolate themselves from 'Jesuitism' and 'democracy' in all of their emergency-calming forms. Those who are called to preserve the tension in the bow must associate only with those like-minded European conspirators who similarly thrill to the disruptive prospect of preparing for an eventual excursion beyond good and evil.

Nietzsche thus concludes his Preface on a cautiously hopeful note. If the tension in the bow can be effectively managed and productively released – without breaking the bow, of course – Europe might yet set its sights on a goal (or target) that will ensure the enduring, global preponderance of its civilisation. While the goal (or target) remains unknown (or at least innominate), we may rest assured that it will not involve the pursuit of truth after the fashion of dogmatism (BGE 43). *That* period in the history of European civilisation is coming to a close. What Nietzsche might mean to suggest here is that a properly managed release of spiritual tension could renew the promise of a genuinely *tragic* (or Dionysian) culture, wherein enduring meaning is created and treasured within the finite, precarious existence of mortal creatures such as ourselves (BT AS 5–6; TI 'Ancients' 4–5). The philosophy of the future, or so we are meant to understand, will be a philosophy of and for real human beings, for whom impermanence, untruth, finitude and decay will no longer count as automatic objections to their worldly existence.

Nietzsche closes his Preface by addressing his best readers by the titles he hopes they (and he) soon will earn. They are – or, more precisely, might soon become – '*good Europeans* and free, *very* free spirits' (BGE P), to whom will fall the task of managing the spiritual tension residing in the bow. He and they will earn these titles, as we shall see, if they are able to optimise the freedom and agency available to them in the still-moral historical context in which they find themselves. They will become the future-oriented subjects of their history only if he is able to guide them towards an understanding of the extent to which they are also claimed by the past and ineluctably marked – though not necessarily maimed – by their history.

The presumptive designation of this 'we' as a vanguard cohort of 'good Europeans' bears noting. Throughout the writings of his post-Zarathustran period, Nietzsche insists that the greatness of European civilisation is uniquely attributable to its irrepressible capacity for innovation, risk, self-overcoming and self-reinvention.[7] Rather than become stagnant and self-assured, resting on its many laurels, European civilisation has responded time and again by rolling the dice, opening itself to a new, unscripted future. Turning confidently in times of decay to its leading artists, composers and philosophers, viz., those whom it has deputised as the guardians and architects of its future (BGE 256), European civilisation has avoided the fate suffered by other civilisations of note. What will qualify Nietzsche and his best readers as 'good Europeans', in short, is their trust in (and will for) a future that need not resemble the past. For the 'good Europeans', futurity always bespeaks the novelty of reinvention, of what Nietzsche calls 'self-overcoming'.

---

[7] I am indebted here to Shapiro 2016: 102–10.

2
Part One: On the Prejudices of Philosophers

Preview

Nietzsche wastes no time in explaining why the dogmatic philosophers whom he ridicules in the Preface are such inexpert swains of truth: they have been led astray – and spared a potentially debilitating encounter with truth – by the prejudices that variously inform and direct their philosophical investigations. In both English and German, a *prejudice* [*Vorurtheil*] is literally a *pre-judgement*, a judgement formed and asserted prior to adequate reflection and credible empirical verification. As Nietzsche mobilises this term in Part One of *BGE*, a prejudice might be understood to be any fixed or foundational assertion that appears to be impervious to challenge and, as a result, neither invites scrutiny nor requires support. In general, prejudices reflect what 'everyone' knows and takes for granted, even if no one – including, apparently, chagrined philosophers – can explain why this is so. If philosophers are to make good on their wish to stand apart from the crowd, they will need at some point to interrogate the crowd-sourced prejudices on which they continue to rely.

In directing our attention to 'The Prejudices of Philosophers', Nietzsche renews and intensifies the approach he pioneered in *Dawn* (1881), which bears the subtitle 'Thoughts on the Prejudices of Morality'.[1] In that earlier book, he sought both to include

---

[1] For the sake of consistency, I have followed Del Caro's practice of translating *Vorurtheile* as 'prejudices'.

himself in the circle of European intellectuals who were determined to bring scientific rigour to bear on questions of morality *and* to expose some of the flaws and failures of his rivals in this endeavour.[2] There as here, he registers his concern that the development of a properly scientific approach to morality has been impeded by the persistence of moral-religious prejudices that have managed, thus far, to defy or elude sustained philosophical inspection.

In his 1886 Preface to the second edition of *Dawn*, Nietzsche attributes the superiority of *his* investigation of the prejudices of morality to his training in classical philology, which, he explains, prepared him to read, think and write more slowly and judiciously than his rivals (D P5). He adverts to a similar advantage in *BGE*, pointing out, for example, that physicists who appeal to the 'conformity of nature to law' are likely to be engaged in (and inured to) the practice of 'bad "philology"' (BGE 22). In both cases, he boasts that his philological training enables him to detect 'bad tricks of interpretation', from which the presence and influence of moral-religious prejudices might be inferred (BGE 22).

The prejudices that most centrally concern Nietzsche in *BGE* are those that have most recently presented themselves for scrutiny. According to his understanding of the movement of history, each successive period sustains itself on the strength of convictions that, for the most part, no one would think to subject to philosophical reflection. Healthy tribes, nations, peoples and cultures are able to maintain their ascendant vitality by dint of their unwavering adherence to convictions whose truth and validity they simply take for granted. In times of historical transition, however, convictions that have begun to exhaust their utility and currency will suddenly become available, *qua* prejudices, for challenge and critique.

One such historical transition, which Nietzsche identifies as a 'turning point in history' (BGE 262), is currently underway, which is why the moral-religious worldview and its enabling

---

[2] For illuminating treatments of Nietzsche's approach in *Dawn* to the question/problem of 'the prejudices of morality', see Franco 2011: ch. 2; Ansell-Pearson 2018: ch. 4; and Ansell-Pearson and Bamford 2020: ch. 3.

PART ONE: ON THE PREJUDICES OF PHILOSOPHERS   35

prejudices have become targets of Nietzsche's critical inquiry. The prejudices he wishes to expose in *BGE* are those that have been chiefly responsible for securing the validity and preponderance of this worldview and discrediting the claims of the rival scientific worldview. Philosophers and philosophically inclined scholars of all types are now free to expose and challenge the prejudices on which the moral-religious worldview trades. While philosophers in predecessor periods might be forgiven for having failed to identify these prejudices as such, Nietzsche's best readers have no such excuse. Inasmuch as they are avowedly allegiant to the emerging scientific worldview, they have no business clinging to the moral-religious prejudices he exposes in Part One.

Summary of sections

Part One of *BGE* comprises twenty-three numbered sections (1–23). The 'will to truth' is introduced rather abruptly, and Nietzsche provides his readers with very little by way of exposition or explanation. As we know from his Preface to *BGE*, the will to truth is that which is responsible for animating the grand, civilisation-defining dogmatisms of Asia (Vedanta) and Europe (Platonism and Christianity). As we also know, the will to truth has very recently taken up residence within the supercharged enterprise of modern science, wherein it funds a successor dogmatism that is not yet widely acknowledged as such. Although he does not say so explicitly, he apparently regards the will to truth not as a prejudice in its own right, but as the authorising, enframing source and condition of the prejudices he surveys in Part One.

Nietzsche begins Part One by availing himself of the unusual latitude that attends his placement in what he later identifies as a 'turning point of history' (BGE 262). Having identified the will to truth as responsible for the 'famous truthfulness of which all philosophers so far have spoken with deference', he suggests that those for whom he speaks have grown 'suspicious' of and 'impatient' with the questions the will to truth has directed them to raise (BGE 1). Signalling their intent to rebel against the will to truth and its restrictive agenda for philosophy, Nietzsche and his 'we' insist on posing several questions *to* the will to truth, especially with respect to the source and legitimacy of its authority. As they do so, we should note, they remain very much under the influence of the will to truth. Their goal is to discover and tell the truth about the will to truth, precisely so that they might face the will to truth with the truth of its own provenance (GM III: 27) – namely, as we shall see, that it rests on an as-yet-unacknowledged *faith* in the redemptive properties of truth (GS 344). In *On the Genealogy of Morality*, Nietzsche explains that 'what compels one to this, to this unconditional will to truth, is the *belief in the ascetic ideal itself,* even if as its unconscious imperative – we must not deceive ourselves about this – this is the belief in a *metaphysical* value, a value *in itself of truth* as it is guaranteed and chartered by that ideal alone' (GM III: 24).

Before we proceed, it may be useful to note that Nietzsche opens Part One of *BGE* by recounting (and formally staging) an instance of *self-overcoming*. From the very dawn of Western civilisation, the will to truth has provided priests, philosophers, scholars and scientists with a compelling impetus for their inquisitions. Although accounts of the purported availability of truth have shifted over time, obliging its dedicated seekers to adjust their methods and expectations, the will to truth has persisted to this day (TI 'True World'). So long as truth-seekers have conducted their inquisitions within circumscribed bounds, the will to truth has granted them the meaning and justification that all human beings seek. As Nietzsche readily volunteers, in fact, he and his target readership should not expect to escape the thrall of the will to truth, which, he advises from the outset, 'will yet seduce us to many a risk' (BGE 1).

In the case of Nietzsche and his best readers, however, the will to truth has reproduced itself in excess of the limits it has set for its clientele among truth-seekers. Rather than simply pose the questions dictated to them by the will to truth, which is how the aforementioned dogmatists eventually grew 'gloomy and despondent' (BGE P), Nietzsche and his 'we' have resolved to pursue their own agenda. *Their* devotion to truth is sufficiently potent, autonomous and transgressive as to steer them into confrontation with the will to truth itself (cf. GM III: 27). '*What* in us really wants "the truth"?', they brazenly ask (BGE 1), thereby confirming that the will to truth has enflamed in them the desire to seek the truth not only about themselves, but about truth itself. Availing ourselves of the literary figure that Nietzsche introduces in this section, we might say that he has become a 'Sphinx' in his own right, viz., a poser of weighty questions, by virtue of having acquired the experience needed by those, for example, Oedipus, who attempt – typically, at great personal expense – to solve the riddle posed to them by the 'Sphinx' (= will to truth).[3] The 'rendezvous' in question, viz. 'between questions and question marks', thus marks the emergence of Nietzsche and his 'we' as intrepid, truth-seeking interrogators of the will to truth.

The will to truth

Although Nietzsche neglects to provide a proper introduction to the 'will to truth' in Part One of *BGE*, his other writings furnish welcome context and illumination. In his speech 'On Self-Overcoming', for example, Zarathustra addresses himself to those who are known to be 'wisest' – namely, those venerable sages whom Nietzsche elsewhere identifies as life-weary degenerates (TI 'Socrates' 1–2). When asked what 'impels [them] and fills [them] with lust', Zarathustra explains, those who are 'wisest' invariably point to the 'will to truth' (Z II: 12), as if that were a philosophically compelling account of the genesis of their supposed wisdom. Bursting their bubble of self-satisfaction, Zarathustra opines that the will to truth is in fact 'a will to the thinkability of all beings', which he immediately proceeds to characterise as the will 'to *make* all being thinkable' (Z II: 12). Arriving at his summary evaluation of the will to truth, Zarathustra speaks directly (albeit by way of apostrophic address) to those who are 'wisest': 'You still want to create the world before which you can kneel: that is your ultimate hope and intoxication' (Z II: 12).

How does such a will arise and persist? According to Zarathustra, those who are 'wisest' are in fact motivated by their 'doubt . . . that [being] is already thinkable' (Z II: 12), which is why their pursuit of truth must take the form of a will or impulse.

---

[3] See Pippin 2019b: 195–8.

Owing to the nagging tenacity of their 'doubt', which Zarathustra regards as well-founded, those who are 'wisest' simply cannot afford the luxury of inquiring or determining – for example, via a rigorous, deliberate scientific investigation – whether or not all beings are in fact 'thinkable'. Inasmuch as the 'wisest' treat the 'thinkability' of all beings as the *sine qua non* of their continued existence, their only viable recourse is to embrace it, uncritically and fanatically, as an article of faith. On the strength of their will to truth, in other words, those who are 'wisest' succeed in *fabricating* the true world before which they are eager to kneel. No other world, and certainly not the real world of flux and becoming, would suffice to assuage their doubts and command their devotion.

If these sages were to keep to themselves, kneeling in silence before the ideal worlds they have created, their will to truth might be dismissed as a relatively harmless response to their all-too-human need for a meaningful existence. As an elaboration of 'will to power', however, their will to truth invariably impels them to find the worship of other worlds – and especially the 'world of life, nature, and history' (GS 344) – to be intolerable. Were these sages to gain access to the levers of political power and cultural authority, their theoretical negation of other worlds would become fully realised throughout their sphere of dominion. In that event, it would (and in fact has) become both dangerous and immoral to kneel before any world other than the ideal world in which 'all beings are thinkable'.

Although Zarathustra honours the will to truth as a creative expression of the 'will to power' (Z II: 12), he also cautions his auditors (and, by extension, Nietzsche's readers) that the will to truth aims to generalise – and, so, to normalise – the anxiety and distress of those who express it. That these sages *need* to kneel before a fabricated, idealised world is no reason to believe that everyone else should or must do likewise. Healthier mortals will kneel before healthier worlds, and the highest among us will kneel before the real world as it is and presents itself.

An instructive elaboration of Zarathustra's teaching appears in Book V of *The Gay Science*, where Nietzsche inquires after the conditions under which science has acquired its impressive currency and cultural authority. Granting that science is defined as an enterprise by its principled opposition to unsubstantiated 'convictions', Nietzsche wonders aloud if this opposition is not itself predicated on

> some prior conviction [*Überzeugung*] – even one that is so commanding and unconditional that it sacrifices all other convictions to itself? We see that science also rests on a faith; there simply is no science 'without presuppositions.' The question whether *truth* is needed must not only have been affirmed in advance, but affirmed to such a degree that the principle, the faith, the conviction finds expression: '*Nothing* is needed *more* than truth, and in relation to it everything else has only second-rate value.' (GS 344)

How might we account for the origin and provenance of this conviction? If it is in fact foundational of the scientific enterprise, it cannot be counted among the trusted results of scientific inquiry. Nor can it be said of this conviction that it passes scientific muster independent of its role in founding the scientific enterprise. According to Nietzsche, neither the supposed 'necessity' of truth nor its purportedly inestimable value has ever been confirmed, precisely because the conviction in question has never been subjected to challenge – until now. The conviction that '*Nothing* is needed more than truth' thus turns out to be the product not of a reasoned, evidence-based scientific investigation, but of an unacknowledged *faith* in the necessity of truth. If Nietzsche is correct in his surmise, the magisterial enterprise of modern science owes its rise and authority to a non-rational, extra-scientific impulse that contemporary scientists and scholars have failed thus far to acknowledge, much less interrogate.[4]

The primary role of this conviction is to ensure that the pursuit of truth is (and remains) a pre-reflective, impulsive expression of *will*. According to Nietzsche's account, creatures such as ourselves have been habituated not simply to appreciate and track

---

[4] Here I follow the general line of interpretation advanced by Havas 1995: 152–72. See also Richardson 2020: 283–303; and Miner 2022: 169–75, 190–5.

the truth, owing to its supposed 'necessity' for our ongoing existence, but also to do so as an expression of volition, wherein one's entire apparatus of drives, passions, affects and other modes of embodiment is activated in a coordinated, directed response. For creatures such as ourselves, the pursuit of truth is not simply useful, but also *vital* – it is that which ensures that we remain disciplined and future-bound, even as the pains and indignities of the present moment threaten to overwhelm us. So it is, Nietzsche suggests, that the conviction in question strikes us as something other than a conviction, or as an obvious exception to the otherwise strict ban on convictions, for we can scarcely fathom what science would be, or what *we* would become, if this conviction were somehow placed under suspicion or, even worse, in abeyance. Borrowing Aldous Huxley's pithy formulation, we might characterise the will to truth as the compulsion of a 'fanatic' who 'consciously overcompensates a secret doubt' pertaining to the genuine value of truth.[5]

Hence Nietzsche's answer to the first question he poses in the initial section of *BGE*: that which is 'in us' and 'really wants "the truth"' is the 'doubt', isolated by Zarathustra, that anything less than 'the truth' will be insufficient to redeem our (seemingly meaningless) finite existence. Incident to this 'doubt' is the corollary suspicion that any meaning we manage to generate for ourselves will fall short of what we require to justify the pains and losses we invariably will incur in the process. We *want* truth, that is, not because its value for creatures such as ourselves has been conclusively demonstrated, but because it is said (and believed) to be a *necessity*, inasmuch as truth alone satisfies our primal *need* for completion, meaning, purpose and direction. As we shall see, in short, the pursuit and possession of truth are believed to redeem the impermanence and imperfection of our mortal, worldly existence.

Returning to *BGE*, we learn that Nietzsche and his 'we' have raised 'an even more thorough question': 'Suppose we want truth: *why not rather* untruth? And uncertainty? Even ignorance?'

---

[5] Huxley 1928: 262.

(BGE 1). Having determined that the will to truth rests on an unacknowledged *faith* in the necessity of truth, and having conjectured that the faith in truth is now ripe for creative interrogation, Nietzsche proposes, first, to expose the scientific will to truth as a disguised 'will to nothingness'; and, second, to accelerate the transition to an 'extramoral' period in which the will to truth shall be pressed into service, or so he presumes, alongside a complementary will to untruth.[6] As he will make progressively clearer to the readers of *BGE*, humanity can no longer afford to invest its faith, blindly, in the necessity and the superlative value of truth. The time has come to determine and prescribe the precise balance of truth and untruth that will secure the preservation of humanity and promote its ongoing enhancement. And although the eventual determination of this balance will fall to the 'philosophers of the future', the preparations for their arrival must begin immediately.

The will to truth and the prejudices of philosophers

Having turned the tables on the will to truth (BGE 1), Nietzsche proceeds to survey the various 'prejudices' that philosophers are only now in a position to recognise (and examine) as such (BGE 2–12). For the most part, we might assume that the prejudices exposed in these sections are shared by Nietzsche's best readers, who, we know, are stranded somewhere between the moral-religious worldview, which they have vowed to renounce, and the scientific worldview, to which they have pledged their (as-yet-uninformed) allegiance. Inasmuch as Nietzsche restricts his focus in *BGE* to these select readers, the prejudices he exposes in Part One are indicative of the moral and religious residues that prevent would-be adherents of the scientific worldview from weaning themselves from the moral-religious worldview.

Nietzsche's introduction-*cum*-interrogation of the will to truth communicates several important points about his aims in *BGE*.

---

[6] I am indebted here to Havas 1995: 164–73; and to Clark and Dudrick 2012: 37–48.

First of all, his readers should form no expectation of escaping the gravitational pull of the will to truth. Unlike the various 'prejudices' surveyed in Part One, all (or some) of which eventually might be dislodged, the will to truth will remain the motivating impulse behind any contributions Nietzsche and his readers will make to the production of a philosophy of the future. Indeed, although 'it is nothing more than a moral prejudice that truth is worth more than appearance' (BGE 34), the will that sustains this prejudice – namely, the will to truth – also sustains the inquiries of those, including Nietzsche and his 'we', who are keen to establish the genuine value of truth (GS 344; GM III: 24). Having shed the 'masks' associated with Platonism and Christianity, the will to truth now animates the project of modern science, promising meaning to all those – including Nietzsche and his readers – who place their faith in the redemptive power of truth (GS 344; GM III: 24). As such, the will to truth is in fact responsible for what is most distinctive about Nietzsche and his 'we'. Whatever they ultimately might attempt and accomplish, they will remain duty-bound agents of the will to truth, even as they perform the 'task' reserved just for them (BGE 230).

Second, the will to truth is not itself a prejudice, but an impulse to satisfy the basic need on the part of human beings for a meaningful existence. As such, the activity of the will to truth lends vitality, force and meaning to the prejudices one holds, permitting and even requiring one to form and hold these pre-judgements prior to (and independent of) reflection and confirmation. The will to truth thus authorises and renders meaningful the worldviews in which these prejudices are embedded. Indeed, Nietzsche's best readers find themselves stranded between the moral-religious worldview and the scientific worldview simply because both worldviews currently offer credible (if limited) accommodations of the will to truth. That his best readers tend to toggle back and forth between these worldviews, appealing now to one and later to the other, might be disorienting (or embarrassing) for them, but it is consistent with the historical setting – that is, the 'turning point of history' (BGE 262) – in which they find themselves.

Third, if philosophers are motivated by prejudices, then it must be the case that there is something un- or anti-philosophical about all philosophers (and philosophies) to date. One of the most influential insights advanced in *BGE* derives from Nietzsche's insistence that 'every great philosophy' so far has been 'the personal confession of its author and a kind of involuntary and unnoticed *mémoires* [or memoir]' (BGE 6). As this passage suggests, in fact, he sees considerable value in the project of divining the hidden motives and commitments these 'memoirs' harbour (cf. GS 348). Of particular interest to his readers is the opportunity to render manifest those involuntary prejudices that have prevented them from embracing more resolutely the scientific worldview. Indeed, the time has come for them to redirect their philosophical reflection towards the very enterprise of philosophy itself, made emblematic, Nietzsche believes, by its reliance on an unacknowledged – and, so, unquestioned – faith in the necessity of truth.

Untruth as a condition of life

While surveying the prejudices of philosophers, Nietzsche also previews his recommendation for a modified (= healthier) expression of the will to truth. In the wake of the collapse of dogmatism, it now might be possible, and perhaps for the first time, to consider the value of *untruth* as a complementary condition of life:

> The falseness of a judgment is for us not yet an objection to a judgment; perhaps our new language sounds strangest in this respect. The question is how far it is life-promoting, life-preserving, species-preserving, perhaps even species-cultivating. . . (BGE 4)

After initially floating the 'supposition' that 'truth is a woman' (BGE P), Nietzsche here clarifies his remit to the readers of *BGE*. In addition to adopting a daringly experimental approach to the pursuit of truth, they will need to cultivate an appreciation of those *un*truths that are proven to be conducive to the preservation and/or elevation of humanity.

As this passage indicates, Nietzsche is generally concerned in *BGE* to prepare his readers to anticipate a future in which goals such as 'species-preservation' and 'species-cultivation' are fully entrusted to human stewardship. So as to contribute to the future he envisions, he recommends that his best readers learn to recognise 'untruth as a condition of life', viz., as complementary to (or coeval with) truth itself, even if doing so 'means offering resistance in a dangerous way to the accustomed value-emotions' (BGE 4). As he hastens to add, no doubt baiting the hook for his curious readers, 'a philosophy that dares this already places itself, solely by those means, beyond good and evil' (BGE 4).

Here we receive an initial characterisation of the affective-somatic transformation that Nietzsche aims to induce in his best readers. He will guide them not only towards a cognitive breakthrough, on the strength of which they will come to view and understand the world differently, but also to a conative upgrade, such that they will experience very differently the world they have rediscovered. Their matriculation through his finishing school will thus prepare them, first, to 'resist' the 'value-emotions' to which they have become 'accustomed'; and second, to do so to a degree, or with an intensity, that lands them in an as-yet-unspecified peril. Although he does not say so in this section, he also expects his best readers to acquire (and become increasingly accustomed to) *positive* 'value-emotions' with respect to untruth, precisely so that they will no longer resort (or assent) to prejudiced or reflexive denigrations of its value. In any event, the suggestion here is that the affective-somatic transformation he recommends to his best readers is meant to produce in them 'value-emotions' that are consistent – and dangerously so – with an experimental embrace of 'untruth as a condition of life'.

Introducing the will to power

Having exposed the tradition of German Idealism as a 'comical' (and insufficiently scientific) dead end (BGE 11),[7] Nietzsche expands his survey to account for some of the 'prejudices' shared in common by philosophers and natural scientists (BGE 12). In particular, he pivots from his critique of 'materialistic atomism' to

---

[7] See Conway 2020: 250–4.

a consideration of alternative 'soul-hypotheses', which he touts as more obviously consistent with the spirit and findings of modern science. As we shall see, his wish to consider (and perhaps retain) the soul-hypothesis in some revised form places him at odds with (what he identifies as) the nihilistic trend in 'modern philosophy' (BGE 54–5)

This pivot leads in turn to his abrupt introduction and subsequent elaboration of the hypothesis of *will to power* (13–23), which he recommends as an elegantly simple, if jarring, corrective to several of the prejudices surveyed thus far. In rapid succession, he demonstrates just how disruptively beneficial this hypothesis might prove to be for philosophers who have been led astray by ill-framed questions and dilemmas pertaining to idealism (BGE 15), immediate certainties (BGE 16), agency (BGE 17), free will (BGE 18–19), the origin of ideas (BGE 20), the *causa sui* (BGE 21) and the conformity of nature to law (BGE 22).

First elaborated in Part II of *Thus Spoke Zarathustra*, the hypothesis of *will to power* asserts that every living being both shares in and articulates a basic will (or impulse) to assert its power by expending its native stores of strength. While recounting his efforts to unlock the mysteries of life, Zarathustra summarises as follows the fruits of his investigation: 'Where I found the living, there I found will to power; and even in the will of those who serve I found the will to be master' (Z II: 12). As if to reward him for his persistent (if invasive) attentiveness, no less an authority than Life itself granted him an audience:

> And Life itself confided this secret to me: 'Behold', it said, I am *that which always must overcome itself.* Indeed, you call it a will to procreate or a drive to an end, to something higher, farther, more manifold: but all this is one, and one secret. (Z II: 12)[8]

As the personified figure of Life proceeds to clarify, it is this emphasis on the non-negotiable *necessity* of self-overcoming that

---

[8] The first reference to will to power in *Zarathustra* appears in Z I: 15. This reference is not explained until Z II: 12.

warrants the hypothesis of will to power. While it is true that sick or distressed organisms will seek to conserve their strength and preserve their diminished vitality – Nietzsche offers a very personal example in *Ecce Homo* – healthy organisms instinctively strive to amass and discharge their strength, even if doing so eventually places them at mortal risk. Indeed, if Nietzsche's readers wish to take seriously the hypothesis of will to power, they will need to begin by acquainting themselves with examples of healthy (or healthier) forms of life, wherein the will to power naturally and amorally trumps the will to self-preservation. As we shall see, the opportunity to do precisely this will arise in Part Five, where Nietzsche bids them to compile a comprehensive 'typology of morals' (BGE 186).

As the personified figure of Life proceeds to explain, the law of the necessity of self-overcoming admits of no exceptions.[9] Even the greatest, noblest and most exotic of life forms eventually will perish, possibly owing to their increasingly risky expenditures of accumulated strength. And just in case Zarathustra was angling for an exemption from this law, the personified figure of Life makes it very clear where he, like every other living creature, stands:

> Whatever I create and however much I love it – soon I must oppose it and my love; thus my will wills it. And you too, lover of knowledge, are only a path and a footprint of my will; verily, my will to power walks also on the heels of your will to truth. (Z II: 12)

Indeed, a central feature of the 'extramoral' period that Nietzsche envisions is its conjectured capacity to celebrate – and, so, justify – human existence on the dynamic model of life represented here by Zarathustra. That life *always* overcomes its transient incarnations, choosing no favourites and granting no exemptions, will be treated in the 'extramoral' period to come not as an objection to the precarious, worldly life of mortal beings, but as an additional charm and seduction.

---

[9] Nietzsche refers to the necessity of self-overcoming as a 'law' in GM III: 27.

In *BGE*, Nietzsche introduces the hypothesis of will to power in the context of his attempt, following Zarathustra, to characterise the basic drive and defining character of life itself. In doing so, he aims to distinguish his approach from those among his rivals, most notably, the (social) Darwinists, who insist that living beings invariably strive to preserve themselves:

> The physiologists should stop and think before putting down the drive for self-preservation as the cardinal drive of an organic being. Anything that lives wants above all to *discharge* its strength – life itself is will to power – : self-preservation is only one of the indirect and most frequent *consequences* of this. (BGE 13; cf. BGE 259, GS 349, GM II: 12)

Three elements of this account warrant our notice. Like Zarathustra, first of all, Nietzsche presents his hypothesis of will to power as demonstrably superior to a rival theorisation of the basic processes of life (cf. GM II: 12). In doing so, he aims to account not only for those distressed and decadent life forms from which his rivals hastily generalise (GS 349), but also for those superlative (but relatively rare) life forms that risk themselves in order to expand their dominion and expend their accumulated stores of strength.

Second, Nietzsche situates his hypothesis of will to power in the emerging depth psychological framework that informs his post-Zarathustran writings (and *BGE* in particular).[10] This framework is intended, in part, to accommodate his claim that an organism discharges its strength, aiming thereby to 'reach its maximum feeling of power' (GM III: 7), by availing itself of an optimised network of unconscious drives and instincts.[11] Third,

---

[10] For detailed reconstructions of Nietzsche's depth psychology, see Parkes 1994: chs 8 and 9. See also Katsafanas 2016: ch. 4; Leiter 2019: 67–78; and Alfano 2019: 255–83.

[11] Clark maintains that this restricted, psychological interpretation of the will to power, as what she calls 'a second-order drive that [Nietzsche] recognizes is dependent for its existence on other drives', is all that he may 'claim knowledge of' (1990: 227). The extensions and applications of this account, especially into the realms of metaphysics and cosmology, may be more famous and influential, but they amount to unwarranted 'generalizations' of his basic psychological thesis (1990: 227).

the will to power is presented here (and elsewhere) as *basic* to life itself, that is, as the very '*essence*' of what lives' (BGE 259; cf. GM II: 12). All other expressions of drive or will, including the adaptive drive for self-preservation, are derivative of the will to power. Nietzsche's hypothesis of the will to power is thus intended to serve as the cornerstone (or foundational principle) of the 'proper physio-psychology' he envisions, which he describes as the '*doctrine of the development of the will to power*' (BGE 23).[12]

As we shall see, the hypothesis of will to power is especially useful in accounting for the uniquely uplifting influence of those exemplary human beings whose labours of self-overcoming motivate an immanent (or 'this-worldly') justification of our mortal existence. Whereas an appeal to self-preservation might adequately account for the behaviour of most human beings, most of the time, especially under normalised conditions of 'distress', only the hypothesis of will to power (or something like it) can explain the risky, norm-busting behaviour of those 'higher' human beings who cannot help but 'squander' themselves as they endeavour to remake the world in their image (TI 'Forays' 44). Nietzsche thus promotes his hypothesis of will to power not only on the strength of its superior explanatory power within the emerging scientific worldview, but also as a hedge against the alarming tendency in science – attributed later in *BGE* to the 'democratic movement' in Europe – to reduce humanity to its lowest common denominator.

We would be remiss, finally, if we did not take note of the rhetorical and dramatic elements of Nietzsche's presentation of his hypothesis of will to power.[13] For the most part, as we have seen, he is content to coax his readers along the path he has blazed for them. Deploying tactical bursts of flattery, presumptive intimacy, inflated hopes and unearned optimism, he gently steers them towards the insights he wishes to impart. On other occasions, however, he is more directly didactic and seemingly unconcerned with the collateral damage he is likely to cause. We find one such

---

[12] For extended treatments of Nietzsche's teaching of will to power, see Clark 1990: ch. 7; Richardson 1996: 16–52; Young 2010: 414–16; Clark and Dudrick 2012: part 2; Emden 2014: 167–83; Katsafanas 2016: 247–56; and Leiter 2019: 50–62.

[13] See Clark 1990: 212–27; Young 2010: 542–8; and Clark and Dudrick 2012: 229–43.

occasion in Part One of *BGE*, where he introduces his unsuspecting readers to his hypothesis of will to power. No longer content simply to nudge his readers in the preferred direction, he bullies them with an extramoral hypothesis which, he implies, they already should have formulated or sampled for themselves. Indeed, if they really are as anti-morality and pro-science as they claim, they should be prepared to entertain, if not embrace outright, the chillingly spare and economical hypothesis of will to power. In this respect, or so we may conclude, his introduction of the hypothesis of will to power is valuable in large part for the sobering jolt it produces in his best readers.[14]

Psychology: the once and future ruler of the sciences

The corrective provided by the daring hypothesis of will to power is especially needful in the domain of psychology, which, Nietzsche laments, 'has gotten stuck in moral prejudices and fears . . . [and] has not dared to enter the depths' (BGE 23).[15] The natural sciences, he thus implies, eventually will take care of themselves, owing to the fearless leadership of figures such as Copernicus and Boscovich (BGE 12), while the social (or human) sciences will require special attention.

Here he asserts that 'psychology [may] again be recognized as the ruler of the sciences, for whose service and preparation the remaining sciences exist' (BGE 23), but *only* if it is purged of the unscientific prejudices and folk superstitions that have prevented it thus far from taking up (something like) the hypothesis of will to power. It bears noting here that Nietzsche considered himself a psychologist with few peers (EH 'Books' 5–6), owing in large part to his daring descents into the aforementioned 'depths' of the soul. Apparently fancying himself the equal of Copernicus and Boscovich, he reserves for himself a similar position of fearless

---

[14] See Young 2010: pp. 414–15.
[15] An example of the retardant effects of morality on the progress of the science of psychology is found in BGE 47, where Nietzsche offers his heterodox explanation of the saintly type.

leadership in the science of psychology and in the human sciences more generally.[16]

In accounting for the current, stalled state of psychological research, Nietzsche alludes once again to the need for his best readers to undergo (and promote in others) an affective-somatic transformation. Attributing the persistent appeal of the discredited moral-religious worldview to the familiarity of its enabling prejudices, he is concerned here not with what contemporary psychologists do and do not yet know, but with what they do and do not yet *feel*. 'A real physio-psychology', he explains, 'has "the heart" against it' (BGE 23).[17] While revealing some of the likely 'unconscious obstacles in the heart of the [psychological] researcher', he identifies three formulations that a 'real physio-psychology' would need to accommodate:

1 A 'doctrine of the reciprocal dependence of the "good" and the "bad" drives';
2 A 'doctrine of the derivation of all good drives from bad ones'; and, finally,
3 A recognition of 'the affects [of] hatred, envy, greed, and [the] lust to rule *as conditions of life*, as [affects] whose presence is fundamental and absolutely essential to the general economy of life' (BGE 23, emphasis added).

As these formulations collectively suggest, any progress towards a properly scientific determination of the conditions under which human life might flourish will depend on Nietzsche's success in promulgating the hypothesis of will to power. Previewing the likely outcome of the investigation he has in mind, he cautions his readers that they might eventually come to experience a kind of 'seasickness', which, he advises, all who can do so should avoid (BGE 23). The guiding insight here, on which he will expand in subsequent parts of *BGE*, is that those whom he recruits into

---

[16] Clark and Dudrick suggest that Nietzsche understands psychology as an 'unnatural' science, inasmuch as 'the object of psychological investigation, the human soul' is neither a 'naturalistic entity' nor a 'metaphysical one' (2012: 139).

[17] See Lampert 2001: 54–60; and Burnham 2007: 43–4.

the circle of his 'we' *cannot* exempt themselves from the dizzying, dangerous voyage that lies ahead, precisely because their will to truth, properly aimed and calibrated, will enjoin them to accept his invitation. As he does throughout *BGE*, Nietzsche thus urges his best readers to persist in the distress and disorientation from which their contemporaries tend to seek relief. Only in this way will they acquire and become accustomed to the 'value-emotions' associated with an acceptance of 'untruth as a condition of life' (BGE 4).

He thus closes this section, and Part One itself, by exhorting his best readers to join him on the perilous adventure that awaits them: '[W]e're sailing straight over and *away* from morality, we're smashing, maybe we're crushing our own remnant of morality by daring to travel there – but what do *we* matter!' (BGE 23). As this passage makes clear, the 'we' Nietzsche plans to assemble in *BGE* will find its meaning, and its optimal configuration, not in a reactive effort to secure the conditions of its self-preservation, but in the surge of freedom and agency that attends the expression of their native will to power. As expected, moreover, the adventure in question is entirely appropriate to their non-negotiable status as agents of the will to truth. Although they seek to obtain 'dangerous knowledge', they do so with respect to the discovery and dissemination of truths (e.g., of human nature) that will call into question (and thereby imperil) their accustomed way of life.

This is why his alluring image of his best readers – as devil-may-care, danger-loving voyagers – suddenly dissolves into an image of those daring psychologists who, as described earlier, are willing to 'resist' what they find in their 'hearts' as they plumb the depths of the soul and map its substructure of unconscious drives and instincts (BGE 23). In other words, the heroic voyage to which he calls his best readers is in fact an *inward* voyage, over the course of which they will be encouraged to regard their supposedly 'good' and 'bad' drives from a novel – and, it must be said, *amoral* – perspective (BGE 23). The development of a 'real physio-psychology', he warns, is bound to encounter 'unconscious obstacles in the heart of the researcher' (BGE 23), which are likely to include the as-yet-unacknowledged moral prejudices that have stranded his best readers midway between the moral-religious worldview they eschew and the scientific worldview they claim to prefer.

The closing image of Part One, wherein his best readers are invited to see themselves as latter-day Argonauts, is meant not only to flatter these would-be adventurers, but also to prepare them to play a lesser role in the production of a philosophy of the future. Rather than participate in the conjectured excursion beyond good and evil, much less lead this effort, Nietzsche's best readers are invited to 'smash' and perhaps 'crush . . . [their] own remnant of morality' (BGE 23). And although his readers might understand their smash-and-crush mission as the first of several (or perhaps many) to be assigned to them, this is not what he says. As we shall see, in fact, he envisions this mission as one that is likely to consume, whether literally or figuratively, the 'we' he is determined to recruit. The reason for this, as he makes clear in subsequent parts of *BGE*, is that an assault on 'our own remnant of morality' eventually must involve or become a *self-directed* assault. The morality his best readers are urged to 'smash' and 'crush' is not only constitutive of their identity – and, therefore, essential to the optimal experience of freedom and agency that is available to them – but also the source of the authority he urges them to seize and wield.

Nietzsche's closing exhortation is as ominous as it is triumphant. The morality he and his best readers are invited to destroy belongs neither to their distant past, for example, as a vestige or souvenir, nor to some unrelated others whose future is of little or no concern, but to *them*, even as they labour, even gleefully, to discredit its diminished claims to cultural authority. As this exhortation confirms (and in fact celebrates), the diseased limb they have vowed to amputate is in fact the very branch on which they are perched. What will happen to them in the aftermath, as they tumble to earth or through the void, is treated here as both unknown and irrelevant. No longer concerned for their safety or the preservation of the *status quo*, they will destroy the very morality that shapes their existence, and they will do so with no assurances of how (or if) they will fare when they accomplish their mission.

This is our first substantial hint of the darker motives that inform Nietzsche's aims in *BGE*. As we shall see more clearly in our consideration of Part Nine, he intends to initiate his best readers – without their knowledge or prior consent – into a Dionysian discipleship, whose members take very seriously the notion that what *really* matters is their 'task', *even if* their performance of this 'task' places them at mortal risk, which, according to Nietzsche, it eventually will do. Indeed, here we receive an initial confirmation that the affective-somatic transformation he offers to induce in his best readers is *meant* to suspend in them their familiar instincts for moderation, risk-aversion and self-preservation. That Nietzsche expects his best readers to become zealots (and perhaps even fanatics) in their pursuit of truth will become a matter of increasing concern as we proceed.

Review

In his survey of 'the prejudices of philosophers', Nietzsche accomplishes three important objectives. First, he accounts for the persistent failure thus far of those hapless dogmatists who have refused to entertain the possibility that 'truth is a woman'. As it turns out, we learn, this failure is by no means random or accidental, for the philosophers in question have been insulated by their training and discipline from a close (and potentially lethal) encounter with the will to truth. Second, he exposes several of the most tenacious prejudices that have stranded free-spirited philosophers, including his best readers, between the moral-religious worldview they have renounced and the scientific worldview they admire. Third, he effectively refines and narrows the target readership for *BGE*, reserving membership in his 'we' for those readers who will venture beyond the comfort zone in which they are permitted to hold their current, misaligned positions.

With respect to all three objectives, the hypothesis of will to power is meant to play a selective role. On the one hand, the hypothesis of will to power is emblematic of a will and commitment to purge one's scholarly practices of all remaining vestiges of the moral-religious worldview, including those prejudices that most recently have been revealed as such. On the other hand, those readers who regard this hypothesis as either too daring or excessively scientific—that is, as insufficiently respectful of the theories and models of human nature that have most recently held sway—might be moved to reconsider the intensity of their enthusiasm for the emerging scientific worldview. Readers such as these will continue, more-or-less happily, to reconcile some scientific advances with their moral-religious commitments, making the best of their occasionally awkward (and ultimately untenable) allegiance to competing worldviews.

Nietzsche concludes Part One on a high note, inviting his best readers to envision themselves as danger-loving heroes and adventurers. At this juncture in the text of *BGE*, the appeal of his conclusion is largely rhetorical. His best readers have not yet proven themselves to be heroic, and he has not yet revealed the full provenance – much less the full cost – of the discipleship in which he has enrolled them. In subsequent parts of *BGE*, he will continue to guide his best readers towards a clearer and more comprehensive understanding of their historical situation, precisely so that they might enjoy the optimal experience of freedom and power that is available to them. For now, he is content to raise their spirits through flattery and other forms of rhetorical amplification, all the while drawing them into the ever more select and intimate circle of his 'we'.

3
Part Two: The Free Spirit

Preview

In Part Two of *BGE*, Nietzsche revisits one of the most influential and beloved teachings of his so-called 'middle' period: the *free spirit*. Whereas his earlier elaboration of this teaching was appropriate to his needs and aspirations as a 'convalescent', especially as he endeavoured to rebound from a near-death experience and a debilitating existential crisis (HH I, P2), his programme of education and training in *BGE* calls for an updated version of this teaching. Not surprisingly, the revised profile he delivers of the free spirit trades on a significant shift in emphasis, which allows him to present his target readership with a more fully contextualised (and mission-specific) version of his earlier teaching.

In *Human, All Too Human*, or so Nietzsche insists, the type of the free spirit was introduced as one '*that has become free*, that has again taken possession of itself again' (EH: hh 1). Not surprisingly, he associates a similar outcome – viz. the achievement of freedom and the attendant experience of self-mastery – with the standard of nobility towards which he steers the readers of *BGE*.[1] In Nietzsche's own case, as he later relates, the freedom of the free spirit was evidenced in his timely recovery from a nearly fatal overdose of modern ideas. Undone and remade by the spiritual afflictions he endured, he finally was free to 'return to [him]*self*' (EH: hh 4). In *Dawn*, he recalls, he was primarily concerned to acquaint

---

[1] See Franco 2011: 44–55; Ansell-Pearson 2018: 29–45; and Abbey 2020: 83–8, 123–8.

his readers (and himself) with the experience of liberation that attends a rigorous, science-inflected investigation of those prejudices that have supported the morality of 'selflessness' (EH: d 2). The 'struggle' he initiated there, directed 'against the morality of unselfing' (EH: d 2), will be taken up and escalated by those among his best readers who join him in the destructive 'task' reserved just for them.

Nietzsche's primary concern in Part Two of *BGE* is to identify more precisely the setting, context and bounds of the freedom to which he and his best readers might realistically aspire.[2] Although he proceeds in *BGE* on the assumption that his best readers have secured a commendable degree of independence and critical distance from the moral-religious worldview, he is determined in Part Two to identify for them the limits of the freedom to which they are now called. In particular, as we shall see, they must *not* confuse themselves with those 'philosophers of the future' whom Nietzsche hails as the freest of the free spirits (BGE 44), for they are bound by the constraints of their historical situation to remain agents of the morality of good and evil *and* of the will to truth.

Notwithstanding the teasing promise suggested by the title of *BGE*, Nietzsche's best readers will not emigrate cleanly beyond the morality of good and evil. To be sure, they might realistically expect to enjoy the *experience* of having done so, but only if they agree to intensify (and weaponise) their residual investments in the morality of good and evil. As we shall see, in fact, a contextualised, period-appropriate version of the free spirit type lies well within their reach, provided that they are willing to affirm the lesser, preparatory role he assigns to them. Alternatively, if they yield to the siren song of modern science, intoxicated by the heady experience of freedom it both promises and delivers, they will eventually be liberated from their pride in humankind and their will for its future.

Complicating this process of contextualisation was the popularity at the time of a cluster of ideals that circulated under cognate

---

[2] According to Lampert, the update in question is required because 'the free minds must advance past their active skepticism to recognition of the possibility of philosophy' (2001: 62).

designations, including the (French) '*libres penseurs*', the (Italian) '*liberi pensatori*' and the (German) '*Freidenker*', all of whom Nietzsche dismisses as nothing more than 'respectable advocates of "modern ideas"' (BGE 44). One notable free thinker was David Strauss (1808–74), 'the first German free spirit' (EH: uo 2), whom Nietzsche savaged in the first of his *Unfashionable Observations* (1873). As Nietzsche explained on that occasion, Strauss peddled a trendy popularisation of modern science in order to celebrate the nineteenth century in Europe as unfailingly and triumphantly progressive, when in fact, according to Nietzsche, Europe (and German culture in particular) had already begun to decline. Behind the mask of the free-thinking progressive, Nietzsche alleged, crouched an opportunistic philistine, who was powerless in any event to deviate from the 'modern ideas' he was so eager to promote.[3]

The case of Strauss is also relevant for its larger and darker implications: Strauss and his fellow free thinkers had become unwitting apologists for a dangerously seductive version of the scientific worldview, which Nietzsche understood to be deeply misanthropic. The 'new faith' Strauss touted was emblematic of the fascination, especially robust among lapsed believers, with the technical promise and explanatory power of modern science. Weary of defending the 'old faith', and newly enamoured of scientific progress, Strauss exemplified the latent nihilism of those late modern free thinkers who, having crowded on to the bandwagon of modern science, would very soon (and very happily) 'sacrifice God for nothingness' (BGE 55).[4]

Convinced that Strauss and his ilk would inadvertently encourage their fellow Europeans to content themselves with the diminished importance and fading dignity of humanity, Nietzsche condemns the free thinkers among his contemporaries as 'incorrigible ninnies

---

[3] For a detailed examination of Nietzsche's case against Strauss, see Church 2019: 35–54.
[4] In the first treatise of *On the Genealogy of Morality*, a 'free spirit' of Straussian ilk is suffered to explain that 'The church repels us, *not* its poison . . . Apart from the church, we too love the poison' (GM I: 9). The 'poison' in question is evidently the 'love' that Nietzsche identified in the previous section as an outgrowth of 'thirst for revenge' that he detects at the core of 'Jewish hatred' (GM I: 8).

and fools of "modern ideas" . . . [who], in their own way, want to "improve" humanity after their image' (EH: uo 2). Impressed by neither the 'image' in question nor the recommended 'improvements' – as if a 'new faith' were preferable simply by virtue of being 'new' or 'modern' – Nietzsche takes decisive steps in *BGE* to distinguish the free spirits among his readers from these better-known free thinkers. He does so, as we shall see, by alerting his readers not only to the limits of their freedom, but also to the opportunities they are uniquely positioned to exploit.

Summary of sections

Part Two of *BGE* comprises twenty numbered sections (24–44). Nietzsche begins by calling his best readers to order (BGE 24–5). After noting (and celebrating) the extent of the folly to which human beings have become accustomed, acknowledging in particular the artful contributions of *science* to the comforting 'simplifications' on which we late moderns rely (BGE 24), Nietzsche sounds a 'serious' note, cautioning his best readers to beware of becoming 'martyrs' to the truth (BGE 25).[5] This admonition is apparently meant to temper the enthusiasm he displayed (and invited) at the close of Part One, where he urged his best readers to suspend any lingering concerns for their future wellbeing as they endeavour to 'crush . . . our own remnant of morality' (BGE 23). As he now undertakes to explain, the dangerous mission he described at the close of Part One has nothing to do with the 'martyrdom' of those who have given their lives, supposedly, for the sake of truth.

The point Nietzsche wishes to convey here is subtle: while the pursuit of truth is most productively conducted by those who display no overriding concern for themselves and their wellbeing, the example set by the 'martyrs' among philosophers is likely to mislead. In an effort to prevent his readers from acting on a

---

[5] A similar transition from cheerfulness to seriousness occurs in Part Eight, where Nietzsche breaks off his 'cheerful Germanifications' to undertake a serious consideration of the 'Jewish problem' in Europe, which he promptly designates as the 'European problem' (BGE 251).

potentially unfortunate misunderstanding of his brief to them, Nietzsche exposes the 'martyrs' among philosophers (and other, kindred 'degenerates') as 'agitators' and 'actors',[6] who, no longer able to smile or laugh at the seriousness of their attachments to their pet truths, resolve to stage the performance, whether it be a 'satyr play' or an 'epilogue farce', at the centre of which they make their *faux* heroic stand (BGE 25). Despite the sympathetic admiration the martyrs in question typically elicit, they deserve to be remembered neither as noble nor as brave. Indeed, the staged spectacles of their martyrdom in fact confirm their cowardice and/or exhaustion. These martyrs retreat, surrender or die *not* to 'sacrifice [themselves] for the truth' (BGE 25), much less to assert their independence, but to bring a contrived end to their increasingly intolerable pursuits of the truth.

The example Nietzsche has in mind here is likely that of the deathbound Socrates, who is widely praised for his unflinching commitment to the pursuit of truth. As is his wont, Nietzsche offers a very different account. That the philosopher should not fear death, as Socrates famously insisted,[7] might be an estimable position to consider and perhaps assert, but it was not made true by the performance in which Socrates serenely anticipated his own death. That the soul is immortal, as Socrates asserted (but failed to establish) in the *Phaedo*,[8] is similarly worthy of philosophical consideration, but it was not made true by the confidence with which Socrates impatiently awaited his hoped-for conversations in the afterlife with the likes of Odysseus and Sisyphus.[9] Indeed, as Nietzsche elsewhere insists in his consideration of another martyr of note,

> Martyrs *harm* the truth . . . Even today, it only takes the crudeness of a persecution to give the most indifferent sectarianism an *honourable* name. – What? Does the value

---

[6] The word here is *Schauspieler*, which is almost always used by Nietzsche as a term of disapproval and/or contempt. See, for example, GS 361.
[7] Plato, *Phaedo*, 61a–e; 2002: 98–9.
[8] Plato, *Phaedo*, 114d–115a; 2002: 150–1.
[9] Plato, *Apology*, 41c; 2002: 44.

of something change when someone gives up their life to it? – (A 53)[10]

So it is, Nietzsche claims, that those who invoke the rectitude and freedom of the martyr actually hinder the pursuit of truth, for they mislead those whose attention the performance in question has been designed to claim.

As the example of Socrates is meant to confirm, philosophical martyrs are *not* the free spirits whom Nietzsche bids his readers to emulate and admire. In fact, he insists, martyrs tend to risk very little, despite their theatrical displays to the contrary. While it may be the case that Socrates did not fear death, which *might* have been considered a praiseworthy achievement on his part, it is evident to Nietzsche that Socrates *wanted* to die and actively lobbied for the verdict and sentence he eventually received (TI 'Socrates' 12). Generalising from his interpretation of the case of Socrates, we might conclude on Nietzsche's behalf that philosophical martyrs only ever *appear* to make the ultimate sacrifice. Exhausted by life and dispirited by their pursuits of truth, philosophical martyrs are eager to be done and grateful for the distraction provided by the spectacle unfolding around them. The real risk-takers are those free spirits who, 'practiced in maintaining [themselves] on insubstantial ropes and possibilities and dancing even near abysses' (GS 347), continue to track the truth without recognition or reward, even (or especially) when the truth hits close to home.

Having warned his readers not to become martyrs to the truth, Nietzsche proceeds to introduce his updated profile of the free spirit type (26–31). In order to accommodate themselves to the contextualised freedom he recommends, and thereby avoid the fate of the philosophical martyrs, his readers must learn when to assert themselves as exemplars of their age and when to withdraw into solitude; when to trust their instincts and when to doubt the 'purity' of their motives; when to advance and when to retreat;

---

[10] According to Nietzsche, '[Jesus] died for *his* guilt – there are no grounds at all for saying, however often it's been claimed, that he died for the guilt of others' (A 27). In other words, Jesus *became* a martyr only under the influence of Paul, the Apostle to the Gentiles. See Bishop 2022: ch. 6.

and so on. In short, they must learn to remain serious in their pursuit of truth, even as they probe the (supposedly solemn) warrant for the truths they (and others) currently espouse.

As we shall see, these sections of Part Two are building up to the potentially sobering realisation that the free spirits whom he invites his best readers to become are simultaneously the *subjects* – and, so, free – and the *objects* – and, so, unfree – of their history. And although they eventually might become as 'independent' as their historical setting will allow, the 'independence' they 'attempt' to enact will invariably be contextualised – and, so, limited – by their ongoing investments in the will to truth and the morality of good and evil (BGE 29). Much like the 'last idealists' whom Nietzsche is similarly keen to enlighten in *On the Genealogy of Morality*, the readers whom *BGE* is meant to educate 'are not *free* spirits by a long shot: *for they still believe in truth*' (GM III: 24).

The self-overcoming of morality

These lessons culminate in the suggestion, elaborated in sections 32–3, that Nietzsche's readers should find themselves 'standing today on the threshold' of a new, '*extramoral*' period in human history, in which it might be resolved that 'the decisive value of an action is exemplified precisely by what is *unintentional* in it' (BGE 32). Unlike the '*premoral* period', in which value was assigned only to the *consequences* of an action, and the current '*moral*' period, in which the value of an action is assigned to the *intention* in which the action is supposed to have originated, the coming '*extramoral*' period will locate the value of an action in the configuration of unconscious drives and impulses in which the action in question *truly* originated. We received an instructive example of the extramoral approach he has in mind when he reduced the question of '*who* [*the philosopher*] *is*' to the (more basic) question of 'the order of rank the innermost drives of his nature stand in relation to each other' (BGE 6).

The terms and tone of Nietzsche's introduction of the coming extramoral period bear noting. Having described the dawning of the moral period as the 'first attempt at self-knowledge' (BGE 32), he wishes to persuade his best readers that the dawning of the extramoral period will involve a second, equally momentous step in the same direction. Having plumbed the depths of the human psyche for the motives, intentions, maxims and plans that account for the origins of our actions – or so we formerly thought! – humanity is now poised on the brink of an investigation of the unconscious drives and impulses to which our motives, intentions, maxims and plans bear witness. In its uniquely extramoral incarnation, that is, the pursuit of self-knowledge will involve a directed effort to map the unconscious substructure of agency and personal identity. Accordingly, the newly aware self will be understood to incorporate (and draw productively upon) those darker and 'devilish' elements that, even now, are treated as extraneous (and even injurious) to selfhood.

As Nietzsche explains later in *BGE*, an important first step across the aforementioned threshold will take place when humanity acknowledges that 'the whole of morality is an intrepid, long forgery that enables us to take some pleasure at the sight of the soul' (BGE 291). Having relied on this 'forgery' to direct our gaze inward, we have managed under the impress of morality to accustom ourselves to the otherwise intolerable 'sight' of the multiplex human soul. By inventing the phantasms (e.g., the 'good conscience') and homunculi (e.g., the 'will') that moralists claim to have discovered, we have steadied our inward gaze and baby-stepped towards the establishment of a properly scientific study of psychology. Having exhausted the value of this exquisite 'forgery', we are now in a position to discard it and press forward towards a fully naturalised account and understanding of the 'eternal basic text [of] *homo natura*' (BGE 230). Despite their dawning recognition of 'untruth' as a bona fide 'condition of life' (BGE 4), Nietzsche and his 'we' will gratefully aim to retire the formerly useful 'forgery' that is morality.

Although Nietzsche does not explicitly invoke the hypothesis of will to power in this section, his best readers will understand (or suspect) that the 'extramoral' period to come will be governed without distraction by the scientific worldview, wherein the hypothesis of will to power (or something like it) will be granted pride of place among explanatory principles. Moreover, as we shall see, he is building towards one of his most extreme statements of this hypothesis (BGE 36), which, if confirmed, is likely to set a forbidding tone for the 'extramoral' period as a whole. Before doing so, however, he takes care to amplify the intimacy of the 'we' that he endeavours to consecrate. Addressing his readers for the first time with an honorific title that will become integral to his efforts to further their education and training, he (presumptively) identifies his 'we' as a band of 'immoralists' (BGE 32). As we shall see, he urges his readers to embrace this title as a *nom de guerre*, which they may exploit to their advantage as they perform the 'task' assigned to them (BGE 226). As it turns out, moreover, their status as 'immoralists' accurately reflects their occupation of what Nietzsche identifies as a 'turning point' in human history (BGE 262). Although he and they belong to the aforementioned 'moral' period, their activity therein might be creatively repurposed so as to accelerate the transition to the envisioned 'extramoral' period. If his best readers accept his invitation to join him as 'immoralists', the transition in question will be officially underway. If their experience reflects Nietzsche's own, finally, their emergence as 'immoralists' will distinguish them decisively from those free thinkers whom he has exposed as nihilists-in-waiting (EH: uo 2).

Convinced that the narrow focus on intentions is itself but a 'prejudice', viz., a cluster of symptoms requiring further interpretation (BGE 32), Nietzsche bids his fellow 'immoralists' to join him in his search for the unconscious (= pre-intentional) springs and levers of human behaviour. They will exhaust the authority of morality, he thus suggests, by exposing its heretofore unacknowledged – and patently immoral – dependence on (and cover for) drives and impulses that in no way qualify as intentional. He thus invites his fellow 'immoralists' to contribute to the 'overcoming [*Überwindung*] of morality' (BGE 32), which he describes as 'the long, secretive work that was reserved for the most subtle and honest, and also the most malicious consciences of today' (BGE 32).[11] As we shall see, moreover, his immediate qualification

---

[11] Nietzsche's reference here to the 'most honest' among his readers, and to their complementary 'malice', anticipates his discussion of 'honesty' [*Redlichkeit*] in Part Seven.

of the endeavour to which he invites them – viz. 'in a certain sense even the self-overcoming [*Selbstüberwindung*] of morality' (BGE 32) – intimates that they will not simply participate in this event, but *host* it as well (BGE 230).[12] In other words, the moral period of human history will conclude, along with the morality it has sponsored, in and through their 'immoral' efforts.[13]

What's in it for them? As Nietzsche's shameless recourse to flattery confirms, his best readers will know themselves to belong, as they no doubt have suspected (or fantasised), to an underground vanguard of misfit heroes, who have been entrusted with securing the future of European civilisation (and of humanity more generally). More to the point: if they join him in mapping the unconscious substructure on which the morality of good and evil trades, they will acquire the self-knowledge he has prescribed to them, and they will stand to gain access to the optimal experience of freedom and power that is available to them. As such, they might yet realise their aspiration to become the free spirits to whom Part Two of *BGE* is devoted. With respect to the audacity and world-historical import of this endeavour, he and his best readers actually might come to resemble the Argonauts and other mythic heroes to whom Nietzsche occasionally compares them. Indeed, his flattery betrays a germ of truth about his best readers: they might yet become heroic in the limited context of the task reserved for them, but only if they complete the programme of education and training found in the pages of *BGE*.

While the specific character of their contributions to the 'self-overcoming of morality' remains as yet undisclosed, the general historical setting of their participation is rounding into view. Morality will 'overcome' itself when its avowed champions turn its residual cultural authority against its generative source.[14] In making their case, Nietzsche and his 'we' will avail themselves of

---

[12] The self-referential scope of their interrogation of the will to truth is apparently meant to anticipate, and perhaps facilitate, the 'revaluation of all values', which Nietzsche elsewhere describes as 'humanity's act of supreme self-reflection made flesh and genius in me' (EH 'Destiny' 1). See Lemm 2020: 34–5, 53–5.

[13] Here I follow Ridley 1998: 124–6; May 1999: 90–2; and Owen 2007: 126–9.

[14] On the proposed use of morality to unseat itself, see Ridley 1998: 124–6; Janaway 2007: 234–9; Loeb 2010: 234–42; van Tongeren 2014: 155–7; and Conway 2014a: 297–304.

psychological evidence confirming the unconscious substructure of morality, on the strength of which they will advance the transition to the extramoral period in human history. As this sketch of an endgame scenario suggests, the close of the moral period will be dependent on the continued rise of an upstart, valedictory regime of morality – identified by Nietzsche as the disciplinary regime of 'Christian truthfulness' (GM III: 27) – wherein truthfulness is valued above all and modelled on the application of scientific rigour.[15] Indeed, once the truth of morality has been disclosed and circulated, resulting in the collapse of the cultural enterprise of morality, the 'moral' period in human history will end and its successor period, as yet characterised simply as 'extramoral', might commence.

Reintroducing the will to power

As if to soften the blow he is poised to deliver, Nietzsche previews the likely outcome of the 'task' he has in mind for his best readers (BGE 34–9). Echoing his prior suspicions of the supposedly inestimable value of truth (BGE 3–4), he declares that 'it is nothing more than a moral prejudice that truth is worth more than appearance' (BGE 34). In place of the supposedly 'essential opposition of "true" and "false"', he wonders if we might instead 'assume stages of apparentness and brighter and darker shadows and overall tones of appearance' (BGE 34). Taking yet another giant step away from the moral-religious worldview, he asks, 'Why shouldn't the world *that concerns us* – be a fiction?' (BGE 34).

As the sequence of these questions confirms, Nietzsche's aim in this section is to escalate the set of challenges he initially posed to his best readers in Part One of *BGE*. Here as there, the goal of these challenges is to position his best readers to determine just how much freedom (from prejudice) they are honestly prepared to accommodate. As we shall see, this determination will enable Nietzsche to assign them to their optimal role and station within the self-overcoming of morality.

---

[15] For extended discussions of this endgame scenario, see Conway 2008: 142–7; and Conway 2014b: 205–11.

Raising the stakes yet again for those readers who wish to move more aggressively towards the scientific worldview, Nietzsche reintroduces his hypothesis of will to power. He begins by urging his readers to 'suppose[e that] nothing were "given" as real besides our world of desires and passions, that we could go down or up to no other "reality" than simply the reality of our drives' (BGE 36). He then bids his readers to consider if 'this given or something like it is not *sufficient* for understanding even ... the so-called mechanistic (or "material") world' (BGE 36). The 'attempt' or 'experiment' he has in mind here is not only 'permissible', or so he asserts, but also 'demanded on the basis of the conscience of *method*' (BGE 36), which, all things being equal, favours simplicity and elegance in its hypotheses and explanations.

Before we proceed, let us take note of Nietzsche's multiple references in this section to the 'attempt' (or 'experiment') he has described for his readers. As we shall see very soon, he introduces the 'philosophers of the future' as 'tempters' (or 'experimenters') [*Versucher*] (BGE 42), which suggests that they are likely to acknowledge a connection with those among his readers who are willing to hazard the 'attempt' [*Versuch*] in question. At stake for Nietzsche's readers, as we shall see, is nothing less than the freedom of the free spirits, which is the basis on which his readers are likely to identify with the 'new' philosophers for whom they are called to prepare. If the 'attempt' [*Versuch*] in question appeals to Nietzsche's readers, the freedom they might expect to enact will resemble – and perhaps rival? – the freedom of those 'philosophers of the future' whom he soon will introduce. If the 'attempt' [*Versuch*] in question does not appeal to Nietzsche's readers, owing either to the audacity of the experiment or to their lingering investments in the authority of the moral-religious worldview, they might expect to be assigned to a lesser station in the free spirit hierarchy. As we shall see, the distinction Nietzsche draws, between 'free spirits' and 'free, *very* free spirits' (BGE 44), may be meant to suggest that his typical readers are not yet equal to the challenge he has set for them in this second encounter with the hypothesis of will to power.[16]

---

[16] I am indebted here to Strong 2003: 545–6.

PART TWO: THE FREE SPIRIT   67

The tough love continues. As his appeal to 'conscience' confirms, Nietzsche once again recommends the hypothesis of will to power as a standard by which his best readers might measure their determination to renounce the moral-religious worldview. He thus concludes this thought experiment by asking his readers to suppose that 'we were to succeed in explaining our entire life of drives as the taking shape and ramification of a basic form of the will – namely of the will to power, as *my* proposition has it' (BGE 36). (To be sure, any such success would represent a significant down payment on his earlier pledge to 'understand [psychology] as morphology and *doctrine of the development of the will to power*' (BGE 23).) In that event, he concludes, we would be warranted in pronouncing 'the world seen from inside' as '"will to power" and nothing else. – ' (BGE 36).

If we bear in mind that Nietzsche rolls out this thought experiment while delivering his updated profile of the free spirit, we might be justified in assuming that the achievement involved in beholding 'the world seen from inside' would be emblematic of a quality and degree of freedom that his best readers are likely to covet.[17] At the same time, however, the radical character of this thought experiment, which expressly denies its subjects access to any external perspectives on the world, might be meant to apprise his best readers – bluntly, to be sure – of the limits of their enthusiasm for the scientific worldview. If they are not yet prepared to regard the world as '"will to power" and nothing else', which, presumably, would require them to renounce any lingering attachments to religion, morality and even sentimentality, they should not expect to complete the envisioned transition to an 'extramoral' period. Indeed, he may mean for this unsubtle thought experiment to inform them that they will never be entirely free of the prejudices that tether them to the moral-religious worldview.

It is difficult to determine how seriously Nietzsche intended this particular thought experiment.[18] He never returned to it with

---

[17] See Lampert 2001: 86–8; and Burnham 2007: 61–5.
[18] See, for example, the discussions by Clark 1990: 212–20; Clark and Dudrick 2012: 229–43; and Pippin 2019b: 210–13.

anything like the anarchic intensity displayed in this section of *BGE*, which might suggest that it was designed and intended for *these* readers, who, we know, he was generally keen to prod and provoke. Although he occasionally makes reference to the will to power later in *BGE* and in his subsequent writings, it never again figures as prominently as it does here. As several scholars have noted, Nietzsche tends to invoke the hypothesis of will to power in *BGE* as a means of startling his best readers, of commanding their attention and, perhaps, of challenging them to measure themselves against the 'extramoral' standard this hypothesis sets for a 'philosophy of the future'.

His goal in doing so, presumably, is to persuade his best readers to exert themselves more forcefully in their efforts to renounce (or neutralise) their remaining moral prejudices and, thereby, to accelerate their progress towards a cheerful embrace of the scientific worldview. In this respect, the hypothesis of will to power might be received as not only promising and worthwhile in its own right, owing to its explanatory power and razored elegance, but also as more generally emblematic of the extramoral outlook he recommends to the readers of *BGE*. As such, his appeals and references to the will to power might be understood as attempts to call his best readers to order, to remind them of the tenacity of their ongoing (if unwanted) investments in the moral-religious worldview, and to bully them towards the scientific worldview they claim to prefer.

Turning to the future

In apparent recognition of the deflationary effects that are likely to attend his renewed attention to the hypothesis of will to power, Nietzsche attempts to raise the sinking spirits of his best readers by sharing with them a premonition of the future of philosophy (sections 42–4). Claiming to glimpse on the horizon the rise of 'a new species of philosophers', whom he honours with the title of 'tempters' (or 'experimenters') [*Versucher*] (BGE 42),[19] he urges

---

[19] See Lampert 2001: 95–6.

his best readers to secure their place in the lineage from which these new philosophers will emerge. Like their predecessors, these 'new' philosophers will be 'friends of "truth"', but they will *not* be 'dogmatists', for they will have no interest in seeking or possessing a 'truth for everyone' (BGE 43). Confident in the judgements they will render, to which 'no one else easily has a right', these 'philosophers of the future' will evince no desire 'to agree with many people' (BGE 43). As we shall see, in fact, Nietzsche expects these 'new' philosophers to legislate and lead in the spirit of the Dionysus who finally appears unmasked in Part Nine of *BGE*.

As we now know, the free spirits whom Nietzsche addresses in Part Two of *BGE* are not as free as his readers may have thought (or hoped). Involuntarily tethered to the moral-religious worldview, they enact their agency within a context whose contours (and limitations) remain largely unknown to them. Nietzsche thus attempts in this section, with as much delicacy and rhetorical finesse as he can muster, to introduce them to a previously unremarked order of rank *among* the free spirits whom he praises. Although he regards and addresses his best readers as 'free spirits', for example, he also celebrates 'the philosophers of the future' as 'free, *very* free spirits' (BGE 44). And just in case his readers might have misplaced the distinction he has introduced, he proceeds to explain that

> These philosophers of the future . . . will not be merely [*bloss*] free spirits, but something more, higher, greater and fundamentally different that does not want to be misunderstood and mistaken for something else . . . (BGE 44)[20]

Nietzsche thus delivers to his readers a firm (but polite) confirmation of their demotion in rank and status. As if to offer them a measure of consolation, he assures them that they clearly outrank those 'wrongly designated "free spirits"', whom he sneeringly

---

[20] In *On the Genealogy of Morality*, Nietzsche once again distinguishes between two orders or ranks of free spirits, explaining there that his best readers, whom he is gently attempting to expose as belonging among the 'final idealists of knowledge', are 'not free spirits by a long shot: *for they still believe in truth*' (GM III: 24).

identifies as belonging among 'the *levellers*' – namely, those who 'want to strive for . . . the universal, green pasture happiness of the herd, with security, freedom from danger, comfort, and easy living for everyone' (BGE 44).[21]

Concluding Part Two of *BGE* as hopefully as possible, Nietzsche audaciously addresses his best readers as the likely predecessors of the 'new philosophers' he has just described (BGE 44). If he has correctly measured his target audience, this concluding bit of flattery might prevent (some of) his best readers from withdrawing from the programme of education and training in which he has enrolled them. Indeed, his goal at this juncture is to persuade his best readers to see in themselves something of the 'new' philosophers whom he has sketched for their edification. In the event that they are able to do so, their will for the future of humanity should remain intact as they prepare to undertake the 'task' that awaits them.

Review

Having encouraged his best readers to think of themselves as would-be heroes and intrepid adventurers (BGE 23), Nietzsche turns in Part Two of *BGE* to a discussion of the constraints and limitations they will be obliged to negotiate. Persuaded of the sincerity of their esteem for the familiar (= positive) features of the 'free spirit' ideal – for example, liberation, independence, cheerfulness, autonomy, self-determination, iconoclasm, intrepidity, etc. – he is concerned in Part Two to educate them with respect to the setting in which they will aspire to this ideal. His central message here is one of contextualisation: while his best readers are optimally positioned to liberate themselves (to some extent) from the prejudices surveyed in Part One of *BGE*, they are not free of the historical and psychological conditions that circumscribe their agency. In no event, moreover, will they be free to suspend or resign their allegiance to the will to truth, though they might yet learn to mobilise this allegiance, and the

---

[21] While Nietzsche does not name any such 'free thinkers', he almost certainly has in mind David Strauss and his ilk.

truthfulness it compels, to their full advantage. Nor will they be free of the morality of good and evil, which, in their capacity as 'immoralists', they nevertheless might endeavour to retire once and for all.

After apprising his best readers of the limits of their freedom and agency, and after assigning to them a preliminary role in the production of a philosophy of the future, Nietzsche once again concludes his discussion on a high note. His best readers are not (and never will become) the 'free, *very* free spirits' who will install a new ideal of humanity, but they might yet become the progenitors of those 'new' philosophers, viz., the 'philosophers of the future', whose approach he claims to spy on the horizon (BGE 44). Hence his closing pitch to his best readers: if they can bring themselves to affirm the more modest, historically appropriate role he has assigned to them, their efforts in pursuit of their appointed 'task' – the nature of which he will reveal to them in Part Seven of *BGE* – will facilitate (and perhaps accelerate) the arrival of these 'new' philosophers. He thus attempts to rally his best readers by inviting them to contribute to the production of the future they mistakenly thought they had already inherited.

4
Part Three:
The Religious Character

Preview

Having apprised his best readers of the setting and bounds within which they might expect to become (and assert themselves as) 'free spirits', Nietzsche turns in Part Three to a consideration of 'the religious character' of those who, under the auspices of European Christianity, have pursued faith – and been rewarded for doing so – by internalising the imperative to sacrifice (BGE 46). His aim in doing so is to demonstrate to his best readers that what they and their contemporaries understand by religion is in fact the normalised expression of a debilitating 'neurosis'.

The title on which Nietzsche settled for Part Three – *Das religiöse Wesen* – is almost certainly intended to confound.[1] The word translated here as 'character' – *Wesen* – is also (and more commonly) rendered as 'nature' or 'essence', either of which would faithfully convey his intention to determine 'what religion is'. As we know from the opening 'supposition' of Nietzsche's Preface, however, a chief aim of *BGE* is to establish his independence from (and opposition to) those idealists who, like Plato, seek 'essences' and 'natures' beyond the real world of flux and becoming. Inasmuch as 'essence' or 'nature' might be understood to endorse the failed efforts of the dogmatists whom he skewers in

---

[1] In his letter to C. Heymons (at Carl Duncker's Verlag) on 12 April 1886, Nietzsche explained that the envisioned third part [*Abschnitt*] of *BGE* was to be called '*Das religiöse Genie*' [The Religious Genius] rather than '*Das religiöse Wesen*' (*SB* 7: 175).

PART THREE: THE RELIGIOUS CHARACTER   73

his Preface, it is unlikely that he intends his investigation in Part Three to yield a perfect, unchanging, suprasensible 'essence' or 'nature'.[2] As Laurence Lampert explains,

> The meaning of the title of chapter 3, *Das religiöse Wesen*, is thus indicated by the first words of the first section: the religious *essence* is to be sought in the religious *being*, not in the objects of religious longing or religious dread.[3]

Hence the appeal of Adrian Del Caro's canny decision to render *Wesen* as 'character': according to Nietzsche, the defining 'character' of a religion – or, at least, of the religion under consideration in Part Three – is revealed in the 'character' displayed by those 'characters' or types (e.g., the saint) whom it has produced in its image. As we shall see, this is a decisive methodological innovation on Nietzsche's part, for it allows him to bracket or ignore the claims made for European Christianity (or any other religion) by its leading champions and apologists. When he subsequently 'consider[s] overall . . . the *sovereign* religions', of which European Christianity is exemplary, he defends his (negative) evaluation by citing the unimpressive specimens these religions typically produce: 'the sovereign religions belong to the major causes that have kept the type "human being" on a lowly level' (BGE 62).

In addition to confirming Nietzsche's rejection of Platonism and its pursuit of otherworldly Forms, the title of Part Three also announces his aim to reclaim the concept of 'essence' or 'nature' that *Wesen* is understood to suggest. Rather than abandon the search for 'essences' and 'natures', he advises, philosophers must learn to look elsewhere – to history, geography, politics, science *and*, most importantly, to 'the real physio-psychology' that he recommends to his readers (BGE 23). As it turns out, they will discover 'what religion is' only if they *begin* – thereby reversing the traditional priority of theory to practice – by bravely facing up to what religion has done (and continues to do), independent of

---

[2] Strauss 1998: 327. See also Pippin 2019a: 114–15.
[3] See Lampert 2001: 102.

what its advocates might promise or preach. Following Nietzsche's lead, his readers will evaluate the religion in question – European Christianity – on the basis of what it has actually accomplished.

According to Nietzsche's account in Part Three, European Christianity is now a religion in name only, for it has abandoned (what he regards as) its essential role in contributing as directed to the elevation of culture. Having lodged an illegitimate claim to independence and sovereignty, European Christianity now presents itself as the highest arbiter of culture, beholden to none, answerable only to itself. In the absence of any meaningful resistance from a cognisant lawgiver or ruling caste, European Christianity now operates free of the customary (and necessarily intrusive) forms of social pressure and political oversight. As a result, the *Wesen* unique to European Christianity – which, as we shall see, takes the form of a 'religious neurosis' – has been propagated to epidemic proportions throughout Europe (BGE 47). If religion is to contribute as expected (and needed) to the production of a 'philosophy of the future', it must be returned to its rightful (= subordinate) place within the order of rank that informs the society it is meant to serve.

Summary of sections

Part Three of *BGE* comprises seventeen numbered sections (45–62). Nietzsche begins his investigation by raising the general question of

> the human soul and its borders, the entire scope of inner human experiences reached so far, the heights, depths, and distances of these experiences, the whole history of the soul *so far* and its untapped possibilities. . . (BGE 45)

Anticipating the 'task' he will assign to his best readers (BGE 230), he presents the 'human soul' as the 'predestined hunting ground' for anyone who, like him, is a 'born psychologist' and naturally thrills to the hunt (BGE 45; cf. GM P7). Lamenting once again the lack of kindred huntsmen among his contemporaries, Nietzsche flatters his readers by suggesting that *they* might yet display the 'courage, cleverness, and subtlety' that are required of those whom he aims to recruit (BGE 45). If his readers are to acquire the aforementioned virtues, of course, they will need to avail themselves of the education and training on offer in *BGE*, to the elaboration of which he now returns. As he does so, he narrows considerably the focus of his proposed investigation of the soul, urging his readers to attend to the myriad ways in which the souls of religious human beings have been formed (and, of course, deformed) by the various historical shapes that have been produced as religious leaders (and their patrons) have imposed their favoured solutions to the 'problem of *science* [*Wissen*] *and conscience* [*Gewissen*]' (BGE 45). Although Nietzsche's wordplay does not translate neatly into English, his point is clear enough: he instructs his readers to zero in on the 'problem' of weighing and balancing the competing demands of reason (or science) and faith (or religion).[4] As he proceeds to explain, these negotiations have marked the human soul as an oft-scarred battleground, over which religious enthusiasts of all and changing stripes have struggled and fought. The outcome '*so far*', as we shall see, is a neurotic, multiform soul at war with itself, which, he believes, is nevertheless poised to contribute to the timely conclusion of the 'moral' period in human history.

The approach Nietzsche adopts as he narrows the focus of his investigation of religion is distinctly and unapologetically *anthropological*.[5] Rather than attend to doctrinal claims and disputes pertaining to theology, or to abstract speculations about the nature and character of the divine, he aims to determine 'the religious *Wesen*' by documenting the various ways in which religion has contributed, as a tool of discipline and control, to the development of European civilisation.[6] He thus endeavours to isolate the 'character' of religion by investigating the 'character' of the

---

[4] Later on, Nietzsche recasts this 'problem' as 'the old theological problem of "faith" [*Glauben*] and "knowledge" [*Wissen*] – or, more clearly, of instinct [*Instinkt*] and reason [*Vernunft*] – thus the question of whether with respect to the valuation of things instinct deserves more authority than rationality [*Vernünftigkeit*], which wants us to evaluate and act according to grounds, according to a "why?"' (BGE 191).
[5] I am indebted here to Emden 2008: 181–99.
[6] See Strauss 1998: 327–30; and Lampert 2001: 109–14.

peoples, nations and cultures it has variously served (or dis-served). Towards this end, he introduces the subjects of his investigation as the *homines religiosi* (BGE 45), thereby suggesting that 'those who are religious' are ripe for the careful scrutiny and precise taxonomic classification that await any newly isolated species or subgroup. Notwithstanding the impediments they place in the path of the intrepid 'hunters' whom Nietzsche rallies to his cause, the *homines religiosi* are useful to him and his readers as study-worthy subjects in whom the 'religious *Wesen*' has attained its full, sickly bloom.

That Nietzsche's readers are likely to belong *among* the *homines religiosi* is treated here not as cause for disqualification, but as an advantage to be exploited. Unlike those scientific methods and approaches that prize objectivity and disinterestedness above all else, Nietzsche's anthropological approach relies on – and in fact celebrates – the first-personal experiences of those who join him. In order to arrive at a comprehensive reckoning of the uniquely human costs and benefits of religion, the 'hunters' whom he recruits must be in a position to understand *from the inside* – and not merely from the clinical distance favoured by traditional scholars – what it means to have suffered under the imposition of a prescribed diet of reason and faith. Hence his forthright admission that those who would join him might need to be 'as profound, as wounded, and as monstrous as the intellectual conscience of Pascal' (BGE 45). Blaise Pascal (1623–62) is of interest here not only for his forthright recognition that aspirants to Christian faith are obliged to 'sacrifice the intellect', but also for his apparent success in reaping from this 'sacrifice' an unexpected spiritual windfall (BGE 229).[7] As this complex appreciation of Pascal suggests, Nietzsche's evaluation of *das religiöse Wesen* is meant to disclose both the damage European Christianity has caused and the (limited) productive uses to which it might yet be put.

Nietzsche proceeds in sections 46–60 to survey the diverse ways in which the *homines religiosi* have negotiated the competing

---

[7] In his letter of 20 November 1888 to Georg Brandes, Nietzsche refers to Pascal, whom he 'almost loves', as the 'only logical Christian' (*SB* 8: 482–3). See also Sommer 2016: 311–12; and Lemm 2020: ch. 2.

claims of reason and faith. Towards this end, he considers the sacrificial faith of Christianity (BGE 46–7); the divergent approaches and sensibilities developed in the Protestant North and Catholic South of Europe (BGE 48; cf. GS 350); the excessive 'gratitude' expressed in the 'religiosity of the ancient Greeks' (BGE 49); the 'passion for God' (BGE 50); the intriguing case of the saint (BGE 51); the grand style of the Hebrew Bible (BGE 52); the crypto-religiosity of contemporary atheism (BGE 53); the antireligious nihilism of modern philosophy (BGE 54–7); the corrosion of the religious instincts by the eclipse of leisure and the emphasis placed on Protestant 'industriousness' (BGE 58); contemporary 'piety' as an expression of the *'fear* of truth' (BGE 59); and the precariousness of loving humanity not for its own sake but 'for God's sake' (BGE 60).

Dissolving the paradox of the saint

In sections 45–52, Nietzsche introduces his readers to the task of determining what we might understand to be the defining 'character' of European Christianity. In his typically breezy fashion, he devotes all of one section to an analysis that transports his whiplashed readers from the origins of Christianity, wherein faith appears under the sign of *sacrifice* – 'of all freedom, all pride, all self-assurance of the spirit' – to the French Revolution, which he brands as 'the last great slave revolt' (BGE 46).[8] He thus introduces in germinal form his influential diagnosis of Christianity, advanced in Part Nine of *BGE* and developed in Treatise I of *On the Genealogy of Morality*, as an exemplar of the 'slave morality', wherein suffering and bondage are hailed as indices of 'goodness' and accepted as down payments on redemption. As we shall see, his account of the psychic economy of sacrifice takes an unexpected turn in Part Eight of *BGE*, where the 'sacrifice of the intellect' is revealed to produce (in some souls) an inducement to continued spiritual growth (BGE 229).

Nietzsche introduces without fanfare the payoff of his anthropological approach to the aforementioned 'problem'. (Indeed, he

---

[8] On the logic of sacrifice, see Bishop 2022: 203–9.

proceeds as if the accuracy of his diagnosis were a settled matter of fact, which, as far as his target readership is concerned, may very well be the case.) As we learn, the sacrifice required of those who aspire to Christian faith is sufficiently severe as to produce in them the 'religious neurosis', which, as he confirms, is 'the religious *Wesen*' that is distinctive of European Christianity (BGE 47). What he means to convey, as we shall see, is that the production of 'neurosis' is a feature, and not a bug, of European Christianity.

At this point in the elaboration of his argument, he is not inclined to denounce Christianity on this basis, for he regards its besetting 'neurosis' as potentially conducive to social cohesion and political stability. Christianity becomes problematic when, as has happened occasionally throughout its history, it escapes the structures designated for its containment and threatens the wellbeing of the society and/or polity it was supposed to serve. According to Nietzsche, the most impactful and dangerous of these outbreaks is currently underway, which, as he later confirms, is a cause for immediate concern: 'a shrunken, almost laughable species, a herd animal, something well meaning, sickly, and mediocre has been bred, the European of today' (BGE 62). His aim in forwarding this grim diagnosis is not simply to shock his readers, who might very well have underestimated the extent of the 'disaster' he describes, but also to chart a realistic way forward. Despite having attained epidemic proportions, the 'religious neurosis' might be exposed (and even battled) as Europe awaits the arrival of those 'new' philosophers who will contain its spread and return religion to its 'natural' or 'essential' role as a tool of discipline and control.

Having identified the historical emergence of what he has already determined to be the 'religious neurosis', Nietzsche links its appearance to 'three dangerous dietary restrictions: solitude, fasting, and sexual abstinence' (BGE 47). (Without saying so explicitly, he has introduced the theme of *religious asceticism* and, by extension, the role of the *ascetic priest* in promoting and normalising the 'religious neurosis' (cf. GM III: 17–18).) Immediately conceding that he cannot in good faith assign cause and effect in the case of this linkage – at least not yet – he cautions his readers to tread very carefully as they move forward (BGE 47). After floating the possibility that the 'religious neurosis' might be indicative of an underlying (but undiagnosed) physiological condition, for example, epilepsy,[9] he warns his readers (and himself) to beware the 'profusion of nonsense and superstition' that obscures their view of the 'religious neurosis' (BGE 47).

Seeking firmer ground and a clearer line of sight, Nietzsche turns to two predecessors of note: Schopenhauer and Wagner, both of whom were determined to investigate the phenomenon of the 'denial of the will' (BGE 47). Building on the insights recorded by these predecessors, Nietzsche narrows his focus yet again, posing the question that lesser historians of religion dare not raise: 'how is the saint possible?' (BGE 47). He surmises here that the standard interpretation of the attainment of sainthood only ever begs the question: if the saint stands forth on the strength of his titanic will, which he is said to exert in control or denial of itself, wherein lies his saintliness? Is the saint's mastery of the will supposed to be the problem (or sin), the solution (or redemption), or both? And why do we permit the saint's achievement, whatever its mechanism turns out to involve, to divert our attention from the (misdiagnosed) neurosis he manifests? That the 'miracle' of sainthood continues to fascinate (and confound) is itself evidence of the extent of the neurosis in question. Like misery, as we shall see, neurosis loves company.

Before we consider Nietzsche's account of 'the religious neurosis', we should note that he does not mean to claim here that *all* religions are or have been expressions of the 'neurosis' he offers to diagnose. Although the 'neurosis' in question antedates the historical emergence of Christianity, originating not in Europe but in 'the orient, the *deep* orient' (BGE 46), he is primarily concerned to track its manifestations within the ambit of European Christianity, whose faithful adherents voluntarily cultivate the ascetic virtues of *selflessness*, even to the point, as in the case of the 'saintly' type, of emptying the self and basking in the admiration of others for having done so.

As we return to the main narrative of Part Three, we learn that the *Wesen* of European Christianity lies in the enormous success it

---

[9] In his next book, he revisits this speculative diagnosis, especially with respect to the various European 'epidemics' that he identifies as outbreaks of 'epilepsy' (GM III: 21).

has enjoyed in propagating and normalising the 'religious neurosis'. Proposing the *saint* as the type in which this 'neurosis' attains its apotheosis, Nietzsche boldly asserts that the protracted misunderstanding (and self-misunderstanding) of European Christianity trades on a surprisingly simple 'error of interpretation' (BGE 47). As he did in his earlier discussion of the martyr (BGE 25), he aims here to distinguish *his* philosophical approach from the 'bad philology' practised by his rivals among the historians of religion. Having previously observed that 'all psychology so far has gotten stuck in moral prejudices and fears' (BGE 23), he notes here that the would-be science of psychology 'suffered shipwreck' when it approached the 'miracle' of the saint (BGE 47). According to him, this so-called 'miracle', which is alleged to have catalysed the sudden conversion of a 'bad human being' into a 'good human being', in fact trades on an unsubstantiated – and now obsolete – belief in 'moral value-opposites' (BGE 47). Once his readers are disabused of this belief, he implies, the 'miracle' in question will dissolve before their very eyes. Rather than prostrate themselves before the aforementioned 'miracle', or the 'saint' who is its supposed host, they will behold and investigate the all-too-human (and all-too-familiar) phenomenon of a soul turned *against* itself, viz., an unfortunate, neurotic soul that derives its optimal experience of freedom and power from its perfection of the virtues of self-denial and self-abnegation.

In order to accomplish this objective, of course, Nietzsche and his best readers will need to update or abandon the standard approach to psychology, which, he observes, has 'placed itself under the rule of morality' (BGE 47). This is the perfect occasion, in fact, to take a preliminary stand 'beyond good and evil', for example, by recasting the saint as an extramoral type – that is, as neither 'good' nor 'bad' nor miraculously transformed – in whom the will to power is acknowledged to have turned *against* itself to productive (albeit short-term) effect.[10] Nietzsche thus accounts for

---

[10] In *On The Genealogy of Morality*, Nietzsche contributes additional detail and context: 'This is a kind of madness of the will in psychic cruelty that has absolutely no equal: the *will* of a human being to find himself guilty and reprehensible to the point of unatonability . . . Oh this insane sad beast human being! What ideas occur to it, what anti-nature, what paroxysms of nonsense, what *bestiality of idea* immediately breaks out as soon as it is prevented a bit from being the *beast of deed*! . . .' (GM II: 22).

the enduring appeal of the saint in terms of the common (and widespread) misinterpretation of the *meaning* of his prowess with respect to 'self-mastery and intentional, ultimate renunciation' (BGE 51). Although the saint might *appear* to have solved 'the riddle' of the soul, which, if true, would warrant the attention the saint has in fact received over the years, the truth of the matter is far less mysterious and, potentially, far more useful to Nietzsche's readers.

As Nietzsche proceeds to explain, the alleged transformation is achieved not by the extirpation – miraculous or otherwise – of the drives and affects that are purported to produce wickedness, but by their creative redirection. The so-called 'saint' has turned his 'wicked' drives and affects against *himself*, eventually deriving a feeling of power (and blissful self-negation) from having done so. He has learned to hate himself, and he is rewarded for his escalating self-contempt by the affirmation and validation afforded him by kindred neurotics. In truth, the 'saint' remains every bit as 'wicked' as before (i.e., when he was said to be a 'bad human being'). (As we shall see, the 'saint' errs not by directing his cruelty inward, but by directing his cruelty towards those affects and passions within himself that are potentially creative and form-giving.) The supposed 'goodness' of the 'saint' is thus a misinterpretation of the (seemingly pro-social) outward expression of his besetting neurosis.

As it is exemplified by the saint, the 'religious neurosis' rounds into view as a two-stage affliction. First, the 'saint' traces his 'wicked' thoughts and deeds to their (allegedly) sinful source in his passions and affects, voluntarily taking on the requisite burden of guilt. Second, the 'saint' anaesthetises himself by directing against himself the full fury of his righteous, sin-seeking will (GM II: 22). Duly narcotised by the '*emotional excess*' he has orchestrated within his troubled soul (GM III: 20), the 'saint' might appear to unsuspecting witnesses to have attained the tranquillity and composure that are associated by pagans with *ataraxia*, by Buddhists with *nirvana*, and by Christians with *beatitude*.[11] Nietzsche thus

---

[11] That Nietzsche may not have been entirely satisfied with his account of the 'religious neurosis' is suggested by the following parenthetical observation: 'religious neurosis *appears* as a form of "evil essence": no doubt. What is it? *Quaeritur* [That is the question]' (GM III: 21).

explains that (and why) the 'saint' has been able – until now – to induce awe and suspicion in those who (mistakenly) infer that his extreme feats of self-denial are evidence of 'a new power, a foreign, not yet vanquished enemy' (BGE 51).[12]

As we shall see, Nietzsche's alternative account of the saint has once again complicated his task in Part Three. He is now obliged to persuade his readers of the morbidity of a religion that is widely acknowledged to be perfectly normal, credibly universal in scope, and eminently functional. To this task he now turns.

The religious instinct

The momentous question the saint elicits from others is withheld for now (BGE 51), and Nietzsche treats this rhetorical break in his narrative as an occasion to renew his opposition to the claim, lodged by social Darwinists and others, that the *homines religiosi* of contemporary Europe represent the apex of human development to date. According to Nietzsche, one need only compare the Hebrew Bible, 'the book of divine justice' (BGE 52), and the Christian New Testament in order to appreciate just how far humanity has fallen from its previously attained heights. What he wishes his readers to understand here is that a people or nation cannot reject the religiosity of its great and noble predecessors *and* expect to become great and noble in turn. Thus begins in earnest his effort to disclose to his readers the general 'character' of religion, which rounds into view in contrast to the (recently diagnosed) 'character' of European Christianity.

What Nietzsche calls the 'religious instinct' might be understood in anthropological terms as an aspiration on the part of a people or nation to grow and thrive through its acceptance of an appropriate burden of obligations (or debts) to venerable, otherworldly others (e.g., ancestors, kings, founders, creators, gods). As

---

[12] The confusion on the part of those who witness the saint is succinctly reconstructed by Lampert: 'Lacking a psychology of their own will to power, [the worldly powerful who encountered the saint] failed to understand the more spiritual forms the will to power could take' (2001: 110). See also Burnham 2007: 79–80; and Acampora and Ansell-Pearson 2011: 84–5.

such, the aim of the 'religious instinct' is to cultivate a binding relationship to the divine, by means of which a people or nation agrees to take on an ever-increasing burden of obligation (or debt), which, when successfully discharged (or repaid), will prove the valour (and value) of the people or nation in question. Do these venerable, otherworldly others actually exist? Despite his popular reputation as a rabid atheist, Nietzsche is obliged by his anthropological approach to leave this question unasked and unanswered. What is crucial for his investigation is what the *homines religiosi* believe to be true.

Nietzsche thus invites his best readers to interpret the 'religious instinct' as indicative of the relative health and strength of the people or nation it represents. On the one hand, a healthy people or nation will instinctively fashion for itself the kind of obligation-laden religion that will challenge it to continue its upward trajectory of growth and self-overcoming. Fearful of dishonouring its monitory elders or disappointing its cognisant deities, and eager to express its gratitude for the benefaction it has received thus far, a healthy people or nation will hold itself to ever higher standards of virtue, success and prosperity, precisely so that it might continue to please those patrons to whom it (believes it) owes its good fortune. Simply put, healthy human beings instinctively desire (and expect to take on) those obligations that will elicit from them the best versions of themselves. The hardships involved in discharging these obligations are understood to be both necessary and acceptable, but only in the event that one's continued growth is either palpable or, if delayed for any reason, credible.

On the other hand, a declining people or nation will instinctively fashion for itself a religion characterised by minimal responsibilities and universal affirmation. In pronouncing themselves sinners, for example, contemporary Christians may *appear* to accept responsibility for their supposedly fallen nature, but they in fact refuse any additional responsibilities that might challenge them to grow and thrive. (It is only as self-avowed sinners, after all, that Christians gain access to the consciousness-blotting narcosis that relieves them, temporarily, of their vexed selfhood (GM III: 20).) Rather than bind themselves to a religion that will burden them with the obligations that are likely to elicit what is best within them, they subscribe to a religion that rewards minimal exertion with blanket affirmation and the promise of eternal salvation. Hence the point of the provocative comparison Nietzsche chooses to emphasise: the Hebrew Bible attests to a people – Nietzsche has in mind the 'kingly' Israelites of the First Temple Period – for whom nothing short of a vengeful god would suffice to prompt them to greatness (A 25), while the New Testament offers teachings tailored to those of whom not too much should (or will) be expected (BGE 52). His assumption here, which he elsewhere articulates and defends at greater length, is that enduring growth, whether in the individual, the collective or the culture, requires a continued escalation of the challenges and obstacles one is expected to face and surmount. In this respect, we may associate the onset of cultural decay with the refusal to accept any additional burdens of obligation (or debt).

The misanthropic atheism of modern philosophy

Nietzsche then pivots to a discussion of the 'atheism' that is practised (if not always or consistently preached) by modern philosophy (BGE 53–60). His stated reason for doing so is to confirm his observation that the 'religious instinct' in Europe has continued to grow, despite the waning appeal of the 'theistic satisfaction' that formerly sufficed (BGE 53).

What this means, as we have seen, is that (some) Europeans apparently yearn to be assigned a burden of obligations (and debts) in excess of what Christianity (= 'theism') currently expects of them. If that were true, the future of humankind (or of European civilisation as its proxy) might yet be secured by leaders and lawgivers who would authorise a post-Christian religion that would satisfy the 'religious instinct' by demanding more of its adherents (and delivering more in turn). Nietzsche thus aims to persuade his readers that the current gulf between the 'religious instinct' and the standard (= Christian) forms of 'theistic satisfaction' is indicative both of an escalating crisis *and* of a potentially promising opportunity for self-overcoming.

Here is what he has in mind: if the rise of European atheism may be traced to the philosophical and religious assaults on God in His traditionally masculine roles as 'father', 'judge', 'rewarder' and confessor (BGE 53), it might be possible to begin the process of mobilising the 'religious instinct' in the service of the social and political ends outlined by Nietzsche in the remainder of *BGE*. While the eventual disposition and content of any post-Christian religion must be left to the discretion of the 'new' philosophers, Nietzsche and his readers might be in a good position to discredit (and perhaps ward off) the nihilism encoded in the grim satisfactions tendered by modern philosophy and science. Indeed, *BGE* itself might be received as a decisive first step in this direction.

In order to demonstrate the complicity of modern philosophy in the refutation of 'European theism', Nietzsche identifies three 'rungs' on the 'great ladder of religious cruelty' (BGE 55). Picking up the thread of his founding insight into the *Wesen* of European Christianity and the neurotic 'character' of the souls it moulds (BGE 46), Nietzsche returns to the theme of *sacrifice*. Initially, corresponding perhaps to what he has called the *premoral* period in human history (BGE 32), the gods were understood to expect (and even demand) the sacrifice of other human beings, including those who were dearest and most beloved. Throughout the subsequent *moral* period, devout human beings have been expected (and willing) to sacrifice what is best and noblest *within themselves* – that is, their 'strongest instincts', their very '"nature"' – so that they might gain or retain the favour of their (somewhat less cruel) gods (BGE 32).[13] In the *extramoral* period to come, Nietzsche speculates, there will be nothing of surpassing value left to sacrifice, with the exception of one's gods (BGE 32).

According to Nietzsche, 'modern philosophy' is implicated in this unhappy regression by dint of the motivation it derives from its 'epistemological skepticism', which, when directed against the 'old concept of the soul', reveals itself to be aggressively '*anti-Christian*' (BGE 54). Echoing his earlier critique of Kant and German Idealism (BGE 11), Nietzsche claims to detect in 'modern philosophy' a quasi-religious fascination with – and fervour for – the systematic disavowal of the soul known to and cared for by

---

[13] Here we recall his assertion that Christian faith begins and develops under the sign of 'sacrifice' (BGE 46).

Christians, viz., the *immortal* soul, whose eternal reward the faithful believe they might yet secure. Hence his wishful attempt to associate the desire on the part of Kant – namely, 'to prove that the subject could not be proven from the standpoint of the subject – nor could the object' – with the Vedantic teaching of the '*illusory existence* of . . . "the soul"' (BGE 54; cf. GM III: 27).

Once modern philosophy succeeds in banishing the soul, he continues, it will have no choice but to direct its 'epistemological skepticism' towards God, whose afterworldly stewardship of the soul is no longer required. It will do so, moreover, efficiently and blithely, as if the sacrifice of God were no big deal. As is the case with the progress of modern science, the (soul- and God-banishing) progress of 'modern philosophy' imbues its eager practitioners with the meaning, purpose and direction they crave. In the long run, however, the pride they have taken in disavowing the supposed bases of human pride will subside. Like their scientific brethren, these modern philosophers will eventually embrace the nihilism they have unwittingly courted all along (BGE 54). What they will *not* embrace, to the disadvantage of late modern European culture, is the prerogative (and attendant responsibility) of philosophers to '*rule*' (BGE 204).

Although the 'death of God' has not yet come to pass – *pace* the hysterical Madman, who over-reacts to his own, similar insight into the advent of European nihilism (GS 125)[14] – the logic of sacrifice is presented here as inexorable.[15] According to Nietzsche, humanity has crossed the horizon of a cataclysmic 'event' of unknown scope and intensity, which will define its prospects for the foreseeable future (GS 343). If the logic of sacrifice maintains its current stranglehold, the 'event' in question may very well place the will for the future of humanity at extreme risk of depletion or even extinction. In that event, Nietzsche worries, we might expect the 'death of God' to precipitate the rise of the 'will to nothingness' (GM III: 28), which might tempt humanity to sacrifice itself

---

[14] See Pippin 2010: 47–62; and Conway 2010: 122–5.
[15] Part of the problem here is the success thus far of the incentive structure that informs the logic of sacrifice: 'But anyone who really made sacrifices knows that he wanted and received something for it – maybe something of himself in exchange for something of himself' (BGE 220).

'for nothingness'.[16] To be sure, all we know right now is that an established way of life, predicated on the validity and centring force of morality and religion, is coming to an end. Familiar structures of meaning and value are crumbling, and replacement structures are not yet in sight. Indeed, although the moral-religious worldview continues to appeal, offering comfort to those who still (wish to) believe, the meaning it confers is noticeably diminished and diffuse.

Here we are reminded that Nietzsche's allegiance to the scientific worldview is presented to his readers as both enthusiastic *and* provisional. While his general intent is to liberate the scientific worldview – and, by extension, its adherents – from the moral and religious prejudices that retard the progress of its development, he is also concerned to steer his best readers away from the nihilism that modern science is currently poised to enact. As an alternative (and antidote) to the 'laboriously won *self-contempt*' that modern science confers upon its faithful adherents (GM III: 25), he recommends a variant of the scientific worldview that is not only purged of unwanted moral and religious prejudices, but also fully infused with nihilism-repelling cheerfulness (GS 343).

Having alerted his best readers to the dawning of an 'extramoral' period, wherein God will be sacrificed 'for nothingness' (BGE 55),[17] Nietzsche pauses to consider how he and they might navigate the nihilism that almost surely awaits them. Returning to the theme of a pessimism predicated on *strength* (BT: AS 1), a pessimism that is at home 'beyond good and evil' (BGE 56), he conjectures that the doomsayers and misanthropes may be wrong after all. This would be the case, for example, if the pessimism he envisions were to yield

> [T]he [inverse] ideal of the most exuberant, lively, and world-affirming human being who has learned to reconcile

---

[16] See Reginster 2006: 39–49.
[17] As this section confirms, Nietzsche's famous pronouncement of the 'death of God' is meant to mark the dawning of an 'event' that will culminate in 'the sacrifice [of] God for nothingness' (BGE 55). Inasmuch as this 'event' has not yet reached its ignominious conclusion, Nietzsche feels warranted to stage the intervention that *BGE* is meant to accomplish.

and come to terms with not only what was and is, but also wants to have it again *as it was and is*, for all eternity, insatiably shouting *da capo* not only to himself but also to the whole play and performance, and not only to a performance, but at bottom to the one who needs this performance – and makes it necessary: because he needs himself again and again – and makes himself necessary – (BGE 56)[18]

Nietzsche's aim in this rousing passage is to prepare his readers for the selective role to be played in the 'extramoral' period by the pessimism he recommends for their consideration.[19] Without discounting the disruptions and upheavals that are likely to follow in the wake of the 'sacrifice [of] God for nothingness', he urges his readers to imagine the type of human being who might *thrive* under the post-theistic conditions of an extramoral period. In its ideal form, this type of human being would experience the retirement of the 'old' morality as an invitation, finally, to affirm without distraction 'what was and is', and to do so for 'all eternity' (BGE 56).

While the conclusion of the extracted passage is admittedly obscure, it may be understood to convey Nietzsche's intimation of what religion might become under the aegis of this alternative ideal. The 'world-affirming' pessimist shouts *da capo* not only to 'himself' and to the 'performance' unfolding around him, but also to an unnamed other, who 'needs' the performance and, therefore, 'makes it necessary'. In doing so, moreover, this unnamed other reveals that he 'needs himself' and, in his efforts to satisfy this need, 'makes himself necessary' by staging and renewing the aforementioned performance.

That human existence is best understood (and most readily affirmed) as a 'play and performance' is an idea that Nietzsche

---

[18] On the relationship of this section to Nietzsche's teaching of eternal recurrence, see Lampert 2001: 116–23, 135–6; Burnham 2007: 83–90; Acampora and Ansell-Pearson 2011: 87–93; and Sommer 2016: 357–61.

[19] In his letter of 29 July 1888 to Carl Fuchs, Nietzsche confides that he would like to be 'described' (but not 'evaluated') some day as 'the inventor of a new kind of pessimism (a Dionysian pessimism, born of strength, which takes pleasure in seizing the problem of existence by the horns)' (*SB* 8: 374–6/Middleton 1969: 304).

consistently associates with the nobles of Greek antiquity, who, he allows, 'used' their Olympian gods as divine (= meaning-conferring) 'spectators' of the otherwise unremarkable human condition (GM II: 23). The belief that their performance was worthy of a divine audience, even if only by merit of their penchant for 'folly', was sufficient for the nobles of Greek antiquity to affirm the 'performance' in which they found themselves emplaced (GM II: 23). Grateful for (or desirous of) divine benefaction, and alert in any event to the whims of their Olympian spectators, the noble Greeks held themselves to an elevated standard of human excellence and found ample meaning in having done so.

A similar experience of religion may be implied by the Latin coda that Nietzsche applies to his description of the alternative ideal: '*circulus vitiosus deus*' (BGE 56). The unnamed other at whom the world-affirming pessimist shouts *da capo*, I suggest, is the god (*deus*) who is responsible for staging and scripting the 'performance' in question.[20] (We might be reminded here of the defiant figure of Prometheus, who was bound by Zeus to the promontory and tormented on a daily basis by liver-devouring eagles.) On this interpretation, the worthy pessimist demonstrates his positive disposition towards life by demanding that the unnamed god authorise a reprise of his performance, despite knowing (or suspecting) that he has in fact invented the divine spectator(s) for whom he performs. (Hence the vicious circle: the pessimist exuberantly affirms life because he understands himself to merit the attention of those divine spectators whom he has conjured for the express purpose of attending to his performance.)[21]

Here we may conjecture on Nietzsche's behalf that the pessimist persists in this (viciously circular) experience of religion because he has acknowledged that untruth – in this case, the fiction of the divine spectators – is a condition of life itself (BGE 4). In that event, a circle that is admittedly vicious (i.e., with respect

---

[20] Nietzsche's reference here to 'the whole play and performance' [*zum ganzen Stücke und Schauspiele*] may be understood to anticipate his reference to 'the Dionysian drama of "the destiny of the soul" – : and he will put it to good use, he will, that great ancient, eternal comic poet of our existence, this we can bet on!' (GM P7).

[21] See Loeb 2010: 194–8.

to logic) would be affirmed by the pessimist as life-enhancing.[22] Unlike the philosophical martyrs, who create diversionary spectacles to mask their besetting exhaustion (BGE 25), the worthy pessimist described here fashions for himself a spectacle in which he is challenged by his divine spectators to perform, grow, improve and eventually affirm in its entirety his post-theistic existence. That these divine spectators might be fabrications, existing only within the confines of the spectacle he has created, is apparently of no lasting concern to the worthy pessimist in question. For all we know, in fact, the worthy pessimist might simply be the unnamed other for whom he performs.

Notwithstanding this hopeful glimpse of a post-theistic future, Nietzsche understands that the 'sacrifice [of] God for nothingness' augurs a potentially cataclysmic outcome. As he explains, the sole remaining motivation for loving humanity is to do so *not* for the sake of humanity, for which modern science and philosophy find no compelling warrant, but for the sake of God (BGE 60). Nietzsche not only applauds this motivation, inasmuch as it arises from 'the noblest and most alienating feeling achieved among human beings', but also praises its unnamed, stammering author, who must remain 'forever holy and venerable to us as the human being who up till now has flown highest and has gotten lost most beautifully!' (BGE 60).

While Nietzsche's tender sentiment may surprise some readers, his reasoning should not. Those who have believed and taught that humanity should be loved 'for God's sake' might have erred in arriving at this desideratum, but they have succeeded, perhaps unwittingly, in erecting an emergency bulwark against the nihilism that impels the progress of modern philosophy and science. Had we not learned to love humanity 'for God's sake', we likely would have already exhausted, with the full approval of modern science and philosophy, our will for the future of humanity. That we are beloved 'for God's sake' may no longer be widely credible, but it has bought humanity sufficient time – or so Nietzsche hopes – to prepare for, and perhaps survive, the coming dark age of European nihilism.

---

[22] See Burnham 2014: 86–9; and Pippin 2019a: 115–17.

The 'new' philosophers

Having exposed 'modern philosophers' as unsuspecting nihilists-in-waiting, Nietzsche turns to a consideration of the 'new' philosophers whose approach he heralded at the close of Part Two (BGE 44). The big pitch here is his promise that the 'new' philosophers will reign in the runaway neurosis by returning religion to its rightful, subordinate place in the cultural order of rank.

The proposed demotion of religion should not be regarded as a strictly punitive measure. Notwithstanding his popular reputation as the arch-enemy of organised religion, Nietzsche acknowledges a limited role for religion within the articulated structure of a thriving culture or society. In order to make this case, he begins with a surprisingly sympathetic appreciation of the benefits we might expect a properly circumscribed religion to confer upon a receptive nation or people. As he explains, religion is best understood as a potentially useful tool or artifice – no less so than the 'political' and 'economic' resources at hand (BGE 61) – in the service of the grander goal of cultural elevation.[23] If properly managed and contained, in fact, religion presents a ruler or lawgiver with an unusually versatile means of serving (and cultivating) multiple constituencies within a social order or polity.

To those who are 'predestined for commanding', religion offers excellent training in the ascetic disciplines required for effective leadership and provides a useful 'means of overcoming obstacles' (BGE 61). By creating a 'bond that binds rulers and subjects together', religion permits a ruler to capture the 'consciences' of those whom he rules and to mobilise them in the service of his larger aims and objectives (BGE 61). To those 'contemplative' types of 'noble descent' who value peaceful solitude, religion grants the desired exemption from the 'necessary *dirt* of all political dealings' (BGE 61). To some of those among the ruled, religion offers the promise of limited social mobility, especially if they belong to those 'slowly ascending classes' that someday might participate in 'ruling and commanding' (BGE 61).

---

[23] See Lampert 2001: 124–8.

To 'ordinary people', finally, religion delivers the pro-social benefits to be wrought from the rigid containment and vigilant management of the 'religious neurosis' itself. Demonstrating his appreciation for the contributions of a docile 'herd' to the achievement of social cohesion and political stability, Nietzsche expresses his admiration for the emotional delicacy displayed by two well-known religions of decadence, Christianity and Buddhism, which variously teach 'even the lowliest to place themselves into a higher illusory order of things through piety, and to firmly embrace their contentment with the real order' (BGE 61). As he later confirms, religion dispenses comfort and hope to those who have none, and it allows for otherwise agitated or neurotic individuals to become productive members of a functional collective or 'herd' (BGE 201; cf. GS 347). As we know, of course, these benefits will accrue only in the event that religion is returned to its rightful, subordinate place in the cultural order of rank.

Having presented the positive case for religion, Nietzsche turns to make the negative case, offering to expose the 'uncanny dangerousness' of those '*sovereign* religions' that refuse to serve as 'a means of cultivation and education and in the hands of the philosopher' (BGE 62). Having asserted their supposed right to 'rule *sovereignly*', the religions in question typically dedicate themselves to the care of those who suffer. While understandable and even laudable, the goal pursued by these 'sovereign' religions is in fact incompatible with the chief objective of any thriving society or polity – namely, to work towards the advancement of culture and contribute thereby to the ongoing elevation of humanity. In an observation that intimates the dark extremes of his 'immoralism', he notes that these 'sovereign' religions have 'preserved too much of *what should have perished*', by which he means that they have 'preserve[d] . . . all who suffer from life as if from a disease' (BGE 62).

This is a problem, he explains, because the preservation of those who 'suffer from life' is a luxury that humankind simply cannot afford. Although we find in 'every other animal species an excess of failures', the '*as yet undetermined*' human animal is *especially* unlikely to produce the kinds of 'successes' that warrant the future – and the *will* for the future – of humankind (BGE 62). Notwithstanding their seemingly noble and potentially commendable objectives, that is, those religions that have presumed to '*rule sovereignly*' have inadvertently succeeded in normalising failure and demonising (what Nietzsche regards as) those human beings who have turned out well. This unfortunate set of outcomes, he believes, only serves to confirm his insistence that the 'nature' or 'essence' of religion lies not in its presumption of independence and sovereignty, but in its service to worthy lawgivers as a tool of discipline and control.

Narrowing his focus once again, Nietzsche indicts European Christianity for its opposition to the most fundamental aims of culture. By acting on its neurotic claim to sovereignty, European Christianity has in fact produced the *opposite* of a culture: 'does it not seem as though a single will dominated Europe for eighteen centuries for the purpose of making human beings into a *sublime abortion*?' (BGE 62). The fundamental issue here is that the project of cultural enhancement requires the presiding legislators to attend to the elevation of the culture's greatest exemplars, and to do so at any tolerable expense. Inasmuch as European Christianity consistently identifies the 'good' man as its supreme product and achievement, it fails at this most basic task of cultural enhancement.

Lest we think Nietzsche to be unusually hard-hearted and cruel, we should note that he places great stock in the humanitarian character of his attack on the current practice of disregarding (and even disputing) the genuine 'character' of religion.[24] Underlying his concern here is his observation that the emergent masses, supposedly beloved and nourished by European Christianity, are actually ill served by its illegitimate assertion of cultural sovereignty. Rather than alleviate the suffering of the poor and dispossessed, for example, by sorting them into properly managed 'herds', Christianity exacerbates their distress by encouraging in them the full bloom of their uncontained, unmanaged, untreated neurosis. That he expects his readers to consider these champions of religious sovereignty alongside kindred idealists is suggested

---

[24] See Lampert 2001: 120–3; and Burnham 2014: 70–2.

by his claim that they have endeavoured to 'stand all valuations *on their head*', thereby 'invert[ing] all love of the earthly and of dominion over the earth into hatred of the earth and the earthly' (BGE 62; cf. BGE P).

The calamity of European Christianity

Nietzsche's harrowing conclusion to Part Three, in which he delivers his summary indictment of European Christianity (BGE 62),[25] is likely to leave some of his readers dispirited and disillusioned. At this juncture in the elaboration of his main narrative, the sheer magnitude of the calamity in question might be received as overwhelming. The appearance on the scene of a mass of 'herd animals' – *not* as an unfortunate accident, but as the outcome intended by those who 'have so far ruled over Europe's fate' (BGE 62) – might be understood to suggest that the collapse of Western civilisation is nigh. Indeed, rather than accept at face value the pieties rehearsed by 'sovereign' Christianity, Nietzsche excoriates its apologists and champions for displaying 'the most disastrous kind of arrogance to date' (BGE 62), for they have attempted a task to which they are by no means equal.[26]

While Nietzsche's ire is perhaps understandable, he is well aware that the priests (and their secular patrons) are not ultimately at fault for the 'disaster' over which they have 'arrogantly' presided. As any worthwhile lawgiver or ruler understands, the value of the priests, as of religion more generally, depends on a strict monitoring of the bounds within which they and it are allowed to operate. That the priestly type has *become* dangerous, productive of those '*sovereign* religions' that have stalled the progress of human development, should not surprise us, for the constraints on

---

[25] He offers similar (and similarly scathing) indictments of Christian morality at GM III: 21 and EH 'Destiny' 4–8.
[26] Channelling the 'rage, compassion, and horror' of those (e.g., Pascal) who would be (rightly) appalled at what Christianity has wrought, Nietzsche addresses those responsible for the calamity as 'oafs' [*Tölpel*] (BGE 62). As Lampert succinctly puts the decisive point, 'When religions reign sovereign, they are "themselves the final goal." When philosophy is sovereign, religion is one "means among other means" to the goal philosophy sets' (Lampert 2001: 131). See also Young 2010: 139–41.

priestly mischief, as on religion more generally, have been relaxed to a dangerous degree in late modernity. The real problem here, to the solution of which Nietzsche rallies his best readers, is the dereliction of duty on the part of those who are supposed to curb the enthusiasm of the priests for the ongoing expansion of their ministry (GM III: 20). For that important task, *new* philosophers are needed, philosophers who will observe the order of rank, keep the priests in check, and reclaim the philosopher's prerogative to determine the future of humankind.

Inasmuch as Nietzsche's readers are not the 'new' philosophers whom he invokes, what might they realistically hope to contribute? If we may assume that his readers are not (yet) prepared to view 'European Christianity with the mocking and disinterested eye of an Epicurean god', and that they are not (yet) in a position to appreciate its 'oddly painful and crude yet refined comedy' (BGE 62), how are they meant to respond to this calamity? At this point in the elaboration of his argument, Nietzsche is content to incite in his readers an intensified feeling of righteous indignation, precisely so that their opposition to European Christianity might become more fully (and productively) visceral. The outrage he invites them to feel and express is apparently catalytic of the affective-somatic transformation he has offered to induce in them. Later on, as we shall see, as their transformation nears its completion, he will prescribe to them the 'task' in which they might channel without reserve the vituperation he has urged them to own (BGE 230).

Review

The symmetry of Nietzsche's claims in Parts Two and Three of *BGE* will not be lost on his best readers. Just as they were identified in Part Two as better suited (*qua* free spirits) to a lesser (but more immediate) role in the production of a philosophy of the future, so religion has been identified, by virtue of its defining 'character', as better suited to a subordinate, instrumental role in the enhancement of culture. In the case of both claims, moreover, an unwarranted assertion of sovereignty has been exposed as both problematic and destructive.

The dissolution of order that characterises late modern European culture has permitted individuals and institutions to expand their dominion in pursuit of a greater (if unearned) share of sovereignty and self-determination. The resulting expansions of dominion, by untested individuals and unworthy institutions, are potentially disastrous for the future of European civilisation. Indeed, the most alarming outcome of the disaster is the looming extinction of those higher human types whose exploits warrant and buoy the will for the future of humanity. Nietzsche thus encourages his best readers to begin the process of reining in these ill-conceived aims at expanded dominion, and to do so precisely by reasserting the legislative prerogative of philosophy.

What Nietzsche has not yet revealed to his best readers is that he regards the recent emergence of a mass of European 'herd animals' as both a calamity *and* an opportunity. As he will proceed to explain in later sections of *BGE*, something may yet be done for and with 'the European of today' (BGE 62), especially if the philosophers of the future share his commitment to a grand project of cultural renewal. In subsequent parts of *BGE*, Nietzsche will respond to this calamity by envisioning an 'extramoral' culture, in which humankind is emboldened to assume control of (and responsibility for) the process of producing, as a matter of volition and design, those exotic, norm-averse human beings who body forth a justification of our mortal, worldly existence.

5
Part Four: Epigrams and Interludes

Preview

Having concluded Part Three of *BGE* with his chilling diagnosis of a 'religious neurosis' run amok, and having identified the mass emergence of the European 'herd animal' as a calamity to be rued (BGE 62), Nietzsche treats his readers to an intermezzo of 'epigrams and interludes'. (That he sees fit to place the intermezzo at *this* juncture, well ahead of the half-way mark, provides further confirmation of the significance he attaches to his diagnosis of the 'religious neurosis' in Part Three.) And although he temporarily dials down the intensity generated by his diagnosis of the unfolding crisis, his programme of education and training continues as planned, its lessons disseminated in the concentrated form of pithy epigrams. While the tone of these epigrams is distinctly lighter, they are nevertheless meant to reinforce the disciplinary regimen in which he has enrolled his best readers. As his readers pause to digest the untimely insights recorded thus far in *BGE*, Nietzsche diverts their focus to the nuggets of wisdom inscribed in these epigrams.

Within the context of Nietzsche's programme of education and training, Part Four of *BGE* amounts to a crash course in the unvarnished candour and unsentimental self-scrutiny that he expects of himself and his best readers. In an apparent recognition of their relative unfamiliarity with the 'youngest' of the virtues in their possession – *honesty* (BGE 227) – he devotes Part Four of *BGE* to an accelerated apprenticeship in the 'extravagant honesty' that others will (correctly) judge to be gratuitously cruel (BGE 230). By placing his readers at the receiving end of a cluster barrage of home truths, which he prudently laces with levity and wit, Nietzsche aims to further their preparations for the 'task' that awaits them.

That Nietzsche's pithy epigrams also display his signature cheerfulness should not be surprising. Building on the subtitle of *BGE*, which promises a 'prelude to the philosophy of the future', he offers these epigrams as timely 'interludes', which, he apparently believes, will fortify his best readers for the arduous journey ahead of them. In particular, he means for his best readers to learn to laugh at their own pretensions and prejudices, even as they continue to take quite seriously the project of girding themselves for the destruction of the 'old' morality. As we have seen, an enlarged capacity for self-directed laughter, verging on self-directed mockery, will be useful to his best readers in the event that they become 'stuck to' a particular idea, truth, role or understanding (BGE 41). As we shall see in Part Nine, moreover, Nietzsche endorses an order of rank among philosophers with respect to the intensity and irreverence of their *laughter* (BGE 294). As one might suspect, he reserves the highest rank for those philosophers who, like Dionysus, direct their laughter against everything that humanity has thus far taken seriously (BGE 295).

In light of the rapid-fire fusillade recorded in Part Four, there should be no expectation that all or even most of these pithy epigrams will be instantly affirmed by Nietzsche's readers, much less immediately incorporated into their habits and routines. Inasmuch as these epigrams subvert conventional wisdom and/or reveal truths as yet unacknowledged in polite society, they may be extremely difficult, at least initially, for his readers to take to heart. Of course, this too is part of his plan. As he notes elsewhere, even the best of his readers are relatively unpractised in the art of slow, careful reading, which he calls *rumination* (GM P8). As part of their education and training in *BGE*, they are invited to acquire (or renew) the habit of tarrying with difficult, unfamiliar, perspective-deranging, paradigm-bending ideas. Towards this end, he packs Part Four with epigrams that are meant to be digested slowly, revisited again and again, considered from various heights and angles, and contemplated over the full term of a lifelong discipleship. (As their

PART FOUR: EPIGRAMS AND INTERLUDES   99

designation as 'interludes' suggests, these epigrams also affirm the need to pause occasionally for diversion, reflection, renewal and recreation.) Ruminating in this fashion will facilitate the (partial) liberation of his best readers and allow them to regard their historical situation from a fresh, new perspective.

Summary of sections

Part Four of *BGE* comprises 122 numbered sections (63–185), each of which contains a single epigram or interlude. Each section conveys a novel observation, which is meant to shed new light on a familiar or well-known topic. The aim in most cases is to challenge or call into question the validity of a commonly held belief or position. In some of these sections, Nietzsche makes his point by rehearsing a bit of scripted dialogue, which is a technique he employs productively elsewhere in *BGE*.

Throughout Part Four, he aspires to a spare, economical, self-contained presentation. The proffered observations appear without introduction, context or supporting arguments. His readers are apparently meant to consider these observations strictly on their own merits, independent of their provenance or popularity, and without any claims to reliable or venerable authority. Are these epigrams presented as the products of empirical investigation? Sustained introspection? Offhand conjecture? Poetic whimsy? Nietzsche does not say. Stripped bare of the usual indices and trappings of received wisdom, his epigrams either land or they do not. In this respect, they are apparently intended to continue the selective process that is meant to separate Nietzsche's best readers from the pretenders in their midst.

Nietzsche's influences

Nietzsche's reliance in Part Four on a collection of pithy epigrams bespeaks the influence of several notable predecessors. As he is quick to acknowledge, he is happily indebted to the 'concise, severe' style perfected by the Roman writers Sallust (86–35 BCE) and Horace (65–8 BCE) (TI 'Ancients' 1). Owing to their influence, he claims, he mounted 'a very serious attempt at *Roman* style, at "*aere perennius*" in style', which, he insists, 'is *noble par excellence*' (TI 'Ancients' 1). Inasmuch as he intends to nudge his best readers towards the 'self-respect' that is indicative of nobility in the twilight period of late modernity (BGE 287), we may interpret his recourse to an epigrammatic style of presentation as an effort to acclimatise his best readers to the nobility of soul to which they might credibly aspire.

The German stylists who influenced Nietzsche include the following writers: Georg Christoph Lichtenberg (1742–99), whom he openly admired for the economy, insight and cleverness he packed into his elegant aphorisms;[1] Johan Wolfgang von Goethe (1749–1832), who, according to Nietzsche, 'disciplined himself into wholeness . . . [and thereby] *created* himself' (TI 'Forays' 49); and Paul Rée (1849–1901), a former friend who conducted similar investigations into the history and psychology of morality. A more immediately recognisable source of influence is the philosopher whom Nietzsche once hailed as his 'educator' [*Erzieher*], Arthur Schopenhauer (1788–1860), who was himself a formidable practitioner of the aphoristic style. By the time he wrote *BGE*, finally, Nietzsche had perfected the art of crafting pithy aphorisms and witty epigrams. Whether writing in his own voice, that of Zarathustra, or that of a fabricated interlocutor *du jour*, he had mastered the art and style on display in Part Four of *BGE*.

As a purveyor of multiple philosophical styles, of course, Nietzsche was also influenced by various French authors of the seventeenth to nineteenth centuries, and especially by those who cultivated experimental approaches that were (and are) well suited to daring explorations of the human psyche. As Thomas Brobjer notes, Nietzsche was influenced, and especially in his fertile 'middle' period, by 'the French moralists (i.e., psychologists) . . . and the Enlightenment *philosophes*'.[2] As Robert Pippin has observed, Nietzsche's tactical delivery of pithy, epigrammatic formulations evinces his debts to those among the French moralists – most notably, Pascal, Montaigne and La Rochefoucauld – who advanced the

---

[1] See Brobjer 2010: 64–5.
[2] Brobjer 2010: 62.

fledgling science of moral psychology by artfully probing the depth and plasticity of the multiform soul.³

As the influence of these predecessors confirms, Nietzsche admires the epigram not only for its spare, economical mode of presentation, but also for its unique capacity to exploit the element of surprise. As we know, epigrams tend to be most effective when, as in an interrogation of core beliefs and basic convictions, extended arguments are neither welcome nor useful. Whether by virtue of a single well-placed word, a rogue image, a naughty wordplay, a daring iconoclasm or a witticism of exquisite subtlety, a well-wrought epigram may pierce the prejudice-encrusted defences of those who, until now, have been determined not to know themselves. In such cases, Nietzsche's aim as an aphorist is to inflict the healing wounds that will spur his best readers towards the level and intensity of self-knowledge he has urged them to attain. In this respect, his tactical deployment of the epigrams collected in Part Four should be understood as supporting his (invasive) efforts to induce in his best readers the affective-somatic transformation that will enable in them an optimal experience of freedom and power. Inasmuch as his epigrams and interludes administer the tough love he is determined to impart, he deserves to be placed in the familiar company of Socrates, Diogenes, Lucian, Voltaire, Montaigne, Marx, Kierkegaard and other philosophical provocateurs.

Like his predecessors among the aphorists, Nietzsche wishes to present himself to his best readers as a credible, authentic source of efficacious wisdom. The epigrams and interludes he delivers in Part Four of *BGE* are meant to attest to the range and depth of his own experiences. No armchair philosopher or idle speculator, much less a would-be 'improver' of humanity, Nietzsche has paid dearly for the wisdom he now dispenses in concentrated bursts of epigrammatic wit. As his best readers are meant to appreciate, in short, he has *lived*, which means that he has suffered and survived myriad slights, losses and disappointments. Both individually and collectively, these setbacks have prompted him to ask (and answer) the difficult questions that a life of unbroken ease and

---

³ See Pippin 2010: 7–21; Brobjer 2010: 62–5; and Hui 2019: 159–64.

tranquillity would have failed to prompt. Wishing to be received, as he once said was true of Epicurus, as 'wisdom in bodily form' (HH II: 224), he offers these aphorisms as evidence of the wisdom his best readers may find embodied in him and, increasingly, in themselves.

As a man of experience and a teller of difficult truths, Nietzsche seeks to address – but not necessarily to quell – the agitations that the previous parts of *BGE* may have raised in his readers. Having urged them to adjust their sights and lower their expectations, precisely so that they might commit themselves to a less glamorous role in the production of a philosophy of the future, he evidently deems it important at this juncture to rehearse for them his credentials as their mentor and guide. The crucial claim on the table here is that he knows what he is doing. He has travelled this path, surveying the terrain it traverses, and he has arrived at the best destination and outcome within his (and their) reach. Having secured for himself the most advantagous situation available within the historical context he and they share, he has optimised his experience of freedom and agency. In short: he is a credible headmaster of the 'school for gentlemen' in which he has enrolled them. He has managed – according to him, largely on his own – to acquire for himself the finish he now offers to apply to them.

Recurring themes and persistent motifs

Although the epigrams and interludes collected in Part Four are rather loosely grouped, some recurring themes and persistent motifs merit our attention:

Depth psychology: Building on his spirited call for a more rigorously scientific approach to the study and practice of psychology (BGE 23), Nietzsche embeds several of his epigrams with the kinds of insights his best readers might expect to reap if, following his lead, they too explore the uncharted depths of the psyche. As he observes, for example, 'Not only our reason, but also our conscience subjects itself to our strongest drive, to the tyrant in us' (BGE 158). Offering a pithy lesson on the multiplicity of the soul and the conflicts internal to it, he stages the following exchange: '"I did that", says my memory. "I could not have done that" – says my pride, and refuses to yield. Finally – memory gives in' (BGE 68). Speculating on the possible continuity of our conscious and unconscious states, he observes that 'Even when we're awake we do things as in dreams: we first invent and create the person with whom we are dealing – and forget it right away' (BGE 138).

Nietzsche's pioneering efforts in the field of depth psychology similarly embolden him to erase or smudge the lines of division that supposedly separate human beings from other animals. His most notable contribution in this respect is his treatment of human interiority as a complex instance of animal psychology. While these lines of division may have been useful in the past, especially in support of long-standing claims to the lordly dignity of humanity, the myth of our separateness from the animal kingdom—that is, of our supposed transcendence (or mastery) of nature—is no longer sustainable. According to Nietzsche, in fact, we late moderns have become dangerously ignorant of – and, so, estranged from – the extent to which we too are creatures of breeding, custom, habit, instinct and disposable animal vitality.

In addition to alerting his best readers to the moral prejudices in which they might be unwittingly ensnared – for example, BGE 64, 118, 122 – Nietzsche also renews his earlier warning about the perils involved in adopting a properly scientific approach to depth psychology. In one of his most famous epigrams, he advises, 'Whoever battles monsters should take care that he doesn't become one in the process. And if you stare for a long time into an abyss, the abyss looks into you, too' (BGE 146). Finally, recalling his earlier characterisation of the will to truth (BGE 1–4), he notes, 'Perhaps no one yet has been truthful enough about what "truthfulness" is' (BGE 177).

Men and women: In various sections of Part Four, Nietzsche turns his attention to the nature of heteronormative romantic love and to the fraught relationships between men and women more generally. Apparently, the proverbial battle between the sexes is both real and enduring, owing to such factors as mutual misunderstanding (BGE 85), mutual self-deception (BGE 131) and the institutional intrusions, respectively, of marriage (BGE 123) and Christianity (BGE 168). Inasmuch as biographers and scholars tend to agree that Nietzsche had very little first-hand experience with requited heteronormative romantic love, it may be the case that his remarks are meant to impress by virtue of the clinical distance that informs them. (Indeed, few scholars would insist that Nietzsche is too close to this subject matter, or too experienced in its nuances, to render an adequately objective claim.)

In several other epigrams, Nietzsche sees fit to offer his views on women (or 'woman'), which some readers have judged to be excessively reliant on tired, demeaning stereotypes. Here we learn, for example, that women are prone to hatred (BGE 84), vanity and self-contempt (BGE 86), shame (BGE 114), 'barbaric' love and revenge (BGE 139), and a 'genius for finery' and (a related) 'instinct for a *secondary* role' (BGE 145). In an epigram that has not aged well at all, he declares that 'When a woman has scholarly inclinations, then usually there is something wrong with her sexuality' (BGE 144). As we survey these epigrams, we would do well to recall that Nietzsche launched *BGE* by supposing that 'truth is a woman'. In the event that his remarks on women strike the reader as crude, anachronistic or amateurish, they nevertheless may admit of productive interpretation as pertaining to the pursuit of truth.

Immoralism: Building on his (presumptive) designation of himself and his best readers as 'immoralists' (BGE 32), Nietzsche devotes several sections of Part Four to an elaboration of the 'immoral' truths to which they are (or soon will be) entitled. As his readers prepare for the destructive task to which he has invited them, they might be pleased to learn that 'there are no moral phenomena at all, but only a moral interpretation of phenomena' (BGE 108).[4] They also would do well to heed his cautionary tale of those 'criminals' who 'diminish' or 'slander' the 'deeds' they once dared to commit (BGE 109). Indeed, they may feel vindicated by his assurance that the telltale 'deed' of the 'criminal' betrays a 'beautiful horror' that a gifted 'artist' might turn to the criminal's 'advantage' (BGE 110). Finally, they are welcome to adopt as their watchword what might have served Nietzsche as an apt epigraph to *BGE*: 'What is done out of love always occurs beyond good and evil' (BGE 153).

---

[4] See May 1999: 107–26; Leiter 2002: 115–25, 156–63; and Janaway 2007: 252–4.

The perils of perspectival familiarity: Several epigrams in Part Four are devoted to the dangers incident to an extended reliance on familiar perspectives and customary frames of reference. Here as elsewhere, Nietzsche's most powerful insights derive their disruptive force from the sudden introduction of a novel or uncommon angle of vision, which, if adopted, would enable his best readers to reorient themselves to the question or problem at hand. An instructive example of this strategy is the following burst of insight: 'You've only been a poor observer of life if you haven't also seen the hand that indulgently – kills' (BGE 69). Building on his earlier suspicions of martyrs and saints, respectively, he thus expounds, 'What? A great man? All I ever see is the actor of his own ideal' (BGE 97). Previewing his advice to his still-virtuous readers in Part Seven of *BGE*, he explains that 'the great periods of our life are to be found where we summon the courage to rechristen our evils as our best' (BGE 116).

As these epigrams confirm, Nietzsche's philosophical interventions are meant to accomplish the kind of intrusive violence that is likely to liberate his best readers from points of view and frames of reference that have grown stale, cramped or dim. These interventions are also meant to accustom his best readers to the various modes of communication he will employ in nudging them towards their optimal experience of freedom and power. As we have seen, his goal for them is to arrive of their own volition at the realisation that they are neither the 'free spirits' nor the anti-Christians they take themselves to be. Having done so, they might become progressively more receptive to his plan for attacking the 'old' morality from *within* its dwindling sphere of contested authority.

Hypocrisy and self-deception: Several of the epigrams collected in Part Four are meant to expose the disjunctions that obtain between what his best readers are likely to expect of (and how they treat) others and what they are likely to expect of (and how they treat) themselves. He thus observes that 'Before ourselves we all pose as more naïve than we are: this is how we rest from our peers' (BGE 100). Expressing a similar sentiment, he notes that 'We may lie through the mouth, but with the face we make in doing it, we end up telling the truth' (BGE 166).

Acknowledging that his best readers are keen observers (and judges) of others, Nietzsche repeatedly encourages them to become similarly knowledgeable (and similarly ruthless) with respect to themselves: 'Whoever does not know the way to *his* ideal lives more carelessly and impudently than someone without an ideal' (BGE 133). Towards this end, he treats his readers to various insights that they might expect to affirm as they establish a healthy measure of critical distance from their most familiar convictions. As this emphasis confirms, he is concerned to acquaint them with the extent to which they do not know themselves, especially inasmuch as they are accustomed to *lying* about themselves and being rewarded (in the currency of social recognition) for doing so. To wit: '"I don't like him." – Why? – "I am not his equal." – Has anyone ever answered this way?' (BGE 185).

Many of the epigrams found in Part Four are clearly meant to accustom Nietzsche's readers to a regimen of self-scrutiny and self-discovery that is significantly more rigorous than any they are likely to have encountered thus far. As he peppers his readers with observations that challenge what 'everyone' supposedly knows about agency and motivation, he adopts a more forcefully didactic approach and tone. In these sections, his readers receive neither fair warning nor soothing caveats for the sudden truths he lobs in their direction. These epigrams challenge standard accounts of motivation, childish pieties about the 'goodness' or 'evil' of human nature, and attributions of altruism and generosity that are traditionally marshalled in praise of civilised, upright, moral human beings. Although these epigrams are formulated in very general terms, in support of a more or less comprehensive model of human interiority, they are also designed to guide his best readers as they attempt the deeply personal (and often painful) soul-searching that he urges them to undertake.[5]

The joys of iconoclasm: Although the epigrams collected in Part Four cover a fairly wide range of topics and themes, a feature that many of them share in common is Nietzsche's unabashed expression of an untimely, anti-modern iconoclasm. Indeed, many of

---

[5] Here I follow Hui 2019: 172–4.

these epigrams afford him the opportunity to display the obvious joy he takes in shattering false images, exploding archaic taboos, sounding out hollow idols, demolishing wobbly pillars of conventional wisdom and generally deranging those views and values that are widely accepted by his contemporaries. Not surprisingly, Christianity emerges as a favoured target in Part Four. In some cases, he swiftly turns the tables, insisting, for example, that 'the devil . . . [is] the oldest friend of knowledge' (BGE 129); that 'people are punished best for their virtues' (BGE 132); and that 'what an age perceives as evil is usually an untimely afternote of what was formerly perceived as good' (BGE 149). In other cases, he takes obvious delight in confounding standard Christian teachings, as when he declares that 'it is inhuman to bless where you are being cursed' (BGE 181), or when he attributes to Jesus the teaching that 'The law was for servants – love God as I love him, as his son! What do we sons of God care about morality!' (BGE 164).

Review

Having subjected his best readers to a potentially terrifying glimpse of the calamity they now face (BGE 62), Nietzsche interrupts the main narrative of his book to deliver a broadside of targeted bursts of insight, wit and wisdom. Retreating in Part Four of *BGE* to the more familiar ground of the here and now, he schools his best readers in the truthfulness they will need to cultivate if they are to contribute meaningfully to the production of a philosophy of the future. As a purveyor of aphoristic wisdom, Nietzsche thus confirms his allegiance to those traditions and schools of philosophy in which real-time practical guidance is judged to be every bit as important as theoretical sophistication. The epigrams and interludes collected in Part Four are thus intended to exert a direct and (eventually) palpable influence on the lives and behaviour of his best readers.

The practical guidance on offer in Part Four of *BGE* is meant to advance the programme of education and training in which he has enrolled his readers. As they continue to adjust their expectations to accommodate the limiting conditions of their unique historical situation, they may put into practice the wisdom encoded in these epigrams and interludes. Rather than await the payoff that will arrive at the end of the book, his best readers should already be involved in the practical matters of reconfiguring their customs and habits, exercising their powers of imagination and creativity, reviving their passions and affects, recalibrating their 'value-emotions', and renewing their commitment to a mortal, embodied, earthly existence.

6
Part Five: On the Natural History of Morality

Preview

Having concluded his lively intermezzo, Nietzsche resumes his elaboration of the challenge at hand. As we recall, he ended Part Three by summoning the unflattering image of 'the European of today' (BGE 62), which he described there as the unfortunate product of the unchecked spread of the 'religious neurosis'. That the emergent mass of 'herd animals' currently has no direction, purpose, place or future is, in Nietzsche's estimation, a regrettable calamity, which he traces to the surging influence of the 'democratic movement' in Europe.[1]

That this calamity need not be the end of the story is the (cautiously) upbeat message he wishes to convey in the remaining parts of *BGE*. Towards this end, he devotes Part Five to a report of his progress thus far towards the realisation of a *natural history of morality*, which he recommends as both complementary to and supportive of the scientific worldview his readers claim to prefer. Much as he did in Part Three with respect to religion, here he recommends an approach to morality that is broadly descriptive and distinctly *anthropological* in nature. (Indeed, what his 'poorly informed and even minimally curious' predecessors have missed is none other than the 'problem of morality itself' (BGE 186),

---

[1] He earlier refers to 'the democratic movement' 'not merely as a declining form of political organization, but as a declining, moreover diminishing form of the human being, as his mediocritization and debasement in value' (BGE 203).

by which he means to designate the immediate context within which – and in response to which – a particular morality rises, falls, and/or evolves.)

Rather than treat and evaluate moralities as competing interpretations of divine will, or as worldly approximations of otherworldly laws and norms, much less as conduits to a desired afterlife or paradise, Nietzsche proposes to treat and evaluate moralities as alternative techniques for 'breeding' particular types or kinds of human beings. As he did in Part Three with respect to religion, he locates the 'essence' or 'nature' of morality in its service as a 'means of cultivation and education' (BGE 62), viz., as a tool of character-building discipline and control.

According to the terms of the anthropological approach he favours in Part Five, moralities are to be classified and esteemed solely on the basis of the quality of the forms of life they promote and/or discourage. To borrow the alternative evaluative language introduced in Part One of *BGE*: practitioners of a 'natural history of morality' would be concerned to reveal the extent to which a particular morality is 'life-promoting, life-preserving, species-preserving, perhaps even species-cultivating' (BGE 4). That a morality might be reliant on falsehoods and fabrications would not be sufficient to motivate an immediate objection either to its implementation or to its continued authority. As we shall see, the anthropological value of a morality is determined by the quality of the human type(s) it actually manages to produce, independent of the means and methods it employs.

The anthropological approach Nietzsche recommends in Part Five will position his readers to dispense with supernatural, theological and metaphysical principles of explanation – including the teleology that he finds (and criticises) in so many contemporary historical accounts of the development of morality – and it will cleave more strictly (but not slavishly) to the evidence that is available in the historical record. Rather than 'find' confirmation of the currency of modern beliefs and contemporary values in the distant past, as is the habit of the 'English psychologists' among his rivals (GM I: 1), his anthropological approach to the history of morality will permit the past to disclose itself on its own terms, even if these terms are offensive or foreign to his late modern readers.² Rather than assume, fatuously, that the 'foundation for morality' awaits his (or anyone's) discovery, for example, he gently reminds his readers that any such 'foundation' would be an unlikely feature of 'a world whose essence is will to power' (BGE 186). As this reminder indicates, he is especially concerned in Part Five to outline an approach to the history of morality that will allow him to document the occasional eruptions of active forces that have altered the landscape of morality (cf. GM II: 17–18).

As Nietzsche explains in his next book, the anthropological approach he recommends in Part Five of *BGE* might be more accurately described as producing a *genealogy of morality*, especially since it is meant to explain how late modern Europeans became ensnared in the crisis he is keen to address.

Summary of sections

Part Five of *BGE* comprises seventeen numbered sections (186–203). In sections 186–7, Nietzsche takes aim at what he calls the 'moral sentiment in Europe now', which, he insists, is at odds with the relatively new 'science of morality' that his contemporaries have recently (and, in his opinion, clumsily) launched (BGE 186). Intending to side, eventually, with the latter against the former, he sets out in Part Five to purge the fledgling 'science of morality' of its residual (and as yet unacknowledged) reliance on the very 'moral sentiment' it has pledged, as yet naïvely, to oppose.

As a first step towards counteracting the unwanted influence of the aforementioned 'moral sentiment', Nietzsche discloses the need to compile a properly scientific '*typology* of morals' (BGE 186), which he envisions as a comprehensive inventory of the types and kinds of moralities that have flourished and perished over the long course of human history. (Ideally, this typology also will include a survey of human and hominid *pre*-history, to the extent that its general trends and patterns may be speculatively reconstructed from the available evidence.) If Nietzsche and his readers are to contribute meaningfully to the typology

---

² On the distinctly naturalistic character of the 'natural history of morality', see Leiter 2002: 11–29; Emden 2014: 204–14; Leiter 2019: 5–14.

he has in mind, they will be obliged to become far more 'modest' than other would-be contributors to the 'science of morality' (BGE 186). As we shall see, he is particularly concerned to preach and practise 'modesty' with respect to the relevance for a proper 'science of morals' of the distinctly modern beliefs and values of its leading practitioners, whose unacknowledged 'good *faith* in the prevailing morality' prevents them from wondering about its provenance (BGE 186). Indeed, the approach he recommends in Part Five will be distinguished from rival treatments of morality by its consideration of the past on its own terms, by virtue of which the (as yet unsuspected) 'real problems of morality' will be rendered manifest (BGE 186).

The imperative of nature

So as to prepare his best readers to undertake the typology he has urged them to compile, Nietzsche offers several untimely insights into the nature and practice of morality (BGE 187–200). We learn, for example, that a morality may be understood on the basis of what it indirectly conveys about its authors and guardians, independently of what it actually prescribes to its adherents (BGE 187). Indeed, a properly historical approach to morality will reveal that moralities are conceived, implemented and repurposed for any number of diverse reasons and objectives, not all of which are conducive to the flourishing of those to whom they are prescribed. In an effort to nudge his readers towards the idea that moralities are always also tools of discipline and control, he urges them to consider each morality as if it were 'a *sign language of the affects*' (BGE 187).[3]

Building on this insight, Nietzsche previews for his readers what their 'typology of morals' is likely to confirm – namely, that 'every morality' involves 'a piece of tyranny against "nature" [and] also against "reason"' (BGE 188), which, if true, will position them to dispute the validity of any (so-called) morality that presents

---

[3] This somewhat obscure reference is clarified elsewhere: Whereas 'the morality of Christian concepts of value . . . [arose] on ground that is morbid through and through . . . master morality . . . is the sign language of successful development, of *ascending* life, of the will to power as the principle of life' (CW E).

itself as a corrective for the 'tyranny' in question. This would be an important advance for Nietzsche to secure, for he vehemently opposes the efforts of those champions of contemporary morality who vow to end the suffering associated with such 'tyranny'. As he makes clear later in *BGE*, the suffering in question is an indispensable catalyst of the growth he identifies as conducive to the amplification of meaning and the subsequent elevation of culture. While it is true, as he puts it there, that the 'creator' within us must be spared any unnecessary suffering, the 'creature' within us *must* be made to suffer if we, as composite beings, are to progress and flourish (BGE 225). To lavish pity upon that within us which remains as yet unfinished is to consign humanity to a legislated mediocrity, which, Nietzsche believes, is itself a kind of suffering that is readily preventable (BGE 225).

A comprehensive survey of actual moralities will reveal, first of all, that contemporary morality, characterised by its aspiration to universal application and its valorisation of *selflessness*, is by no means the only (or the best) species of morality; and, second, that a direct relationship obtains between the elevation of a people or nation and the rigour of the morality that serves it. Hence Nietzsche's praise for those moralities that enforce (what he deems to be) a kind of tyranny: any achievement of growth, power, self-overcoming and the experience of freedom presupposes the presence of constraints against which an organism, an individual, a clade, a tribe, a people, a nation or a culture may engage in productive, upbuilding struggle. He cites poets, composers, orators and artists as experts on this point: their best, most creative efforts are the products not of *laissez aller* (i.e., letting themselves go), but of their strict, protracted obedience to those laws, norms and regulations that elicit from them their latent creative genius. 'What is essential and inestimable in every morality', he thus decrees, 'is that it is a long compulsion' (BGE 188).

This anthropological approach to the 'science of morality' thus reveals the narrowly circumscribed conditions under which human beings might reasonably expect to survive and thrive. Foremost among these conditions is what Nietzsche labels 'nature's moral imperative', which, he explains, is addressed to 'peoples, races, ages, classes – but primarily to the whole "human" animal, to *humankind*' (BGE 188). According to the terms of 'nature's moral imperative', he explains, 'Thou shalt obey, anybody at all, and for a long time: *otherwise* you will perish and lose all respect for yourself' (BGE 188). The second of these unwanted outcomes is not simply an afterthought on Nietzsche's part. Unlike other animals, for whom survival is sufficient, the human animal also must endeavour to thrive, which it can do *only* if it acquires sufficient self-respect to project its will into the future.

We thus arrive at the chief justification for the 'natural history of morality' that Nietzsche outlines in Part Five of *BGE*. Nature *may* be considered a trusty teacher or guide, as various moralities have insisted (BGE 9), but only *indirectly* so – owing not to any native impulse towards philanthropy or human-centred hospitality, but to 'her wasteful and *indifferent* magnificence, which is outrageous but noble' (BGE 188).

Nature teaches us, in other words, by showing us no particular favour whatsoever, thereby compelling us to tyrannise ourselves in the face of its (or her) staggering indifference to human aspiration and artifice. According to Nietzsche, 'nature's moral imperative' comes to us directly from those among us who mandate the anthropogenic tyranny our survival requires. Finally arriving at the 'immoral' conclusion of his case for protracted, compulsory obedience, he observes that 'slavery, it seems, in the cruder and finer sense of the word, is also an indispensable means of spiritual discipline and cultivation' (BGE 188). As this section makes clear, moreover, the obedience that nature's indifference ordains also produces in us the self-respect that funds any credible project of cultural elevation. (As we shall see, however, the typical yield reaped by nature from an entire 'people' – 'six or seven great men' (BGE 126) – is no longer sufficiently productive of self-respect to warrant the future of humankind.)

Other lessons follow from this crucial insight into the 'natural' imperative to obey: the importance of calculated fasting (BGE 189); the ignoble origin of the insistence, on the part of Socrates and of contemporary utilitarians, that those who are 'bad' are merely in error (BGE 190–1); the unacknowledged complementary role of 'invention' (or fabrication) in any process of cognition (BGE 192); the formative role of dreams in structuring and enriching our waking experience (BGE 193); the diverse meanings attached by individuals and peoples to the experience of ownership (BGE 194); the 'inversion of values' wrought, supposedly, by the Israelites of the Second Temple period (and the founding role of this 'inversion' in launching 'the *slave revolt in morality*') (BGE 195); and the centrality to any morality of unseen causes and forces whose exertions must be inferred from observable behaviours that are not otherwise fully explained (BGE 196).

Having (indirectly) introduced himself as 'a psychologist of morality' (BGE 196), and having forewarned his readers of the 'inferences' to follow, Nietzsche turns his attention to some of the most common and persistent of the misunderstandings that continue to delay the progress of a properly anthropological approach to the 'science of morality'. As we learn, those moralities in which 'predatory' human beings are classified as 'pathological' (rather than, say, as 'healthy' or 'tropical') evince a measure of 'timidity' that is inconsistent with the growth and elevation of a thriving people or culture (BGE 197). Equally 'timid' are those risk- and danger-averse moralities that counsel their adherents against indulging any strong or ennobling passions, as if a homespun collection of prudential platitudes were an acceptable substitute for a science of morality (BGE 198).

Resuming his discussion of the 'imperative' to obey, Nietzsche submits the 'fact' that 'among human beings obedience has so far been practiced and cultivated best and longest' (BGE 199). As a result, he explains,

> [T]he need for obedience is now innate in the average person, as a kind of *formal conscience* that commands: 'Thou shalt unconditionally do something, and unconditionally not do something'. . . (BGE 199)

Claiming that 'the herd instinct of obedience is inherited best and at the expense of the art of commanding' (BGE 199), he speculates that the extreme case would be one in which 'the commanders and those who are independent are the very ones who will be lacking; or they will suffer inwardly from bad conscience and first need to deceive themselves in order to command' (BGE 199).

As it turns out, this is no idle hypothesis on Nietzsche's part, for it describes the situation on the ground in the late modern Europe of his day. Those who are believed to command typically do no more than relay the wishes of other or higher authority figures. This command deficit is matched on the other side by the surplus obedience of 'the herd man in Europe today', who 'gives himself the appearance of being the only permissible kind of human being' (BGE 199). According to Nietzsche, however, all is not (necessarily) lost. Citing the example of Napoleon's tyranny over Europe, he insists that 'the appearance of one who commands unconditionally [would] strike these herd-animal Europeans as an immense comfort and salvation' (BGE 199). Apparently, the emerging mass of European 'herd animals' would be relieved to accept the yoke designed for them by a commander who finds meaning and joy in compelling the obedience of others.

Why might this be so? By way of preparing his readers to consider his bold plan for cultural renewal, Nietzsche offers the following psychological profile of the aforementioned 'herd man of Europe today':

> Someone from an age of disintegration, in which races are mixed together, who as such embodies the heritage of multiple origins, that is, conflicting, and often not only conflicting drives and value-standards that fight one another and rarely give each other any peace – such a human being of late cultures and refracted lights will on average be a weaker human being: his most basic longing is that the war that he *is* simply come to an end. . . (BGE 200)

In addition to providing welcome insight into the causes and consequences of the aforementioned calamity, this passage reveals the silver lining that Nietzsche spies in an otherwise dark and angry cloud. According to him, the current situation is sufficiently chaotic that the emerging mass of European 'herd animals' is likely to welcome the unambiguous commands issued by a strong, uncompromising, charismatic leader.

They would do so, he adds, because the leader he has described will succeed not by *ending* the 'war' that contemporary Europeans have become, but by rebranding this 'war' as a previously unacknowledged 'stimulus and spur to life' (BGE 200). Simply put, the kind of leader Nietzsche has in mind will model to the 'Europeans of today' – and, so, justify in the process – a life of *productive* internal conflict. The irony here is that the freedom associated with the morality of *laissez aller* will actually prompt those who have been liberated to crave the direction that only a tyrant can provide.

Before closing this line of inquiry, Nietzsche teases his readers with the prospect of a leader who not only confers meaning upon the spiritual suffering of the masses, but also displays 'a genuine mastery and subtlety of waging war with oneself' (BGE 200). And although he does not exactly promise that some such figure will emerge to redeem the 'herd animal Europeans of today', he does note, intriguingly, that such leaders tend to 'appear in exactly the same ages when that weaker type with his longing for peace steps to the fore' (BGE 200). The intended implication is clear enough: those who join Nietzsche in preparing for the production of a philosophy of the future may expect to be rewarded for their efforts by the arrival of a leader 'predestined for victories and for seduction' (BGE 200; cf. GM II: 24).

The moral neurosis

Having made his preliminary case for the match he has proposed, Nietzsche pivots to his conclusion. In doing so, he previews an important lesson that he expects the prescribed 'typology of morals' to confirm. In an effort to isolate the basic psycho-dynamic principles that govern the internal maintenance of the 'herd', he declares that the social machinery of the 'herd' is simply inimical to the 'love of the neighbor' that is (dishonestly) promoted by the champions of Christian morality (BGE 201). The primary concern of the 'herd', he reveals, is to preserve the community it shelters. The problem, as we shall see, is that the goal of preserving the community as constituted, *qua* 'herd', does not merit the measures taken to preserve it.

Here's why: once the herd has defended itself against the threats posed by external enemies – typically, by retreating, surrendering, capitulating or otherwise submitting – it naturally seeks to secure itself against the threats posed by internal enemies. Owing to its pathologically risk-averse constitution, however, the herd understands its internal enemies to include any of its members whose expression of strong drives or vibrant passions might 'bring about the destruction of the community's sense of self' (BGE 201), for example, by standing out and casting an oppressively long shadow. To guard against any such transgression, the herd brands as *evil* any type or token of self-expression 'that elevates the individual beyond the herd and causes fear in neighbors' (BGE 201). The essence of the herd morality may thus be distilled into the following 'imperative of herd timidity': 'we want that some day there should be *nothing any more to fear*' (BGE 201).

Connecting his analysis in Part Five to his investigation of the 'character' of religion in Part Three, Nietzsche attributes to the 'herd animal morality' a steadfast refusal to acknowledge any other (much less any *higher*) types or kinds of morality: 'it says stubbornly and ruthlessly, "I am morality itself and nothing besides is morality!"' (BGE 202). As Nietzsche's readers will no doubt have noticed, this outrageous (and patently ahistorical) claim bespeaks a spiritual affliction that is related, by virtue of its unchained narcissism, to the 'religious neurosis' diagnosed in Part Three of *BGE*. Just as the 'religious neurosis' achieves full bloom in its unwarranted assertion of cultural 'sovereignty' (BGE 62), so the 'herd animal morality' reveals *its* besetting neurosis in its fantasy of having consolidated a monopoly in the business of morality (BGE 202).

In both cases, a potentially serviceable set of cultural practices has been permitted to exceed the boundaries established for it within the (formerly sturdy) order of rank. In both cases, moreover, the trespass in question is traced to the collapse of the order of rank, which Nietzsche prefers to characterise in terms of a dereliction of duty on the part of those philosophers who are supposed to reinforce its structure and police its internal boundaries. In both cases, finally, the prescribed remedy involves a restoration (and likely fortification) of the collapsed order of rank. Just as the 'new' philosophers will contain the epidemic outbreak of the 'religious neurosis' by treating all 'sovereign' religions as handy tools of discipline and control, so will they 'force' all moralities 'to bow first of all to the *rank order*' (BGE 221),[4] which they will determine by reckoning the relative value of the 'characters' each morality is known to produce.[5] Needless to say, the 'herd animal morality', which neurotically hails itself as the one true morality, will find itself at or near the bottom of the restored order of rank.

The 'new' philosophers: commanders and legislators

Prompted by the threat he associates with the rise and virulence of 'the democratic movement' in Europe, Nietzsche devotes the final section of Part Five to an extended invocation of those 'new' philosophers whom he earlier introduced and praised (BGE 203). What is new in this context is that Part Five has made the case for a productive, win–win match between the emergent mass of European 'herd animals' and the 'new' philosophers whom he envisions. Speaking for all those who still remain even minimally hopeful of the renewal of European culture, he insists that 'there is no choice' but to anticipate and prepare for the arrival of 'spirits who are strong and original enough to stimulate opposing valuations and to revalue "eternal values"' (BGE 203). They will do so, he promises, by reinstituting (and subsequently policing) a viable, future-bestowing order of rank, the resurgence of which will not only reignite 'the will of millennia', but also direct its progress along '*new* [i.e., ordered, goal-directed] rails' (BGE 203).

That Nietzsche remains resiliently hopeful is a function of his faith in the particular intervention that he believes these 'new' philosophers will stage: they will 'teach human beings the future of humanity as its *will*, as dependent on a human will' (BGE 203).

---

[4] Presumably, the 'new' philosophers will be considerably more adept at making (and enforcing) this case than the 'moral pedant' to whom Nietzsche refers in BGE 221. I am indebted here to Lampert 2001: 213–14; and Burnham 2007: 158–9.

[5] Although Nietzsche does not explicitly diagnose a 'moral neurosis' in *BGE*, he later confirms the neurotic kinship of religion and morality: 'Moral judgment has this in common with religious judgment, that it believes in nonexistent realities . . . Moral judgment, like religious judgment, belongs to a level of ignorance where even the concept of the real, the distinction between the real and the imaginary, is lacking: So that "truth" at such a level indicates nothing but things that today we call "fantasies"' (TI 'Improvers' 1).

They will do so, he explains, by 'prepar[ing] great risks and overall experiments [*Gesammt-Versuche*] of culture and cultivation', which will be applied, apparently, to the undisciplined, uncultivated mass of European 'herd animals' (BGE 203). His choice of words in this passage reminds us of his wish, voiced earlier in *BGE*, to cast himself and his best readers as worthy predecessors of those 'experimenters' and 'tempters' [*Versucher*] who, he promises, will lead European humanity on its thrilling voyage beyond good and evil (BGE 42). His own hopes for the future thus arise from the connection he posits between the self-directed 'experiments' he and his best readers will conduct and the grand cultural 'experiments' to be inaugurated and supervised by the philosophers of the future.

Nietzsche's aim here, which is easily misplaced behind the soaring rhetoric of his conclusion, is to interpret the recent emergence of an unformed mass of European 'herd animals' as a sign that humankind can no longer afford to entrust its future to 'the monstrous fortuity' that has guided its erratic, just-in-time development thus far (BGE 203). As we are now in a position to understand, the problem with relying on the 'monstrous fortuity' of nature is the lamentable inconsistency of nature's production of those higher human beings – for example, free spirits, exotic exemplars, great individuals, geniuses of the heart, etc. – whose exploits embolden humanity to project its will into the future. In an extended fallow period, like that of late modernity, the will for the future of humanity will ebb as metaphysical (and eschatological) comforts once again become increasingly appealing. Under such conditions, humanity is in danger of believing itself to be inadequate on its own merits to warrant a future worthy of the sacrifice and hardships involved in securing the terms of its production.

Indeed, this is the (limited) sense in which humanity now must aspire to take its place, soon to be vacated by God, at the command centre of the cosmos. By seizing control of nature's 'breeding' project (GM II: 1), and compensating in the process for the indifference of nature, the 'new' philosophers described by Nietzsche will undertake the willed production of those 'higher' human beings whose norm-shattering exploits catalyse the elevation of culture. In their capacity as 'legislators and commanders', the philosophers of the future will do for humankind what we have become convinced over the past two millennia that only God could accomplish on our behalf. Under their legislative guidance, the '*as yet undetermined animal*' (BGE 62) will finally receive its optimal determination.

No longer reliant upon the grace of God and the promise of a table-turning passage to the afterlife, the philosophers of the future will assure mortal, worldly human beings that their finite existence is justified and worthy of affirmation. In doing so, they will finally answer the question of 'which type of human we should *breed*, should *will*, as being of higher value, worthier of life, more certain of a future' (A 3). In other words: to prepare for the arrival of the 'new' philosophers is to prepare for their efforts to authorise the single greatest upheaval and redirection in the history of human civilisation. On the strength of their efforts to 'force the will of millennia upon *new* rails' (BGE 203), humankind will either emancipate itself from 'the monstrous fortuity' on which it has been reliant *or* perish in its attempt to do so.[6]

Nietzsche thus hopes to persuade his best readers to receive the recent emergence of a mass of European 'herd animals' not only as a calamity, never to be repeated, but also as an opportunity to liberate humankind from the 'grisly reign of nonsense and accident' (BGE 203). Although he leaves the details of this liberation to the philosophers of the future, his matchmaking efforts betray his lingering weakness for a social structure in which the emergent mass of European 'herd animals' is collected at (and as) the base of a pyramidal class- or caste-stratified polity. Indeed, despite acknowledging the limitations of the aristocratic forms of order that have served thus far to elevate humanity and enhance the human type, he remains confident that something like an 'aristocratic society' will figure prominently in the plans of the 'new' philosophers (BGE 257). Presumably, the herd animals in question

---

[6] In order to 'force the will of millennia upon *new* rails' (BGE 203), the 'new' philosophers will need to overpower the 'single will [that has] dominated Europe for eighteen centuries' – namely, the will to 'mak[e] human beings into a *sublime abortion*' (BGE 62). On the darker implications of what Nietzsche proposes in this section, see Burnham 2007: 131–4.

will receive direction, purpose, meaning, form and 'breeding' in exchange for their (unspecified) contributions in support of the deliberate, timely, willed production of exemplary human beings. After revealing the source of his hopes for the future, Nietzsche concludes Part Five with a preview of what the 'natural history of morality' is likely to disclose – namely, *'the total degeneration of human beings* down to . . . the perfect herd animal[s]', which he characterises, derisively, as 'dwarf animals of equal rights and claims' (BGE 203). And although he regards this outcome as deplorable, alerting his best readers to the unprecedented 'nausea' (or 'disgust') they are likely to endure as they compile the prescribed 'typology of morals', he nevertheless dangles before them the prospect of a 'new *task*' (BGE 203), which he apparently believes will compensate them for the discomfort they are certain to experience.

Here two additional points bear noting. First of all, Nietzsche informs his best readers that their inquiries into the 'natural history of morality' will acquaint them with an alternative (and venerable) measure of human flourishing, in comparison to which contemporary Christian morality will be exposed as a vector of degeneration. Having glimpsed this alternative measure of human flourishing, his readers are likely to realise that the emergence of 'the perfect herd animal', hailed by 'socialist clowns and flatheads' as 'their [ideal] human of the future', in fact attests to the recession or loss of the kind of future to which they would be inclined to attach their will (BGE 203). Second, he envisions the exercise of compiling a 'typology of morals' as both preparatory *and* initiatory. It is meant to endow his best readers with a scholarly, truth-intensive momentum that will carry them forward towards the 'task' he has reserved for them, the content of which he will reveal to them in Part Seven of *BGE*.

Review

Nietzsche's contribution to the newly emergent 'science of morality' involves an unsentimental study, predicated on an unprecedented historical (and pre-historical) sweep, of the diverse kinds and types of moralities to which the historical record attests. The expected results of the prescribed 'typology of morals' include the following: therapeutic, sanity-restoring outcomes for those involved in the study; welcome insight into the historical diversity of moral types and kinds; a preliminary acquaintance with those healthier forms of life in which the will to power is visibly dominant; the recovery of lost or neglected moral wisdom; an understanding of the various ends and objectives to which moralities have been employed; a sober reckoning of the opportunity costs associated with the pursuit of a moral monoculture and a morality of universal scope; an appreciation of contemporary morality as an historical aberration; and, finally, the dawning of a prospective sense of 'what could yet *be cultivated in human beings*' (BGE 203).

The large-scale civilising project that Nietzsche envisions in Part Five is meant not only to amplify the frequency of the emergence of 'higher' human types, but also to encourage 'ordinary' human beings to see themselves as party to a stable, sustainable species, reliant only on itself for the justification and meaning it seeks. To date, the obstacles and challenges humankind has encountered in nature (including human nature) have sufficed to elicit our best, most creative genius. From this point forward, however, humanity must take active, prospective control of this process of development. According to Nietzsche, the 'new' philosophers whom he foresees will incorporate into the formative apparatus of culture the precise impediments and challenges that will vouchsafe the continued survival of humanity (or over-humanity) in the 'extramoral' future to come.

7
Part Six: We Scholars

Preview

Thus far in *BGE*, Nietzsche has identified a *crisis* (viz. the emergence of an unformed mass of European 'herd animals'), presented a *diagnosis* (viz. the unchecked assertion of neurotic claims of cultural sovereignty) and proposed a *solution* (viz. the rise of a new breed of philosophers, who, having reclaimed the lordly prerogative to *create values*, will grant these 'herd animals' the direction, purpose and meaning they currently lack). Apparently, as we have seen, this solution will authorise the 'new' philosophers to employ the emergent mass of 'herd animals' in an effort to produce, as a matter of design and volition, those 'higher' human beings who, to date, have only ever emerged as accidental, unanticipated 'lucky strikes'. Aiming to circumvent (or correct for) 'the law of nonsense in the overall economy of humanity' (BGE 62), Nietzsche sketches a future in which the 'new' philosophers will mobilise the emergent mass of 'herd animals' in the service of their (as yet unspecified) efforts to execute this ambitious plan.

To be sure, the consolidation of a philosophy of the future is still a long way off. Nietzsche's more pressing concern is to steer his best readers towards the conditions under which they might productively express their anti-Christian animus and their pro-science enthusiasm. This they will accomplish, he advises, only if they constitute themselves as a mutually supportive collective (i.e., a 'we') under his tutelage, and only in their capacity as *scholars*. Perhaps sensing the temptation on their part to overstep their age and barge headlong into the future he has sketched for them, he aims in Part Six to ground his readers in the twilight period of late modernity and restrict their attention to the optimisation of the scholarly gifts at their disposal. They will know and feel themselves to be 'free spirits', he assures them, but *only* in the event that they situate themselves, as scholars, in the residually moral period that has produced them. Still, the breathtaking glimpse he provides of an 'extramoral' future, wherein humankind finally accepts responsibility for its own destiny, may serve to rally his best readers to the comparatively modest role, *qua* scholars, to which he assigns them.

Summary of sections

Part Six of *BGE* comprises nine numbered sections (204–13). Having entrusted his best readers with the preparatory task of producing a 'typology of morals', Nietzsche is concerned in Part Six to acquaint them with a scholarly (or scientific) context that has become increasingly free of theological, doctrinal and ecclesiastical constraints. While the freedom they enjoy no doubt appeals to them, which may account for their interest in *BGE*, the collapse (or erosion) of familiar norms and boundaries will introduce a new set of challenges, of which they are mostly ignorant. Indeed, Nietzsche is particularly concerned in Part Six to investigate what it means to be a scholar in an age in which 'only the herd animal receives and dispenses honors' (BGE 212).

In sections 204–5, he takes note of, and prepares his best readers to criticise, the recent (and alarming) development wherein scientists and scholars have declared their 'independence' and asserted their 'emancipation' from philosophy, as if they were free to proceed without the benefit of philosophical training, direction and rigour (BGE 204). (Although Nietzsche does not say so here, we may assume that the renegade scholars in question are similarly unwilling to acknowledge the status of psychology, 'for whose service and preparation the remaining sciences exist' (BGE 23).) This unwelcome departure from the order of rank among scholarly types is a consequence, he explains, of the increasingly pervasive 'democratic movement', whose levelling influence he charted in Part Five of *BGE*. The not-so-subtle subtext here is that his best readers will need to distance themselves from this emergent ideal of emancipation and, in the process, close 'the gates to the rabble man's instinct' (BGE 204).

Of course, if the emancipated scholars in question are unimpressed by philosophy as it is *currently* practised, their disdain is entirely understandable:

> Especially the sight of those mishmash philosophers who call themselves 'philosophers of reality' or 'positivists' is capable of planting a dangerous mistrust into the soul of a young, ambitious scholar: those are at best scholars and specialists themselves, it is palpable! – (BGE 204)

Philosophy in the modern period has lost its way, Nietzsche explains, because philosophers have forsaken their obligation to lead and abandoned their right to command. This dereliction of legislative duty is in fact symptomatic of the 'self-contempt' that Nietzsche claims to detect in those philosophies that take great pride in discrediting everything from which humankind as a whole derives its sense of pride. Elaborating on his previous indictment of the 'epistemological scepticism' that animates 'modern philosophy' (BGE 54), he draws a damning conclusion:

> Philosophy reduced to 'epistemology', in fact nothing more than a timid periodism and doctrine of abstinence; a philosophy that does not even cross the threshold and scrupulously *denies* itself the right to enter – that is philosophy in its last throes, an end, an agony, something that arouses compassion. How could such a philosophy – *rule!* (BGE 204)

As we know from Parts Three and Five of *BGE*, Nietzsche lodges a related complaint against those 'modern philosophers' who stand idly by as religion and morality, respectively, assert their presumptive claims to independence and cultural sovereignty. He finds even more disturbing the negligence of those philosophers who actively endorse these claims. Although he makes no explicit reference in Part Six to a 'scholarly' strain of the neurosis he diagnosed in Parts Three (religion) and Five (morality), his readers will no doubt appreciate the gravity of his concern with those scholars who similarly assert unwarranted claims to independence and sovereignty.

After acknowledging the myriad 'dangers' that impede the development of the philosopher in late modernity (BGE 205), Nietzsche offers his readers an initial glimpse of his distinction between two types or grades of philosopher: those scholars with whom we are most familiar, whom he subsequently designates as 'philosophical laborers' (BGE 211); and those *real* philosophers in whom he locates a risk-taking intensity of creative vision and energy (BGE 205). Whereas the former type of philosopher is faintly praised for living 'cleverly and off to the side', the latter type 'lives "unphilosophically" and "unwisely", above all *uncleverly*' (BGE 205). Recalling his earlier designation of the 'new' philosophers as 'tempters' or 'experimenters' [*Versucher*] (BGE 42–4), he explains that

> the real philosopher . . . feels the burden and the duty of a hundred experiments and temptations of life [*Versuchen und Versuchungen des Lebens*]: – he constantly risks *himself*, he plays *the* dicey game. . . (BGE 205)[1]

Several implications of this provocative claim bear noting. First, the 'burden and the duty' accepted by the real philosopher are to be contrasted with the arrogant frivolity of the 'emancipated' scholar. As we shall see, in fact, the weight of this 'burden' and the solemnity of this 'duty' uniquely prepare the genuine philosopher to legislate, command and create new values. Second, the 'experiments' this philosopher conducts, unlike those attempted by most scholars, pertain to the matter of how one actually *lives*, which suggests a determination, perhaps along the lines sketched by Nietzsche in Part One of *BGE*, to balance the claims asserted,

---

[1] A *Versuch* is an *experiment* or an *attempt*, but it also may involve a *temptation*. Nietzsche called his 1886 Preface to the new edition of *The Birth of Tragedy* 'An Attempt at a Self-Criticism' [*Versuch einer Selbstkritik*]. See Sommer 2014: 135–8; and Conway 2014a: 246–8.

respectively, on behalf of the value of (ascending) life and the value of truth.² Third, the 'experiments' the genuine philosopher conducts are ultimately *self*-directed, undertaken at considerable 'risk' to his life and person. Fourth, the 'game' this philosopher plays qualifies as 'dicey' because it obliges him to gamble with his own existence and, apparently, that of humankind as a whole. (As such, the 'real' philosopher described here betrays a noteworthy affinity for the Dionysian teachings that Nietzsche will reveal in Part Nine of *BGE*.) Fifth, the 'experiments' this philosopher conducts will be received by some as 'temptations', which is a cue to Nietzsche's readers to determine whether or not *they* are enticed by the prospect of the genuine philosopher.

Having sketched for his readers the 'real' philosopher, whom he implicitly identifies as 'a genius', viz., 'a being that either *begets* or *bears*' (BGE 206), Nietzsche delivers a sober, unflattering account of those lesser scholars who would (or do) celebrate their 'emancipation' from the yoke of philosophical leadership:

> [T]he scientific human . . . [is] an ignoble kind of human, with the virtues of someone who is not dominating, not authoritative and not even self-sufficient . . . (BGE 206)

Utterly unprepared to lead and command, these scholars are in fact ripe for continued co-optation by forces and agents in the service of the 'democratic movement'. To be sure, the 'emancipated' scholars in question will flatly reject any such characterisation of their scientific agenda. They will point on the one hand to the uselessness, scholasticism or obsolescence of philosophy, and on the other hand to the momentum and excitement surrounding their own research. The sciences, they will insist, require no external supervision or guidance, as is evidenced by the superior explanatory power of the scientific worldview. Unaware of the extent to which they are influenced by 'modern ideas', and clueless more generally with respect to the ways in which scholars are used and abused by those who wield political power, they will

---

² On the potentially productive tension between the will to truth and the will to value, see Clark and Dudrick 2012: ch. 3.

mistake the (very real) rush of emancipation for an achievement of sovereignty and self-determination. As such, these scholars may be expected to continue to discover (what they claim to be) evidence – whether in nature, religious teachings, or ancient texts and artefacts – in support of the rudderless 'emancipation' in which they revel. And here we confront 'the worst and most dangerous thing of which a scholar is capable': as an unwitting champion of the 'mediocrity of his type', this scholar 'instinctively works [towards] the annihilation of the extraordinary human being' (BGE 206). Marshalling an image he introduced in his Preface to *BGE*, Nietzsche warns that this kind of scholar will endeavour either to 'break' or 'slacken' the 'bow' in which the tension of the spirit thrums, acting out of a familiar sense of 'compassion [or pity]' for those who suffer from the accomplishments of their betters (BGE 206).

Despite acknowledging that 'objectivity' is or would be a welcome trait in a scholar, Nietzsche cautions us to look more closely at what it is that we honour in those whom we hail as 'objective' (BGE 207). He is concerned in particular that we 'put a stop to the exaggeration with which the de-selfing and de-personalising of the spirit is being celebrated recently as if it were a goal in itself, as redemption and transfiguration' (BGE 207). The scholar who has attained a desired measure of 'objectivity' is useful, to be sure, for example as a 'mirror', but he does not qualify thereby as an '"end in itself"' (BGE 207). Nietzsche is similarly unimpressed by those scholars who, 'trained to twitch with every No, indeed even with a decisively firm Yes', hide behind the mask of the 'skeptic' (BGE 208). Demonstrating once again the diagnostic acuity he has displayed throughout *BGE*, Nietzsche exposes scepticism as 'the most spiritual expression of a certain complex physiological condition that in common language is called weakness of the nerves and sickliness', which he proceeds to specify in its most extreme forms as a 'degeneration' and subsequent weakness of the 'will' (BGE 208).

Nietzsche's readers will note the similarities that obtain between his diagnosis of the 'skeptic' and his earlier demystification of the 'miracle' associated with sainthood (BGE 47). In both cases, he deploys a sophisticated (and properly scientific) psychological analysis to debunk and displace a popular (but unsubstantiated) prejudice. In both cases, moreover, an achievement of supposedly positive moral worth – viz. the conversion of the saint, the self-mastery of the sceptic – is explained more simply and comprehensively in terms that suggest a morally neutral (and distinctly all-too-human) response to physiological distress. Nietzsche is furthermore concerned here to develop his method of psychological analysis into a larger criticism of late modern European culture as a whole. In short, the sceptic is by no means an isolated case, for the 'disease of the will' he manifests has spread, albeit 'unevenly', across the whole of Europe. The situation is sufficiently dire, or so Nietzsche maintains, that it might take 'an increase in the menace of Russia' to compel Europe to acquire the '*one will*' it currently lacks (BGE 208).

The implication here is that the 'new' philosophers whom Nietzsche heralds at the conclusion of Part Six will be *genuine* (as opposed to *nominal* or *opportunistic*) benefactors of science, precisely inasmuch as they will restore something like the traditional order of rank among learned disciplines. In doing so, they will unleash the explanatory power of modern science while also blunting its most dangerous and reductive tendencies. Until the sciences are returned to their rightful positions of subordinate rank, subject to the direction and determinations imposed by the 'new' philosophers, scholars will continue to take their cues from the mob mentality and levelling aspirations of the 'democratic movement'. As we have seen, of course, this path leads inexorably to nihilism and the will to nothingness.

Nietzsche elaborates on this last point in *On the Genealogy of Morality*. Expanding on his characterisation of scientific research as dependent on those who determine its form, direction and agenda, he explains that

> Science . . . first needs a value-ideal in every respect, a value-creating power, in whose *service* it *may believe* in itself – science itself is never value-creating. (GM III: 25)

What this means, he believes, is that scientists and scholars are invariably (if not consciously or voluntarily) subservient to those who establish the values – for example, health, utility, productivity, flourishing, creativity, etc. – that inform and direct their scholarly endeavours. Under proper guidance and sponsorship, scientists and scholars happily devote themselves to the tasks, experiments and projects that have been set before them. In the absence of such structure, 'emancipated' scholars take their cues from opportunistic authorities *du jour* who merit neither their consideration nor their obedience. Even worse, these 'emancipated' scholars will not be sufficiently aware of their service in the thrall of these bogus authorities to muster a credible measure of resistance or even scrutiny. Boasting of their 'emancipation', they will think of themselves as free agents, boldly pursuing 'pure' science or edgy scholarship, when in fact they compound the problems and calamities created by the charlatans from whom they unwittingly (or fawningly) take their direction.

Nietzsche closes this section by raising significantly the stakes of his defence of the rank ordering of learned disciplines. As we late moderns prepare to exit the era of 'petty politics' and enter the era of 'grand politics', we can scarcely afford to allow the various sciences to continue to determine their own goals and aspirations (BGE 208). Scholars will quickly become the unwitting dupes and pawns of political schemers, and they will all-too-readily lose sight of the question of what will (or should) become of humanity. In their respective adumbrations of the 'new warlike age' that Europe has entered (BGE 209), sections 209 and 210 set the stage for the influential distinction Nietzsche draws in Section 211 – namely, that between 'philosophical laborers', viz., those earnest (if desultory) types who lack the imagination and prerogative to lead, and those *'genuine'* philosophers, identified by Nietzsche as *'commanders and legislators'*, who will *'create values'* (BGE 211).

Philosophers as legislators

Nietzsche's initial aim in drawing this distinction is to place the 'philosophical laborers' alongside the scientists and scholars whom he has discussed throughout Part Six. Like their counterparts and brethren in other scholarly fields, the 'philosophical laborers' are obliged to take their cues from those others who frame their discipline and set the agenda for their scholarship. As such, to be sure, these labourers perform a valuable service to their respective fields, 'press[ing] into formulas a huge body of valuations . . . [derived from] former value-*positings* and value creations that have become dominant' (BGE 211).

As Nietzsche explains elsewhere, the 'labor' thus described is appealing to the scholars in question inasmuch as it accommodates the '*impoverishment of life*' that he identifies as the physiological 'presupposition' of contemporary scientific research (GM III: 25). These 'philosophical laborers' belong among the scholars he has discussed and diagnosed, apparently, because they too manifest the telltale symptoms of a tired, exhausted, twilight culture: 'the affects cooled down, the tempo slowed down, dialectic in place of instinct, *seriousness* stamped on the faces and gestures' (GM III: 25). In short, we should form no reasonable expectation that these 'philosophical laborers' will *create* the values that are needed to inaugurate a new, 'extramoral' period in human history or to found a culture that thrives beyond the reach of the morality of good and evil.

Those self-identified philosophers who are inclined to protest this apparent demotion in status may take some comfort from Nietzsche's insistence that even Kant and Hegel might be understood to have served, nobly, as 'philosophical laborers'. Of course, this surprisingly deflationary appraisal of two of the most influential figures in German (and European) philosophy only piques our interest in the 'genuine philosophers' whom Nietzsche intends to elevate above the disciplinary fray. Who are they? Are they recognisable at all as philosophers? Indeed, if they are distinguished by virtue of being 'commanders and legislators' (BGE 211), are they perhaps more familiar to us on the model of military leaders (BGE 200), or that of political or religious lawgivers?

Having raised the question of whether such philosophers have ever existed or might do so in the future (BGE 211), Nietzsche revisits the questions of what a philosopher is and what a philosopher might be expected to accomplish (BGE 212). Beginning anew, he accounts for the philosopher as '*necessarily* a human of tomorrow and the day after tomorrow', who 'has always found himself to be in contradiction to his today'

(BGE 212). Philosophers have served as 'extraordinary promoters of humanity' *not* because they are 'friends of wisdom', as is commonly alleged, but because they have agreed and been suffered to serve as the 'bad conscience of their time' (BGE 212). It is in this capacity, he explains, that philosophers have criticised the signature values and practices of their age.

Although philosophers are best known for the unsettling, probing questions they pose, criticism is neither the goal nor the entirety of the cultural labour they (intend to) perform. What typically goes unnoticed, Nietzsche explains, is that the destructive, iconoclastic inquisitions they conduct are intended as preliminary to their efforts to introduce new values for a new (or dawning) period in the history of a nation, people, or even of humankind itself. Summoning an appropriately grisly image to convey the intimate linkage between their labours of 'No-doing' (or negation) and 'Yea-saying' (or affirmation), he explains,

> [Having] applied their vivisecting knife to the very chest of the *virtues of their age*, they [have] revealed what their own secret was: to know of a *new* greatness of humanity, of a new, untrodden path to making it greater. (BGE 212)

As the paradigm case of Socrates confirms, philosophers are not typically appreciated in their own time for their intended contributions to the enhancement of humanity. Owing to the challenges they pose to a fading *status quo*, which Nietzsche likens in this passage to invasive surgery (or autopsy), philosophers are typically received not as benefactors, but as malefactors. Indeed, they are often accused of having caused the social disarray or cultural decay they profess to diagnose. Unlike other contributors to the enhancement of humanity, philosophers cannot illuminate a new way of life without first documenting the exhaustion of the old way of life. Very soon, as we shall see, Nietzsche will urge his readers to 'practice vivisection' on themselves (BGE 218).

Shifting his focus from what philosophers have done in the past to how they might operate in the present, that is, if faced with 'a world of "modern ideas"' (BGE 212), Nietzsche boldly takes matters into his own hands. Speaking on behalf of an unnamed contemporary philosopher, who, he cautions, may or may not exist, he forwards and defends a new, alternative standard of 'greatness' (BGE 212), which is apparently meant to guide his readers towards a deeper appreciation of the distinction he has drawn between 'philosophical laborers' and 'genuine' philosophers. As he sees it, the current problem is that contemporary scholars are encouraged – and, it must be said, all too eager – to confine themselves to narrow research specialities, wherein they are shielded from the larger and more pressing problems that impend the future of humanity.

In an effort to arrest (and perhaps reverse) this unwelcome trend, Nietzsche proposes – again, speaking on behalf of the unnamed contemporary philosopher – to redefine 'greatness' in terms that are more obviously suggestive of those creators of value whom he hails as 'genuine' philosophers:

> In the face of a world of 'modern ideas' that wishes to banish everyone to a corner and 'specialty', a philosopher, if there could be philosophers today, would be forced to posit the greatness of humanity, the concept of 'greatness', precisely in its extensiveness and multiplicity, in its wholeness in plurality: he would even determine value and rank according to how much and how many different things someone could carry and take upon himself, how *far* someone could extend his responsibility. (BGE 212)

This rich passage clarifies a great deal and adumbrates some of Nietzsche's subsequent insights. First of all, the philosopher he has in mind would stand resolutely, much as Nietzsche himself does in *BGE*, against the wisdom supposedly encoded in 'modern ideas'. This philosopher would find and honour greatness not in the 'weakness of the will' that is celebrated in the 'ideal of an idiotic, renunciatory, humble, and selfless humanity' (BGE 212), but in the 'strength of will' that prompts the best among us to aspire to the most comprehensive set of experiences and perspectives that is consistent with the attainment of 'wholeness in plurality'.

Second, Nietzsche explicitly links this new, alternative standard of 'greatness' to an *enlarged* (rather than a diminished) burden of responsibilities. Instead of urging his best readers to renounce or shed their responsibilities, which they might have understood the 'malicious' title of *BGE* to promise or recommend, he in fact encourages them – albeit indirectly – to become *more* responsible, and more extensively so, than ever before. The suggestion here is that the modern soul is uniquely equipped, first of all, to accommodate an unusually broad range of disparate responsibilities; and, second, to discover its optimal carrying capacity by adopting a daring regimen of self-directed experimentation, especially with respect to the range and heft of the burdens it might bear. As we shall see in Part Six of *BGE*, Nietzsche is particularly concerned to persuade his readers to expand and diversify their portfolio of *scholarly* responsibilities and, as a result, to find their own greatness as seekers and tellers of brutal, inconvenient truths. In doing so, they will continue and intensify the 'great hunt' he has invited them to join (BGE 45).

Third, the model of 'greatness' identified here (and attributed to the unnamed contemporary philosopher) takes into account what Nietzsche has identified as the non-negotiable multiform character of the modern soul. In many respects, as we have seen, the modern soul is a motley amalgamation of unruly instincts, drives and affects, which represent a chaotic tangle of inheritances from various moral, intellectual, scholarly and spiritual disciplines. Although the modern soul is typically at odds with itself, and often hopelessly so, in some rare cases it may be disciplined to 'wholeness in plurality'. In such cases, the chief defect of the modern soul – namely, its involuntary allegiance to multiple and conflicting impulses and imperatives – would become its primary asset and source of appeal. Rather than give up on the modern soul, declaring it to be a lost cause, the unnamed contemporary philosopher fashions for it a standard of 'greatness' that is appropriate to its unique structure and its non-negotiable placement in a twilight period of European history.

Fourth, Nietzsche not only *speaks* in this section on behalf of the unnamed contemporary philosopher, but also *legislates* on his behalf. Having questioned, rhetorically, whether a genuine philosopher is even possible today, he concludes this section by reprising in slightly altered form the period-appropriate standard of 'greatness' that he earlier attributed to the unnamed contemporary philosopher:

> [T]he philosopher will reveal something about his own ideal when he posits: 'the greatest should be the one who can be most solitary, most hidden, most deviating, the human who is beyond good and evil, the master of his virtues, the one whose will is superabundant; precisely this should be called *greatness*: being able to be just as manifold as whole, just as broad as full.' (BGE 212)

Although it is likely that Nietzsche's readers have suspected all along that *he* is the unnamed contemporary philosopher for whom he claims to speak, this extracted passage resoundingly confirms their suspicions. The revised standard of 'greatness' posited in this passage incorporates several telltale elements of the finish that Nietzsche has offered to apply to all those who matriculate through his school for gentlemen: solitude, concealment, deviation, residence beyond good and evil, self-mastery and superabundance (as opposed to weakness) of will. Moreover, these telltale elements are linked in this passage to the standard established earlier in this section by the unnamed contemporary philosopher: 'as manifold as whole, as broad as full'. As it now appears in its newly revised form, in other words, this period-appropriate standard of 'greatness' will be attained by those who complete the programme of education and training on offer in *BGE*.

When received by Nietzsche's readers, this new standard of 'greatness' will land with the force and authority of a legislation. As it does so, his readers will realise that a *third* type of philosopher – neither labourer nor commander but akin to both – now merits their consideration. And although they are not likely to be surprised to learn that Nietzsche regards himself as a (kind of) legislator, albeit not on the grand scale he has reserved for the 'new' philosophers, they might be (pleasantly) surprised to learn that he also includes *them*, at least potentially, in the third type he has introduced (via exemplification) in this section. Indeed, the 'strength of will' he has displayed in this section is apparently meant to entice his best readers to stay the course, precisely so that they too might attain the standard of 'greatness' he has defined in this passage. Like him, they too eventually might legislate – though not on the grand scale – for they too might glimpse possibilities for 'greatness' in the twilight period of late modernity. In short: *he* is the link that will join them to the future they have dared to envision and pledged to produce.

Why, then, does Nietzsche belabour the ruse of speaking for an unnamed contemporary philosopher who may or may not exist? His goal here is not simply to be clever, but also to acknowledge his own limitations with respect to the production of a viable philosophy of the future. Although he has credibly propounded a new, period-appropriate standard of 'greatness', his success in establishing this standard is dependent on his ability to draw his best readers into the circle of his idealised 'we'. Hence the cagey, tentative and indirect approach he adopts in this section: he may yet *become* (and be remembered by name as) the contemporary philosopher he has channelled in this section, but *only* if he succeeds in cultivating generations of readers who will instantiate his standard of 'greatness' and carry his teachings into the 'extramoral' period to come. If he fails to do so, his experimental legislative forays (in *BGE* and other post-Zarathustran writings) will be no more impactful than those of the unnamed contemporary philosopher he has conjured for the occasion. By adopting this particular strategy of indirection, Nietzsche confirms to his best readers that his legacy is in their hands. He will 'become what he is' – and thereby avoid the fate he openly fears (EH 'Destiny' 1) – only if they make it so.

Scholarly virtues

Is Nietzsche entitled to speak, even if provisionally, on behalf of the 'philosophers of the future'? Of course not. By his own admission, he has no business attempting anything in excess of his preparatory efforts in anticipation of their arrival. Yet he cannot (or will not) help himself. Gambling that the leaders whom humanity so desperately needs might be impressed by a calculated display of audacity, representative of a humanity worth saving from itself, he outlines a period-appropriate model of 'greatness' that might strike them as a useful precursor to the new ideal they will see fit to install. If he is successful in this risky venture, the 'philosophers of the future' might elect to renew (in some unspecified form) the innovative, experimental agenda established by the 'good Europeans'. Indeed, here we may be meant to recall the similarly audacious efforts of that irrepressible pessimist, who, in shouting *da capo* to the god he has conjured for the occasion, presents himself as worthy of the divine spectator for whom he performs (BGE 56).

To be sure, Nietzsche's calculated act of transgression is also meant to impress his best readers. In their capacity as 'philosophical laborers', they are neither called nor expected to create new values or to legislate a vision for the future of humanity. At the same time, however, they need not resign themselves to the drone-like existence sought and attained by most contemporary scholars. Indeed, those who are inclined might follow his lead by aligning their own scholarship with the *tertium quid* he models to them in this section. As scholars, in other words, they might endeavour to stake out a position somewhere in between the legislative heights reserved for the genuine philosophers and the dreary lowlands occupied by the 'philosophical laborers'.

How might they go about this? Alert to the need for a new ideal and a restoration of the order of rank, they might distinguish themselves from other (= lesser) scholars by resisting the familiar temptation to assert their sovereignty. They might do so, as we have seen, by confirming the pride of place among scholars that is reserved for genuine philosophers, while simultaneously refusing to claim this place or occupy it in the interim. Having become involuntarily adept at deferring their gratification, they will patiently await the arrival of those for whom they prepare. Acutely aware of their limitations with respect to leadership and legislation, they will humbly decline any opportunity to stray from their established areas of specialised expertise. Rather than lodge a specious claim to independence from the order of rank, they will content themselves with the achievement of self-restraint, which, Nietzsche suggests, would be a timely contribution to the production of a philosophy of the future.

As we know, of course, Nietzsche has consistently cast a sceptical eye on the traditional forms in which the scholarly virtues – for example, patience, humility and self-restraint – have been cultivated, practised and defended. He insists, for example, that 'our feelings of devotion, of sacrifice for our neighbor, and the whole morality of self-renunciation must be mercilessly called to account and taken to court' (BGE 33). Here we should note, however, that he does not say that he expects or favours any particular outcome of the prescribed interrogation and judgement. In keeping with his general theme of attending carefully to historical context, he aims instead to determine the uses to which these scholarly virtues might best be allocated. Although he questions the continued viability of the 'whole morality of self-denial', he nowhere states that its value is now exclusively or categorically negative. As we know, in fact, he offers in *BGE* to school his readers in the tactical redeployment of unwanted virtues and involuntary moral obligations.

The scholarly virtues displayed by Nietzsche and his best readers should not be confused with the timidity and selflessness for which he criticises the 'philosophical laborers' among their contemporaries. He and his best readers will subordinate themselves not as an expression of servility or self-contempt, but as an outward sign of their allegiance to the order of rank among scholars. As he has urged them to affirm, the prerogative to wield 'science as the hammer of philosophy', to borrow Burnham's formulation, is not theirs to claim; it must be reserved for those 'new' philosophers who will set the agenda for scholarship in all disciplines and fields of scientific research. In this respect, his finishing school for gentlemen is meant to prepare his best readers to serve as knights of a vacant throne. If he has trained them well, they will expose and turn away all pretenders to this throne, while resisting any (neurotic) temptation to seize it for themselves. As described, in fact, Nietzsche and his best readers are (or soon will become) model scholars, inasmuch as they honour (or soon will do so) the order of rank at no penalty to their experience of freedom and power. By dint of this simple act of self-restraint, they will inaugurate a much-needed reversal of the larger cultural trends that have landed late modern European culture in its present state of disarray. We might think of them (and him) as having embarked upon an apprenticeship in philosophical legislation and command.

Hence the irony of Nietzsche's takeaway lesson in this section: he bids his readers to be audacious in their untimely displays of patience, humility and self-restraint.[3] In daring to affiliate themselves with a project that is both grand and world-historical, they will affirm the need to subordinate themselves to those whose guidance they await. Rather than aspire to goals and objectives that lie beyond their reach, or limit themselves to the unambitious objectives of traditional scholarship, they will seek to accomplish nothing more and nothing less than what is possible for them. What his best readers are meant to realise, and subsequently to enact, is that playing a supporting role in a world-historical endeavour is preferable to playing a leading role that requires them to pretend that they are more powerful or more fully liberated than their historical situation allows. In repurposing the scholarly virtues of patience, humility and self-restraint, Nietzsche and his best readers will begin the process of clearing the cultural space in which the new philosophers will establish a new, meaning-conferring order of rank.

What a philosopher is (and does)

Having renewed his call for a 'new' breed of philosophers, and having suggested how a 'genuine' philosopher might coax a 'tomorrow and the day after tomorrow' from the uninspiring 'today' of late modern European culture (BGE 212), Nietzsche pivots in the final section of Part Six to the question of what a philosopher is (BGE 213).

He begins by sounding a note of caution, reminding (or informing) his readers that only those with the requisite 'experience' can meaningfully answer this question (BGE 213). Those without the requisite experience should take 'pride' in *not* knowing and, as a result, in not burdening the future with unfounded anticipations and unwarranted expectations (BGE 213). (Indeed, a further benefit of the self-restraint Nietzsche and his best readers

---

[3] Here I follow Lampert, who attributes to Nietzsche the cultivation for himself (and recommendation to others) of the 'audacious modesty of a nonskeptical philosopher who has the whole future of humanity on his conscience' (Lampert 2001: 193).

exercise is that they will be less likely to clutter the aperture to the future with naïve speculations about the 'commanders' and 'legislators' for whom they prepare.) Implicitly laying claim to some measure of the requisite 'experience', Nietzsche proceeds to offer a (self-serving) sketch of the philosopher, which culminates in his insistence that genuine philosophers, like artists, understand that their 'feeling of freedom' reaches its peak when they 'no longer do anything "voluntarily" and everything "necessarily"' (BGE 213). As expected, he proceeds to deliver a sober (and potentially dispiriting) reckoning of all that is required to bring the philosophical type into existence: 'Many generations must have done the preliminary work for the origin of a philosopher' (BGE 213).

The bad news here is that the production of the philosophers of the future, which Nietzsche has forwarded as his preferred solution to the current crisis, may require centuries of concentrated, focused effort. These philosophers will not arrive on the scene any time soon, and Nietzsche's best readers must reconcile themselves to a protracted period of potentially thankless preparatory effort. The good (or better) news is that the conditions that are required to produce the philosophical type are neither easily nor quickly undone. Even in late modernity, he suggests, we may detect and perhaps repurpose the remnants and fragments of neglected and forgotten orders of rank. Indeed, the fatal flaw of the 'democratic movement' is its habitual underestimation of the preparations for and preconditions of the noble achievements it seeks to level. Owing to this fatal flaw, the 'democratic movement' tends towards premature pronouncements of victory over all that is grand and rare. Simply put, the subversion of the most obvious material and social testaments to the rise of nobility does not automatically suffice to extinguish the noble soul, which both antedates and survives the outward indices of its abiding self-respect.

The even better news here, which Nietzsche intends as the chief takeaway from Part Six, is that a narrow path remains open to a future beyond good and evil, a path along which his readers may count on him to conduct their passage. Apparently, that is, Nietzsche's 'experience' is sufficiently broad and diverse as to certify the value not only of his closing sketch of the philosophical type, but also of his understanding of the conditions under which one might expect this type to emerge (BGE 213). One such condition is unmistakable: philosophy is possible only as the 'cultivated' product of an established order of rank and a viable constellation of mutually reinforcing norms and institutions (BGE 213). In short, the solution he proposes to the problem of the emergent mass of European 'herd animals' is to lay the foundation for a new civilisation, viz., a pan-European order to rival and even surpass the empires of bygone periods.[4] He thus bids his best readers to begin the preparations that some day, centuries or even millennia hence, will culminate in the willed production of the 'genuine' philosophers whom he has described.

Review

Although they have dedicated their lives to the practice of disciplined scholarship, Nietzsche's best readers have failed as yet to appreciate the precise ways in which their scholarly prospects are limited. Notwithstanding their pledge of allegiance to the scientific worldview, for example, they continue to ply their scholarship in observance of norms, procedures and methods associated more closely with the moral-religious worldview. In Part Six of *BGE*, they learn that their status as scholars confers upon them advantages *and* disadvantages, opportunities *and* constraints, liberties *and* obligations, with respect to the undisclosed 'task' Nietzsche has reserved for them. As such, they will need to become scholars who, having acknowledged their limitations, voluntarily restrain their scholarly ambitions, thereby clearing and preserving the legislative space in which the 'new' philosophers eventually will generate new values.

---

[4] See Emden 2008: 299–308.

8
Part Seven: Our Virtues

Preview

In Part Five of *BGE*, Nietzsche urged his readers to begin the process of compiling a proper 'typology of morals' (BGE 186), which, among other outcomes, would provide them with a more comprehensive grasp of the multiple, overlapping moral traditions that have contributed to the formation of their historically specific experience of identity and purpose. In Part Six of *BGE*, he encouraged his readers, *qua* scholars, to cultivate (and model to others) a recognition of the order of rank among scholarly disciplines, the restoration of which would acknowledge the authority of the 'new' philosophers whom he and they await (BGE 213). By displaying the neglected scholarly virtues of patience, humility and self-restraint, his readers would begin the process of reversing the dangerous trend among scholars towards unwarranted assertions of sovereignty and independence.

Nietzsche's efforts to recover these neglected scholarly virtues leads naturally to his discussion of 'our virtues' in Part Seven of *BGE*. As it turns out, the exercise of the virtues disclosed in Part Six serves to illuminate the enlarged space in which other, related virtues may be retrieved and repurposed. Of particular interest to Nietzsche in Part Seven of *BGE* is the virtue of *honesty* [*Redlichkeit*], which he describes as the 'virtue from which we cannot get away, we free spirits' (BGE 227). As this clever juxtaposition of freedom and unfreedom is meant to confirm, Nietzsche is concerned in Part Seven to steer his best readers into a more productive relationship to the morality of good and evil. Although they are not free to 'get away' from the honesty that motivates their practice of truth-seeking and truth-telling, they *are* free to choose the targets and amplify the intensity of their inquisitions.[1] In particular, as we shall see, they are welcome to indulge the anti-Christian and pro-science impulses that have piqued their interest in contributing to the production of a philosophy of the future. If they elect to seek and tell the truth about Christian morality, exposing the illusions and fabrications on which it trades, they may succeed not only in claiming for themselves the optimal experience of freedom and agency that is available to them, but also in accelerating the arrival of those 'new' philosophers whose legislations they eagerly await.[2]

What becomes increasingly clear in Part Seven of *BGE* is that Nietzsche understands his assault on contemporary morality as originating in and proceeding as a recognisably *moral* challenge to the continued authority of the morality of good and evil.[3] That his best readers are creatures of 'duty' and obligation, possessed of a full complement of unmistakably moral virtues, is presented here not as a regrettable (much less disqualifying) feature of their historical situation, but as the seat of their most formidable comparative advantage. As we learn in Part Seven, they are in fact tasked with working *within* the collapsing framework of contemporary morality, precisely so that they might turn its residual authority against its generative source.[4]

Summary of sections

Part Seven of *BGE* comprises twenty-five numbered sections (214–39). Nietzsche begins by conceding that he and his best readers are and must remain creatures of (moral) virtue. While

---

[1] See Richardson 1996: 26–7; and Lemm 2020: 24–33, 167–8.
[2] I am indebted here to Sommer 2016: 632–4.
[3] I am indebted here to the related interpretations developed by Owen 1995: 89–93; Ridley 1998: 115–26; May 1999: 137–8, 177–80; and Hatab 2008: 164–71. See also Conway 2014b: 207–13.
[4] Here I follow Lampert 2001: 219. See also Ridley 1998: 124–6; May 1999: 88–94; Owen 2007: 126–9; and Conway 2014a: 302–9.

this concession is likely to be poorly received by those readers who wish to escape the present moment – not to mention the morality – in which their virtues root them, he urges them to adopt an updated (and more faithfully scientific) understanding of their relationship to the morality they have pledged to retire. Just as they should not be confused with either their clueless contemporaries or their 'grandfathers', so the virtues at their disposal should not be assumed to be those practised (or revered) by either cohort (BGE 214). As 'Europeans of the day after tomorrow' and the 'first-born of the twentieth century' (BGE 214), he and his readers are likely to find themselves in possession of virtues that may be repurposed to reflect their unique status and the task reserved just for them.

Revisiting the virtues

Effectively renewing his earlier invitation to join the 'great hunt' (BGE 45), Nietzsche bids his readers to conduct a daring inventory of the virtues in their possession, urging them to search for their virtues even 'in [their] labyrinths! – where, as is well known, so many different things lose themselves' (BGE 214; cf. BGE 29). As this not-so-subtle remit confirms, Nietzsche wishes for his readers, whom he elsewhere diagnoses as 'strangers' to themselves (GM P1), to become more familiar with those precincts of their souls, including the labyrinthine realm of the unconscious, which they have prudently learned to ignore or disown. As they strive towards an ever more comprehensive understanding of themselves, for example, as situated in a particular historical context, they will discover the precise limits within which they might enact their freedom and agency. They will do so, to be sure, at great danger to themselves. As Nietzsche has already warned them, they might 'lose' themselves as they explore the labyrinth, and they might fall prey to 'some cave Minotaur of the conscience' (BGE 29)

And although an enlarged repository of self-knowledge might be a valuable possession in its own right, Nietzsche's primary aim in Part Seven of *BGE* is to introduce his best readers to those virtues, powers, affects and other modalities of embodiment that will be most useful to them in pursuing the task he has reserved for them. As they become better acquainted with themselves, in short, they are likely to discover that they in fact command an impressive range and intensity of virtues, which, he assures them, they may put to good use in the service of their pro-science and anti-Christian allegiances. In Part Eight, as we shall see, he describes the German soul in particular as riddled with 'passages and inter-passages', as well as 'caves, hideouts, and dungeons' (BGE 244). 'The Germans', we learn there, 'know the secret paths to chaos' (BGE 244).

Despite confirming that their contributions to the production of a philosophy of the future will not deliver the total liberation they may have wished to secure for themselves, Nietzsche signals to his best readers that the virtues already in their possession – namely, the titular 'our virtues' – are more useful and versatile than they presently know or believe. The suggestion here, on which he does not adequately expand, is that the morality of good and evil replicates itself – and, so, prevails – by estranging its adherents from the complexity and wealth of their full moral inheritance. Habituated to atone for their supposedly fallen nature, and for the lapses manifested thereby, Nietzsche's readers are not yet adequately acquainted with the full range and plasticity of the powers at their disposal. Indeed, some of the virtues in their possession may remain as yet unknown (or innominate), while those that *are* known, especially if they occasion embarrassment or chagrin, may be productively repurposed. Still others may yet be acknowledged (and decommissioned) as counter-productive. And so on. In Part Seven of *BGE*, in short, the 'great hunt' becomes a bona fide treasure hunt.

The important point here is that the inventory Nietzsche urges them to undertake must be conducted on a rigorously scientific basis. This means that the virtues in their possession must be discovered (or rediscovered) and assessed in practice, as dictated by an innovative regimen of risky, self-directed experimentation (GS 34). Rather than continue to help themselves to lazy recitations of the 'good' and 'evil' they supposedly harbour, advancing the former while arresting the latter, they will need to hazard an ambitious, ruthless exteriorisation of their heretofore hidden interiority. As they disgorge all manner of passions and affects, manifesting virtues and vices alike, they may try on novel modes of embodiment while cycling through an ever-expanding range of combinations and intensities. To be a creature of virtue, he thus wishes for them to understand, is to be variously enabled, richly embodied and diversely empowered.

On the one hand, Nietzsche wishes to acknowledge that the possession of any virtue represents a distinct measure of unfreedom (or imposed/internalised tyranny). Following Aristotle (among others), Nietzsche regards virtues as indices of inheritance and involuntary habituation, of a cast of mind or character that was not chosen and which is revisable only with great effort.[5] To be a creature of virtue, in short, is to be claimed by one's past and limited in one's orientation to the future.[6] As such, the possession of any virtue is a sign that one remains an object (or artefact) of history, even as one strives to establish oneself as a subject (or author) of history.

On the other hand, Nietzsche hints to his best readers that they will be pleasantly surprised by the (previously unknown or underestimated) virtues they will discover deep within themselves. As he surmises, their as-yet-unacknowledged virtues are likely to be fully compatible with their 'most secret and cordial inclinations, their most ardent needs' (BGE 214), which means that the exercise of these virtues need not be as constraining (or demeaning) as they presently fear. When properly reconsidered, that is, 'our virtues' not only reflect the unfreedom to which they faithfully attest, but also disclose the freedom and agency to which Nietzsche's best readers might credibly aspire. Despite being historically conditioned to remain creatures of virtue, they might yet learn to enact their virtues in novel forms and patterns of expression.[7]

---

[5] See Solomon 2003: 121–7; and Acampora and Ansell-Pearson 2011: 148.
[6] Here I follow a general line of interpretation pursued, variously, by Leiter 2002: 279–83; Janaway 2007: 236–9; Owen 2007: 128–9; Loeb 2010: 234–7; and Acampora 2013: 192–7.
[7] See Janaway 2007: 249–54; Owen 2007: 63–5, 126–9.

The many colours of virtue

The good news for Nietzsche and his best readers is that they need not labour in vain: the virtues he and they possess are uniquely suited to the (as-yet-unnamed) task that awaits them. Alerting them to a conclusion that their 'typology of morals' eventually will deliver with bracing clarity, he explains that

> [W]e modern human beings . . . are determined by *different* moralities; our actions shine alternately in different colors, they are rarely unequivocal – and there are enough cases in which we perform *multi-colored* acts. (BGE 215)

Concerned that his best readers might cleave as yet to an unduly narrow (and monochromatic) appreciation of the moral inheritance in which they share, Nietzsche attempts to acquaint them with the many 'colors' (= combinations and intensities of virtue) in which they might yet 'shine'. Indeed, although he does not say so explicitly, he means to caution them against any overly simplistic (or deflationary) account of the virtues in their possession. Two concerns are relevant to his motivation. First, he is aware that his best readers are likely to be ashamed and perhaps contemptuous of their residual investments in the morality of good and evil. Second, he knows that contemporary morality maintains an interest in denying the historical complexity that a proper 'typology of morality' will readily confirm.

Building on his earlier challenge to those who 'assume there is an essential opposition between "true" and "false"' (BGE 34), Nietzsche issues a similar challenge to those who see 'actions' as either good or evil (BGE 215). As is often the case when he avails himself of an aesthetic trope, he wishes to disabuse his best readers of their tendency to think (and act) in terms of binary oppositions. In particular, as we shall see, it is not a question of being *pro* or *contra* morality, especially in the event that one can (and must) be both. Similarly, it is not a question of being *pro* or *contra* any particular virtue, for each of 'our virtues' might shine forth, diversely and differently, depending on the person, situation, setting and context in question. Having earlier wondered if it might 'suffice to assume stages of apparentness and brighter and darker shades and overall tones of appearance' (BGE 34), his goal here is to persuade his best readers to understand the possession and exercise of virtue as a matter of intensity, degree, combination, variegation, shading and complementarity.

Much as a painter mixes and blends the colours of her palette to create new hues, tints, textures and variations, so Nietzsche's best readers might experiment with novel manifestations and enactments of the virtues in their possession. As he allows, they may be pleasantly surprised, and perhaps even revitalised (= 'shining' anew), by the shades and colours they are able to produce. In any event, they will discover that they are in fact diversely related to the morality they currently claim to oppose. Indeed, they will find within themselves a confirmation of the complexity, diversity and plenitude that their 'typology of morals' has previewed (and will reveal) more generally.

Nietzsche thus proposes to translate a non-negotiable reality (or necessity) into a strategic advantage. Much as he views the recent emergence of an unformed mass of European 'herd animals' as both a calamity to be addressed and an opportunity to be exploited (BGE 62), so he regards the motley moral inheritance of 'modern men' (and his readers in particular) as both a source of confusion and a potential boon for would-be assassins of morality. While it is true that 'modern men' are 'determined' in potentially confusing ways by multiple, overlapping moral traditions (BGE 215), they nevertheless may aspire to exploit the wealth and complexity of their moral inheritance, from which they may yet distil the 'high spirituality' he recommends to them (BGE 218). The assigned 'typology of morals' will provide them with a map of the moral inheritance they have received, which they may adopt as a guide in their experimental efforts to reconfigure and repurpose the virtues in their possession. He thus explains, in admittedly 'flattering' terms, that the 'high spirituality' he recommends to them 'exists only as the last spawn of moral qualities' (BGE 219).)

The many costumes of virtue

Before elaborating on the 'different moralities' that have 'determined' him and his best readers (BGE 215), Nietzsche assures them that their disdain for the virtues commonly associated with

Christian morality is warranted (216–28), but only partially so. Confirming the validity of their grievances, Nietzsche rehearses some well-known elements of his more general critique of morality. Moral judgements are often expressions of revenge, lodged by a weaker party against a stronger party (218–20). An 'unegoistic morality' that presumes its universal appeal constitutes 'a seduction and injury of the higher, rarer, more privileged' among us (221). For this reason, he explains, 'moralities must be forced to bow before the [order of rank]' (BGE 221), which, when accomplished, would afford 'the higher, rarer, more privileged' among us the additional protections they require.[8] Pity is an outward (and therefore misleading) expression of self-contempt (222). And so on.

In general, he allows, morality has taught us to suspect, second-guess and even despise ourselves. This is why he recommends that his readers – whom he addresses as 'you psychologists' – should 'study the philosophy of the "rule" in its struggle against the "exception"', which he immediately converts into the directive to 'practice vivisection on the "good man", on *"homo bonae voluntatis"*... *on yourselves!*' (BGE 218). Implying thereby that their 'vivisecting knives' are at the ready – which, if true, would link them to the philosophers identified earlier as 'extraordinary promoters of humanity' (BGE 212) – Nietzsche urges them to direct against themselves the cruel scrutiny they displayed in their earlier examination of the *homines religiosi* (BGE 45), of which *homo bonae voluntatis* is presumably a subspecies. On the strength of this directive, the 'great hunt' (BGE 45) officially turns inward.

Likening moralities to disposable 'costumes' (BGE 223; cf. GS 365), Nietzsche suggests that although our current capacities

---

[8] The claims asserted in BGE 221 are attributed by Nietzsche to an unnamed 'moral pedant and purveyor of trivia', who, he suggests, may not deserve the 'laughter' he is likely to receive in response to the bold claim that Nietzsche sets off with quotation marks. Nietzsche's point here is not that the 'pedant' is wrong or misguided in what he believes, but that his tactics are not likely to draw 'the laughers [to] *his* side'. Of course, if the 'moral pedant' is sincere in his determination to 'honor and distinguish a selfless man', he may be chagrined at the outcome of the '*rank order*' of moralities he has demanded. According to Lampert, Nietzsche attributes his own views to an unnamed 'moral pedant' because he knows himself to be inclined, at times, towards moral pedantry (Lampert 2001: 213–14).

for freedom and agency have been determined by diverse moralities, none of these moralities exerts a proprietary claim on us. He thus reveals that our relationship to morality (and moralities) is rooted in our various performances of them: we try on 'different moralities' as an actor might don and discard costumes at the direction of a troupe leader.[9] Owing to the motley character of the moral inheritance in which we share, we have learned to play many roles convincingly – for example, morphing instantaneously from libertine to prig, as Fitzgerald has Nick say about Tom – without disappearing permanently into any of them.

Although the impermanence of our relationship to morality is often cited as a disadvantage to us, especially in comparison to those historical settings – real or imagined – in which moral roles have been significantly more constant and reliable, Nietzsche wishes to illuminate its potential advantages (BGE 218). In particular, the performative character of our relationship to morality potentially affords us a welcome measure of critical distance from the moralities we serially display. As is his wont, Nietzsche describes this critical distance in terms of our capacity to *laugh* at each of our variously costumed selves. In a passage that is meant to announce an important pivot in his discussion of 'our virtues', he remarks,

> [W]e are ... prepared as no period before us for the carnival of great style, for spiritual carnival laughter and high spirits, for transcendental heights of the highest nonsense and Aristophanean mockery of the world. Perhaps we will discover right here the realm of our *invention*, that realm where even we can still be original, perhaps as parodists of world history and buffoons of God – perhaps, even if nothing else of today has a future, our *laughter* still has a future! (BGE 223)

This passage yields some important clues and clarifications pertaining to Nietzsche's aims in Part Seven of *BGE*. First of all, he confirms his readers' suspicion that he and they have been dealt

---

[9] See Parkes 1994: 364–72.

a motley, mediocre hand to play. Obliged to become versed and fluent in multiple moralities and moral poses, the 'hybrid' Europeans among his readers are masters of none (GS 352). Somehow, then, his best readers must transform their otherwise undistinguished capacity to cycle through various 'costumes' into their signature 'invention'. They will not create new values or discover a new morality, but they may yet fashion for themselves a novel use and application of the multiple moralities (and fragments of moralities) at their disposal. In short, their involuntary share in the hybridity that characterises late modern European culture must become their strongest suit.

Second, their performance of multiple moral roles has enabled them to become practised in detaching themselves from the roles they play. Although they are not free not to play the roles assigned to them, they *are* free not to become permanently identified with any of them. Whereas representatives of predecessor periods were expected to apply themselves in all sincerity to the moral and social roles to which they were assigned, Nietzsche's best readers know themselves to be nothing more than 'costumed' repertory performers. As an appreciation of the contextualised freedom they enjoy, he suggests that their (self-directed) laughter might lift them to the heights attained by the great critic Aristophanes, in which case they might credibly assert themselves as 'parodists of world history and buffoons of God'.

Why might Nietzsche imagine that his best readers will find this outcome to be desirable?[10] As we know, he has been concerned throughout *BGE* to apprise his readers of the limitations arising from the non-negotiable historical conditions of their agency. If they have taken this lesson to heart, they may be warming to the idea that their actual contributions to the production of a philosophy of the future might be significantly less grandiose than they originally thought or hoped. That their '*laughter* still has a future' might, in this context, sound just about right to them, especially if they have begun the process of accommodating themselves to

---

[10] On the possibility that the passage in question delivers a 'heavy dose of irony', see Acampora and Ansell-Pearson 2011: 156–7. For the related claim that 'mere laughter is not enough', see Lampert 2001: 215.

the lesser role and station he has reserved for them. Also, being compared to Aristophanes might strike them as an agreeable fate.

However, the real payoff here is related to the prospect of an *authentic* existence, which Nietzsche dangles before his readers in this passage.[11] Despite acknowledging their compulsory performance of multiple moral roles and poses, which might lead some to despair of ever being or feeling *original*, Nietzsche locates the germ of *their* originality in their raucous, irreverent, full-throated laughter. Indeed, the prospect of attaining an authentic presence in a slavishly inauthentic period, even if one's originality is limited to the reverberations of one's laughter, might simply be too inviting to decline. That their *'laughter* still has a future' might be appealing, in other words, inasmuch as it means that they have successfully inscribed themselves into history not simply as objects (or victims), but as subjects in their own right, that is, as having made an *original* contribution to the production of the future. Indeed, they might be content to offer their laughter as the calling card that will attract the attention and favour of the 'new' philosophers whose approach they await.[12]

As satisfying as this might be, however, it need not exhaust the full extent of the contributions his best readers will make to the production of a philosophy of the future. Although morality is currently employed as a tool to diminish the strong and empower the weak, this is not its only or even its best use. If Nietzsche's readers have taken seriously his call to prepare a 'typology of morals' (BGE 186), they might already appreciate that not all moralities are designed to prosecute a campaign of levelling. Moreover, the historical situation in which they find themselves, which he describes as a 'semi-barbarism', affords them access to 'secret passages everywhere' (BGE 224), including those passages that will lead them to examples of what he later will identify as vestiges of the 'master' morality (BGE 260). While their situation is by no means ideal, it is one that his readers may yet turn to their advantage.[13]

---

[11] Some important challenges to the ideal of authenticity are raised and considered by Katsafanas 2016: 217–19.
[12] For an instructive discussion of the various uses and contexts in which Nietzsche recommends or extols laughter, see Alfano 2019: 216–32.
[13] See Janaway 2007: 236–9.

Before he reveals wherein this advantage might lie, however, Nietzsche must complete his potentially dispiriting account of who he and his best readers are and have become:

> We human beings of 'historical sense': we also have our virtues as such, it cannot be denied – we are unpretentious, selfless, modest, courageous, full of self-overcoming, full of devotion, very grateful, very patient, very accommodating – for all that perhaps we are not very 'tasteful.' (BGE 224)

As he explains, the 'historical sense' on which his readers pride themselves is reduced, by their 'semi-barbarism', to 'the taste and tongue for everything' (BGE 224). Lacking a settled sense and taste of their own, his contemporaries name as a virtue their willingness to submit to the tastes of others (cf. EH: bge 2). Indeed, this phoney, commitment-averse cosmopolitanism is nothing more than a dressed-up expression of the philistinism that prevails throughout the *Reich* (TI 'Germans' 4). According to Nietzsche, he and his best readers bear witness to an unmistakably 'ignoble' taste.[14]

And now the good (or less troubling) news: owing to the 'democratic mingling of classes and races', and the disintegration of traditional class boundaries and social structures, Nietzsche notes, '*Moderation* is foreign to us; let us admit it to ourselves . . . we semi-barbarians . . . are only in *our* bliss, where we also most of all – *are in danger*' (BGE 224). Apparently, that is, he means to confirm here that he and his best readers share in the 'neurosis' that he documented in previous parts of *BGE*. They too wish to assert their independence and sovereignty, albeit not necessarily after the fashion of those whom Nietzsche has diagnosed. If they are to indulge their share in the 'neurosis', in other words, they will do so not in opposition to the order of rank, but in response to those who refuse to respect it. Having earlier urged his readers to exercise patience, humility and self-restraint, he now illuminates for their edification

---

[14] In his letter to Overbeck on 24 March 1887, Nietzsche complains that 'Englishmen' such as Lecky 'lack the "historical sense" and a few other things besides. The same is true of the much-read and – translated American Draper' (*SB* 8: 49/Middleton 1969: 265).

the limited sphere in which they may express *without reserve* their anti-Christian animus and their pro-science advocacy. So long as they remain focused on their truth-telling 'task', they may vent the full fury of the 'semi-barbarism' that is their rightful inheritance. As guardians and propagators of the 'magnificent tension of the spirit in Europe' (BGE P), they may 'bend the bow' even further by turning morality against itself. Like Wagner's Siegfried, in fact, they may delight in destroying those remnants of the past that hold at bay the brighter future that awaits their liberating efforts.

'We immoralists!'

Having disclosed the truth of their historical situation, Nietzsche leads his danger-loving, semi-barbarian readers on a training raid directed against two hoary assumptions about human nature: 1) that human beings naturally and instinctively seek pleasure and avoid pain; and 2) that suffering should be avoided and can be abolished (BGE 225). Reprising a familiar theme, he reminds his best readers of what he and they already know: 'The discipline of suffering, of *great* suffering . . . has created all the enhancements of humanity [so far]' (BGE 225). He apparently means to suggest here that suffering *becomes* great when it contributes meaningfully to the realisation of an end or objective that restores to humanity its will for the future.

This additional specification is instructive, for it positions Nietzsche to distinguish between two kinds of suffering that are often confused or conflated. Claiming that 'in humans, *creature* and *creator* are one', he explains that *pity* is customarily shown to the 'creature' within us, despite (what he offers as) the fact that enhancements of the human type *require* that suffering be visited upon the creaturely (i.e., unfinished) elements of human nature (BGE 225). While some forms of suffering might be mitigated with no net penalty to the cause of human enhancement, other forms – most notably, those directed by the 'creator' within against the 'creature' within – are simply non-negotiable. (Having earlier exposed pity as an expression of 'self-contempt' (BGE 222), Nietzsche apparently means to indicate here that those who valorise or preach pity are guilty of generalising without warrant from their own experience of misery.) If pity is to be considered valuable or worthwhile, he adds, its expressions must be reserved for the *creative* (i.e., finish- and form-giving) elements of human nature, which he here reveals as the genuine victims and intended targets of Christian morality. If human beings are to continue to ennoble and elevate themselves, creaturely suffering must be accorded its rightful role in the machinery of moral enhancement. To take steps towards the abolition of creaturely suffering would be to ensure (and perhaps accelerate) the ongoing diminution of humanity.

Rather than tarry any longer with a problem that invites and rewards philosophical 'naïvete', Nietzsche abruptly reminds his best readers of the exalted status of the 'we' to which he and they belong. As he indicated earlier (BGE 32), he and they are (or soon may become) 'immoralists', which is the *nom de guerre* he confers upon those who seize the residual authority of morality and turn it against its generative source (BGE 226).[15] In their resolve to wield morality itself as a tool, moreover, they will anticipate the efforts of those 'new' philosophers who will corral the 'sovereign' religions (e.g., European Christianity) that currently refuse to contribute to 'the overall development of humanity' (BGE 61). Apparently intending to activate his best readers as 'immoralists', Nietzsche now escorts them into the very heart of the book (BGE 226–30),[16] where he not only explains how they might turn their (unwanted) virtues to their strategic advantage, but also reveals the specific 'task' he has reserved for them.[17]

As we track their march into the heart of the book, let us bear in mind the immediate context of this fateful journey: Nietzsche has just now explained why he does not pity the creaturely elements – those that that remain unfinished and unformed – within the human soul. Rather than pity his best readers for the loneliness and disaffection he knows they will experience as a

---

[15] The 'two fundamental negations' that are expected of the 'immoralist' are specified at EH 'Destiny' 4.
[16] Here I follow Lampert 2001: 226–31.
[17] In his letter of 29 July 1888 to Carl Fuchs, Nietzsche laments that he has not yet been 'characterized . . . as an *Immoralist* (the highest form, till now, of "intellectual rectitude", which is permitted to treat morality as illusion, having itself become *instinct* and *inevitability*' (*SB* 8: 374–6/Middleton 1969: 305).

consequence of taking up the task he has reserved for them, he shows them how to turn this experience – and this suffering – to their advantage. In other words, he ministers to the creative elements within them while prescribing additional suffering for their creaturely natures. He does so, presumably, by employing his formidable artistic talents to 'transfigure' – that is, render meaningful and tolerable – the cruelty he lovingly directs towards them (BGE 229).[18]

He begins by delivering one of his clearest statements concerning the limitations imposed on his best readers by the historical situation in which they find themselves:

> *We immoralists* . . . are spun into a harsh yarn and shirt of duties and *cannot* get out – in this we are 'human beings of duty,' we, too! Occasionally, it is true, we dance in our 'chains,' and between our 'swords'; more often, no less true, we gnash our teeth and feel impatient about all the mysterious harshness of our fate. *But we do what we will* – the oafs and appearances speak against us, 'those are human beings *without* duty' – we always have the oafs and appearances against us! (BGE 226, emphasis added)

What begins as a backhanded compliment to his ineluctably encumbered readers – they may 'dance', he allows, but only ever in their 'chains' and between their 'swords' – quickly morphs into an unexpected recipe for their improbable success. Immediately after conceding that he and they 'gnash [their] teeth' and chafe under the burden of their 'fate', he attests to the (contextualised) freedom they may enjoy as 'immoralists': notwithstanding the 'harsh yarn and shirt of duties' in which they are obliged to enact their constrained agency, they 'do what [they] will', which, as we shall see, involves them in disclosing the truth about human nature, Christian morality, modern science and truth itself.

Elaborating on his earlier account of the as-yet-unacknowledged strategic advantage that accrues to him and his best readers, Nietzsche

---

[18] We are reminded here of Nietzsche's earlier praise for those leaders who are able to rebrand suffering as a previously unknown 'stimulus and spur to life' (BGE 200).

explains that he and they are 'immoralists' *not* because they are in fact free from moral duties and obligations, but because others, whom he calls 'oafs', believe this to be true of them.[19] The 'oafs' believe this, as we know, because they are largely unaware of the complexity and hidden wealth of the moral inheritance they share with Nietzsche and his best readers. As far as these 'oafs' are concerned, one is either moral or one is not. The possibility of a moral challenge to the authority of Christian morality, which is what Nietzsche urges his best readers to undertake (BGE 221), is and will remain for the 'oafs' a non-starter.[20] Herein, Nietzsche suggests, lies an advantage that he and his kindred 'immoralists' might exploit.

By adopting the name and title awarded them by those 'oafs' who 'speak against' them (BGE 226), Nietzsche and his best readers may position themselves to capitalise on the inevitable misunderstandings of their intramural challenge to morality.[21] They oppose the 'old' morality not from without, as the 'malicious' title of *BGE* might lead the 'oafs' to suppose, but from within, viz., as newly empowered agents of the newly emergent disciplinary regime of 'Christian truthfulness' (GM III: 27). In opposing themselves to the 'immoralists', the 'oafs' in question will fail to realise that they have picked a fight with 'human beings of duty', whose unacknowledged virtues – especially pertaining to truth-seeking and truth-telling – they cannot match. Exploiting the element of surprise, Nietzsche and his fellow 'immoralists' may perform their duties and exercise their virtues while also sowing consternation among the 'oafs' arrayed against them. As we shall see, in fact, the ensuing skirmish will reveal the name-calling 'oafs' to be the true immoralists, inasmuch as they repeat (and probably believe) the founding lies of Christian morality. They will be exposed as such, viz., as immoral champions of an obsolete morality, by those –

---

[19] See Solomon 2003: 50; and Conway 2014a: 287–92.
[20] The demand for a moral challenge to morality is attributed by Nietzsche to a 'moral pedant' who may in fact be Nietzsche himself (BGE 221).
[21] Whereas the 'philosophers of the future' represent a 'higher, greater' type of free spirit 'that does not want to be misunderstood and mistaken for something else' (BGE 44), the 'merely' free spirits among Nietzsche's readers will need to turn to their advantage the misunderstandings and mistaken identifications that are their lot. See Conway 2014a: 302–7.

Nietzsche and his 'we' – whom they mistakenly supposed to have no moral allegiances (and no corresponding 'duties') whatsoever.

A new task

Duly apprised of their status and calling as 'immoralists', Nietzsche's readers are finally prepared to reconsider their signature virtue: *honesty*, which, as we have seen, is a 'virtue from which [they] cannot get away' (BGE 227). Nietzsche furthermore recommends honesty as a virtue that his best readers may yet cultivate, amplify and repurpose to productive effect. As 'one of the youngest' of the virtues in their possession, 'still quite immature, still frequently mistaken and misconstrued, still barely aware of itself', descended from neither the Socratic nor the Christian table of virtues (D 456), honesty is likely to be relatively unknown, untested, unexplored and, *therefore*, ripe for development and creative redeployment.[22]

Honesty is by no means the only virtue that Nietzsche and his best readers possess, but it merits particular notice as the most powerful and pliable of the period-appropriate virtues at their disposal. Owing to the recent convergence of science and morality, the virtue of honesty has been recast in the mould of scientific rigour (GS 344; GM III: 27). Within the ascendant disciplinary regime of 'Christian truthfulness', in other words, the virtue of honesty not only compels one to tell the truth and keep one's promises, but also enjoins its bearers to root out hypocrisy, dogma, illusion, prejudice, mendaciousness and other kindred species of moral rot. So long as Nietzsche and his 'we' express themselves as scholars, 'hardened by the discipline of science' (BGE 230), what they say will be taken seriously even if what they say is unpopular.

As Nietzsche tells the story, the practice of honesty is now (or soon will become) unbound, unrestrained and unlimited, which is precisely what modern science demands of its practitioners. The historical advantage that accrues to Nietzsche and his fellow

---

[22] I am indebted here to White 2001: 63–6; Lampert 2001: 219–23; Burnham 2007: 163–4; Franco 2011: 184–7; Brusotti 2013: 272–5; Ansell-Pearson and Bamford 2020: 58–66; and Lemm 2020: 31–7. See also Conway 2014b: 207–9.

'immoralists' is that they may exercise the virtue of honesty in the service of their withering challenge to the cultural authority of morality itself. As 'semi-barbarian' representatives of the decadence of late modern European culture, in fact, they are not constrained by considerations of measure, taste, decency, refinement and other factors that have limited the pursuit of truth in predecessor periods (BGE 224). According to Nietzsche, in other words, it is now both morally obligatory *and* personally satisfying to expose the lies and illusions on which Christian morality continues to trade.

Having closed Part Five of *BGE* by teasing his readers with the promise of 'a *new task*' (BGE 203), and having devoted Part Six to an explanation of why they, *qua* scholars, are uniquely positioned to accelerate the approach of the '*genuine*' philosophers whom he has breathlessly described (BGE 211), Nietzsche finally reveals the 'task' that awaits him and his best readers:

> To translate humankind back into nature; to master the many vain and gushing interpretations and connotations that have so far been scribbled and painted over that eternal basic text [of] *homo natura*; to ensure that the human being henceforth stands before human beings even as it stands today, hardened by the discipline of science, before the *other* nature, with undaunted Oedipus eyes and sealed Odysseus ears, deaf to the luring songs of old metaphysical bird-catchers who have all too long fluted in their ears, 'you are more! you are higher! you are of a different descent' – that may be a strange and insane task, but it is a *task* – who would deny it! (BGE 230)

He and they will complete this task, he proceeds to explain, by debunking the myriad fabrications – whether they be religious, philosophical or even scientific in provenance – which currently impede our investigations of human nature and cloud our understanding of the human condition more generally.

As characterised here, the 'task' in question would appear to be chiefly subtractive (or destructive) in scope.[23] As such, it fits neatly within the 'No-saying, "*No-doing*"' remit of Nietzsche's

---

[23] See Leiter 2002: 74–7. See also Acampora and Ansell-Pearson 2011: 161–5.

post-Zarathustran writings (EH: bge 1). Having previewed in his *Zarathustra* a viable future incarnation of humanity, keyed to the ideal-in-waiting of the 'great health' (GS 382, GM II: 24), Nietzsche now assigns his best readers the task of scouring the 'eternal basic text [of] *homo natura*' of its multiple layers of accumulated accretion.[24] In urging his readers to join him in asserting 'mastery' over the (dubious) interpretations of human nature that continue to obscure its 'eternal basic text' – an allusion, perhaps, to the economy and astringency of the hypothesis of will to power – he renews his offer to guide them towards the optimal experience of freedom and power that is available to them. They will not create new values, and they will not become the 'legislators and commanders' whose approach he heralds (BGE 211), but they nevertheless may advance the cause by debunking the noxious interpretations that have attached themselves like barnacles to the 'eternal basic text [of] *homo natura*'.[25]

That his best readers are uniquely suited to this task is presented by Nietzsche as a happy coincidence of their philosophical disposition and the circumstances of their historical situation – not to mention their good fortune in having been enrolled in his finishing school for gentlemen. Referring to himself and his best readers as 'hermits and marmots', he intimates that they have grown weary of (and disaffected from) *all* attempts to characterise human nature, including those interpretations that count in their estimation as nothing more than 'worthy word-pomp' (BGE 230). Disinclined 'to don such moral word tinsel and tassels' (BGE 230), they will content themselves with the task of discrediting all such interpretations and dissolving the accretions they support. Owing to their historical placement in the ascendant disciplinary regime of 'Christian truthfulness' (GM III: 27), they may raise questions

---

[24] Nietzsche elsewhere describes his 'No-Saying, "*No-Doing*"' task as authorising '[his] assault on two millennia of anti-nature and violation of humankind' (EH: bt 4).

[25] At some point, presumably, the task of 'translating humanity back into nature' must give nature itself – that is, that which is not conventional but natural in *homo natura* – its due. In that event, Nietzsche and his 'we' may be in a position to disclose the active, kinetic, quasi-agential properties that Nietzsche occasionally attributes to nature. For a characterisation of the task as both subtractive (or destructive) *and* creative (or constructive), see Lemm 2020: 31–43.

and illuminate problems that simply never occurred to (most of) their predecessors. In doing so, moreover, they may avail themselves of a scientific curiosity that virtually knows no bounds. Having cautioned his readers that the will to truth would continue to 'tempt [them] to many a venture' (BGE 1), Nietzsche authorises his 'we' to seek the truth about human nature itself. This may explain why he describes this task as possibly 'insane' (BGE 230), especially if it leads his best readers to entertain the possibility of a human nature oriented to, and dependent on, both truth and untruth.[26]

As Nietzsche explains, one of the most important steps in this direction will oblige him and his best readers to turn a deaf ear to a familiar – and, to Nietzsche's way of thinking, patently false – refrain: 'you are more! you are higher! you are of a different descent!' (BGE 230).[27] As they do so, of course, they will need to be equally careful to refuse the invitation to self-contempt that contemporary science breeds in its most ardent practitioners.[28] That human nature is neither 'more', nor 'higher', nor 'of a different origin', is hardly sufficient warrant for the conclusion, increasingly popular among scholars and scientists, that human existence is *therefore* meaningless (or insufficiently meaningful) (GM III: 25). Indeed, although they will approach their task as scholars, they will employ an approach to scholarship – viz. a 'gay science' – that affords them abundant good cheer and a buoyant will for the future of humankind. They will find *their* meaning not in the misanthropic materialism of contemporary science (GM III: 25), but in taking up their task and contributing thereby to the production of a philosophy of the future.

Despite acknowledging that this task *may* be 'strange and insane', Nietzsche ventures neither an affirmation nor a denial of

---

[26] See Clark and Dudrick 2012: 37–55.
[27] The objectionable refrain in question – 'you are more! you are higher! you are of a different descent [*du bist mehr! du bist höher! du bist andere Herkunft!*]' (BGE 230/ KSA 5: 169) – is notably similar to the description Nietzsche earlier provided of the 'philosophers of the future', who are 'something more, higher, greater and fundamentally different [*etwas Mehreres, Höheres, Grösseres und Gründlich-Anderes*]' (BGE 44/ KSA 5: 60). It also bears noting that Nietzsche himself implores the readers of *Ecce Homo* not to 'mistake' him for someone else (EH P1).
[28] See Havas 1995: 177–81; Ridley 1998: 120–6; and Conway 2008: 140–7.

this possibility.²⁹ His intention here is to shift his readers' attention from the reasonableness (or sanity) of the task at hand – which he treats as beside the point – to the importance (and desirability) of having a task – *any* task – at all. Here two points bear noting. First, Nietzsche understands a 'task' not on the model of a chore or an agendum, but as a goal- or aim-directed endeavour that engages the affects, focuses the attention, concentrates the intellect, galvanises the will and produces sufficient meaning to justify one's continued existence as a mortal, worldly creature. Simply having (and affirming) a task, he thus suggests, will distinguish him and his best readers from their aimless, blindly striving contemporaries.

Second, he treats this task not as the product of a simple choice, volition or preference, but as a vocation or destiny, that is, as a claim selectively impressed upon those to whom offers of enrolment are extended. Indeed, although one eventually must choose whether or not to accept one's appointed task, one's choice in the matter is only ever in response to the summons one has received. In this respect, a task may be understood as a historically specific possibility that presents itself for affirmation only to those whose talents and virtues are uniquely suited to its pursuit and elaboration. In his own case, he explains, the task reserved for him – which he identifies as 'the revaluation of all values' – emerged slowly and imperceptibly as the product of internal processes, both psychological and physiological, of which he was mostly unaware. In order 'to become what one is', which is his preferred designation of the process of permitting oneself to grow into one's task, 'one must not have the faintest notion what one is' (EH 'Clever' 9). As this admonition confirms, moreover, he is well aware of the potential harm he may visit upon (some of) those readers whom he has urged to aspire to an enlarged repository of self-knowledge.

That Nietzsche regards his best readers as *worthy* of the task he discloses is itself intended as a mark of distinction. Having a task – as opposed, say, to having a job or a chore – presupposes a will for the future, which in turn requires the volitional resources needed to project one's will into the future. A task thus constitutes

---

²⁹ The question he poses here – 'why knowledge at all?' – may remind us of the importunate questions he earlier posed to the will to truth (BGE 1).

a burden, to be sure, but one that not just anybody can or will bear. One must be strong enough for it, and one must be summoned to its performance. By dint of his efforts to persuade his best readers that they have been selected for the task he has disclosed, Nietzsche sets the stage for his claim, in Part Nine of *BGE*, that his best readers may yet partake of an epoch-appropriate standard of nobility, as evidenced by their acquired capacity for *self-respect* (BGE 287). Accepting the task assigned to them, arriving thereby at the determination that they are worthy of this vocation, would be a significant down payment on the 'self-respect' that may yet certify their share in nobility.

Nietzsche concedes that it might be difficult to distinguish the 'extravagant honesty' that he and his readers will display from more familiar expressions of 'cruelty' (BGE 230). Rather than deny the charge of cruelty, moreover, he emphasises instead the productive role of honesty – and, so, of cruelty – in a period that stands in desperate need of it and in the context of a task that absolutely requires it. Having urged his readers to 'rethink cruelty and open [their] eyes', and having revealed that 'in every wanting-to-know there is a drop of cruelty' (BGE 229), he is not inclined to allow the 'knowers' among his readers to become ashamed of the cruelty that informs their efforts to assert their 'intellectual conscience and taste' (BGE 230).[30] (Apparently, that is, Nietzsche's programme of education and training in *BGE*, wherein 'psychology [has been] handled with avowed hardness and cruelty' (EH: bge 2), has acquainted his best readers with the cruelty they will be authorised in turn to dispense.) In addition to anticipating the chilly reception that he and they are likely to receive as they pursue the task reserved for them, Nietzsche thus makes allowances for the cruelty their 'extravagant honesty' is likely to impart. In doing so, as we shall see, he points his best readers in the direction of the Dionysian discipleship he will later claim to represent (BGE 295).[31]

---

[30] According to Nehamas, Nietzsche finds the 'risk' of 'physical cruelty of the worst sort' to be 'desirable', even though he 'does not in any way think that [the 'physical cruelty' in question] is desirable' (1985: 218–19).

[31] As Lampert observes, '*Beyond Good and Evil* attains one of its greatest summits when the argument of "Our Virtues" climaxes as a case for cruelty. . .' (2001: 208). See also Strauss 1998: 188–90; and Burnham 2007: 165–7.

But why, exactly, will their expressions of 'extravagant honesty' elicit allegations of cruelty? The simple answer here is that cruelty is likely to play a discernible role in the (overdetermined) truth-telling in which his best readers will be engaged. Inasmuch as Nietzsche and his 'we' intend to escalate the 'magnificent tension' that resides in the European spirit (BGE P), we might expect their tension-averse contemporaries to denounce their efforts as gratuitously cruel. In their determination to negate the lies and fabrications on which Christian morality trades, Nietzsche and his 'we' will no doubt be received (and reviled) as wanton merchants of cruelty, especially as they express their considerable enjoyment in doing so. As immoderate 'semi-barbarians', they may on occasion become excessive – and, yes, excessively cruel – in their denunciations of those who disseminate and/or consume untruths.[32] If nothing else, their aforementioned laughter may be received as cruel, especially if they channel Aristophanes as they expose (and ridicule) the lies that prop up the 'good' man as the apex specimen of human flourishing (BGE 218).

From these outward displays of cruelty, Nietzsche intimates, we may infer that he and his 'we' have mustered the *will* 'to treat things profoundly, manifoldly, thoroughly: as a kind of cruelty of the intellectual conscience and taste' (BGE 230). Having become productively cruel to themselves – which, as we know, is the desired outcome of the affective-somatic transformation he has offered to induce in them (BGE 218) – they are now free to become productively cruel to those others who instinctively recoil from 'the eternal basic text [of] *homo natura*' (BGE 230). Whereas the 'saint' targets the 'creator' within himself, gaining thereby only a temporary (and prohibitively costly) feeling of freedom and power (BGE 47), Nietzsche and his 'we' direct their inward cruelty towards the 'creature' within, viz., that which remains unfinished in them and others.[33]

That Nietzsche's best readers are likely to be (and to be seen as) cruel thus suggests that the dutiful performance of their task will

---

[32] Solomon notes that 'truthfulness is not primarily service to others. It is first of all self-overflowing' (2003: 153). See also Lemm 2020: 36–7.

[33] With respect to the self-referential scope of the *Redlichkeit* cultivated and practised by Nietzsche's best readers, see van Tongeren 2014: 157–60.

grant them expanded access to their full complement of affects, passions and instincts, as well as the modes of embodiment they variously animate. Vented under the period-appropriate sign of *honesty*, their native cruelty will fortify their truth-telling efforts and align them ever more closely with the newly ascendant regime of morality. In other words: by taking up their appointed task and allowing themselves to be remade in its image, Nietzsche and his 'we' may secure for themselves the affective-somatic transformation that *BGE* is meant to induce.[34] As we have seen, their will for the future of humanity will find its fullest expression in the passion, craft and good cheer they display while performing their assigned task.

In telling the truth about Christian morality, puncturing the illusions that even now sustain its (diminished) cultural authority, they will feel revitalised, purposeful, self-directed and effective. In doing so, moreover, they will approach (and perhaps attain) the optimal experience of freedom and agency that is available to them. So long as they are immersed in the performance of the task Nietzsche has reserved for them, they will feel themselves to be emancipated from the constraints of the morality of good and evil, even as they channel the authority and currency of this morality in its final, fading form.[35] For the first time in their lives, they will want and wish to be moral, and they will revere themselves for participating wholeheartedly in the irreducibly moral task assigned to them.[36] Not unlike Wagner's Siegfried, they may gleefully lay waste to any target within their reach, regardless of the status of the traditions, precedents, customs and norms they break along the way (CW 4). Of course, if they stray from the lane into which Nietzsche has guided them, attempting to do either too much or too little to produce the desired philosophy of the future, they will squander the comparative advantage he has helped them to secure for themselves.

---

[34] Lampert links (what I have called) the *affective-somatic transformation* of Nietzsche's readers to Nietzsche's efforts to rehabilitate cruelty and strip it of its unwarranted and counterproductive moral accretions (2001: 225–9).

[35] See Richardson 2008: 26–7; and Lemm 2020: 32–5.

[36] See Janaway 2007: 249–54; and Owen 2007: 63–5, 126–9.

Here we may go even further. In the restricted context within which they pursue their task—that is, exposing the truth of morality and reckoning its costs to the future of humankind—they will know and feel themselves to be worthy heralds of the 'new' philosophers whose approach they await. As they endeavour to 'translate humanity back into nature', they will display an acquired (or resurgent) will for the future of humanity, which will empower them to affirm the historical setting in which they perform their appointed task.[37] It is for this reason that Nietzsche finally addresses his 'we', in the context of urging them to become known (and remembered) for their 'extravagant honesty' (i.e., their 'cruelty'), as 'free, *very* free spirits' (BGE 230), which is an honorific designation he has reserved thus far for the 'philosophers of the future' (BGE 44). So long as they occupy the sweet spot he has isolated for them, they will be known to themselves and 'eulogised' by others as the 'free, *very* free spirits' whom he hailed at the conclusion of his Preface to *BGE* (BGE 230). If Nietzsche is successful in *BGE*, we may expect the (merely) 'free spirits' among his readers to grow into the 'free, *very* free spirits' whose 'extravagant honesty' both intrigues and entices the 'new' philosophers whom they await.

In sections 232–9, Nietzsche apparently changes course, electing to gather and disseminate his various thoughts on women, which at one point he intended to collect in a separate, free-standing part of *BGE*.[38] Here we might note that Wagner's Siegfried, whom Nietzsche has encouraged his best readers to emulate in a limited context, found the meaning of *his* revolutionary heroism in his efforts '*to emancipate woman* – "to redeem Brünnhilde"' and, thereby,

---

[37] Lemm offers the intriguing suggestion that at (or beyond) its limits, the 'task' entrusted to Nietzsche's best readers 'produces knowledge that changes the nature of the human being. Only when the will to knowledge becomes self-reflective and takes on the features of nature as will to power, does knowledge release nature's creative potential for the generation and creation of life within the human being and realize the extraordinary forces of metamorphosis [*Verwandlung*], of overcoming and self-overcoming' (Lemm 2020: 16).

[38] In his letter to C. Heymons (at Carl Duncker's Verlag) on 12 April 1886, Nietzsche explains that *BGE* would 'contains ten parts or sections', one of which he planned to call '*Das Weib an sich*' (*SB* 7: 175).

to ensure that '*misfortune is abolished*' (CW 4). In light of his enduring allegiance to *this* Wagner, who boldly conjured the barbarian hero Siegfried, Nietzsche may be understood in these concluding sections of Part Seven to be similarly interested in contributing, proximately, to the 'emancipation of woman' and, ultimately, to the destruction of the morality that holds women hostage.

Review

Nietzsche's inventory of 'our virtues' culminates in his identification of *honesty* as a virtue that may be mobilised and repurposed to particularly good effect. In their subtractive efforts to disclose the truth about human nature, Nietzsche and his 'we' may vent without measure or reserve (and with an exceedingly good conscience) their anti-Christian animus. Among the 'many vain and gushing interpretations and connotations that have so far been scribbled and painted over that eternal basic text [of] *homo natura*' (BGE 230), they are likely to find any number of fictions and fabrications that are cited, solemnly, in support of the validity of Christian morality. Each accretion they dissolve, each layer they erase, each supernaturalism they banish, will mark a victory for science and a loss for the 'old' morality.

9
Part Eight: Peoples and Fatherlands

Preview

Having identified *honesty* as exemplary of 'our virtues', Nietzsche turns in Part Eight of *BGE* to a domain and subject matter about which, he believes, precious little honesty has been available to his best readers – until now. It is time to tell the truth about politics and the role of Europe (and Germany) in forging a new world order for a new period, which, as we know, will be characterised by 'the *compulsion* to grand politics' (BGE 208).[1]

Here we encounter once again Nietzsche's knack for translating a lamentable calamity into an unanticipated opportunity. As we now know, the calamity in question may be traced to the deterioration of those 'conditions' under which particular peoples, nations, classes and castes have been bound to the '*determinate milieu*' from which they formerly derived an enduring sense of meaning, place, order and identity (BGE 242).[2] Accordingly, the opportunity he wishes to promote arises from his appreciation of the uniquely 'supra-national and nomadic' quality of 'the *developing European*' (BGE 242). Simply put, or so he notes, the European 'herd animals' whose emergence he documents have been bred to labour under the direction and surveillance of lordly others. To date, however, the only yoke offered to them, consisting of the

---

[1] See Strong 1975: 137–45; Conway 2014b: 207–13; and Drochon 2016: 80–96.
[2] He describes 'our Europe of today' as 'the showplace of an absurdly sudden experiment of radical class mixing and *consequently* race mixing' (BGE 208).

minimal constraints exerted by the 'democratic movement', has failed to endow them with the meaning, direction and virtue they have been promised. If that promise is to be kept, another kind of yoke will be needed.

Critics of Nietzsche's plan to emigrate beyond good and evil will find much in Part Eight to confirm their suspicions and cement their opposition. As we shall see, the political consequences of moving beyond good and evil apparently involve a cold, unsentimental reduction of European peoples and nations to their constituent quanta of 'force', which Nietzsche-inspired lawgivers are invited to rearrange – with no overriding concern for traditional norms or moral constraints – into the configurations they deem best suited to the overarching goal of returning Europe to a dominant geopolitical position. In the realm of politics, that is, moving beyond good in evil is presented as a necessary condition of entering into (and prevailing in) 'the great play and struggle of forces' (BGE 251), which may simply be another way of characterising 'the world seen from inside' – namely, as '"will to power" and nothing else' (BGE 36). Nietzsche thus conceives of the disintegration of European culture as a problem to be solved by a novel (and presumably scientific) approach to cultural engineering.

While Nietzsche's blueprint for a new European order is likely to put his best readers in mind of familiar versions (or caricatures) of *Realpolitik*, a potentially crucial difference here is that his proposed reconfiguration of Europe is designed not to improve its geopolitical standing in matters pertaining to military might, colonial expansion or commercial dominance, but to revive and amplify its contributions to the elevation of culture. Situating himself in direct and hostile opposition to the philistinism of Bismarck's *Reich*, Nietzsche avers that might makes right *only* if the might in question is amassed and deployed in the service of cultural advancement (TI 'Germans' 4). That his blueprint for a new European order will be received as immoral, viz., as cruel and coldly utilitarian in its calculations, is of no concern to him, so long as it is understood to guide the 'new' philosophers in producing a Europe in which political power is but a means to the more glorious end of cultural advancement.

PART EIGHT: PEOPLES AND FATHERLANDS   171

Summary of sections

Part Eight of *BGE* comprises sixteen numbered sections (240–56). The distinction embedded in the title of Part Eight is meant to suggest two possible outcomes for Germany (and, as it turns out, for Europe). If Germany continues along its present course, Nietzsche believes, it will remain nothing more than a 'fatherland', which, he intends to demonstrate, is in fact a cultural dead end. If the Germans instead aspire to play a leading role in the reconfigured Europe he envisions, they may expect to transcend the limitations of their current fascination with the *Reich* and become, once again, a genuine 'people' with a renewed commitment to the elevation of culture.

Hence his intriguing assessment of the Germans, which is prompted, as he explains, by his appreciation of the music of Richard Wagner: 'they are of the day before yesterday and the day after tomorrow – *they still have no today*' (BGE 240).[3] Owing to this vacancy, the Germans tend to live in a past and for a future that each remain unproductively disconnected from the actual circumstances of their present situation. Determined to win for the Germans the 'today' they persistently lack, Nietzsche attempts in Part Eight to chart a course from their current, self-congratulatory fatherlandishness to the status of a genuine, world-historical people.

Although he does not say so explicitly, he apparently means to suggest here that the Germans have no 'today' because they are not yet prepared to confront the 'contradictions' they would be urged to face by their resident philosophers (BGE 212). Rather than take such 'contradictions' to heart and rise to the occasion of the current crisis, the Germans instead relax into the philistinism of the *Reich*, which Nietzsche identifies as a prime symptom of cultural decay (BT: AS 6; TI 'Germans' 4–5). It is as if the Germans exist in a persistent fugue state, estranged from the geo-political challenges of the present by their dreamy idealisations of the past and future. While frozen in this state, the Germans regard

---

[3] Nietzsche revisits this characterisation of the philosopher, with specific reference to himself, in both EH 'Wise' 2–3 and CW P.

their resident philosophers not as trusty stewards of the German soul, but as threats to its security – which, in some sense, they are and must be.

The key insight here is that standing in 'contradiction' to one's 'today' need not have the exclusively corrosive effect that champions of the *Reich* apparently fear. While it is true, as we know, that philosophers 'appl[y] their vivisecting knife to the very chest of the *virtues of their age*', it is equally true – at least according to Nietzsche – that they do so in order to prompt humanity towards the '*new* greatness' they uniquely anticipate on its behalf (BGE 212). If Germany were to heed the 'contradictions' embodied by its native-born philosophers, it would acquire a 'today' to which its past and future could be productively (and realistically) joined. As delivered by Nietzsche and his 'we', the 'today' in question would be sufficiently rich and lively as to launch Germany into a future worthy of its past. The point here is to engage the *status quo* in productive contestation and, thereby, to acquire the momentum to chart an ever grander future for Germany and Europe.

In sections 240–1, Nietzsche attests to the enduring appeal for him (and for the 'good Europeans' more generally) of the 'fatherlandishness' that is stirred in them by Wagner's music (BGE 241). Rather than denounce outright the music of Wagner, Nietzsche's goal in Part Eight of *BGE* is to model to his best readers a particular way of appreciating Wagner and the fatherlandish feelings he excites in them, precisely so that they might aspire to a more productive ideal of their Germanity. Narrowing his focus to the '*democratic* movement' underway in Europe (BGE 242), Nietzsche revisits his claim that the recent emergence of a homogeneous mass of European 'herd animals' is both a genuine calamity *and* an auspicious opportunity. Emphasising once again the 'skill and power for adaptation' that distinguishes the type of the '*developing European*' (BGE 242), he proposes to turn the democratic impulse to the advantage of the revitalised, reunified Europe he has in mind. As it turns out, 'the democratization of Europe' is not only 'leading to the production of a type that is prepared in the subtlest sense for *slavery*', but also creating 'an involuntary arrangement for the cultivation of *tyrants*' (BGE 242). In other words, he is counting on the 'democratic movement' in Europe to give rise, inadvertently, to its *other* – namely, a tyrannical type equal to the task of imposing form and order on to the emergent mass of European 'herd animals'. In that event, the recent surge of the 'democratic movement' in Europe could be harnessed to facilitate the win–win match he earlier proposed on behalf of the 'new' philosophers (BGE 203).

The German soul

Having alerted his readers to the siren songs of the fatherland (BGE 241), Nietzsche turns to an account of why their best future *as Germans* coincides with their conjectured future as 'good Europeans' (BGE 243–4). Notwithstanding the multiple vexations that complicate his relationship to his fellow Germans, here he confirms his allegiance to a particular ideal of Germanity. Indeed, his hopes for the future of Germany – and, so, of Europe – are rooted in his idealised depiction of the German soul, which he characterises as multiply conflicted and seductively at odds with itself (BGE 244). (As we have seen, it is the 'contradictory nature' of the German soul that accounts for Nietzsche's offer to bestow upon the Germans a 'today' replete with the 'contradictions' embodied by its leading philosophers.)

Elaborating on his earlier account of the labyrinthine structure of the late modern soul (BGE 214), he describes the German soul as riddled with 'passages and inter-passages', as well as 'caves, hideouts, and dungeons', and 'secret paths to chaos' (BGE 244).[4] According to Nietzsche, in fact, the capacity of the German soul to accommodate diverse, competing impulses is the source of the 'profundity' that it was once customary to attribute to the Germans, 'as a distinction' (BGE 244). At its world-historical best, that is, the German soul translates its capacity for internal conflict into excess creative energy, to which its most significant cultural triumphs bear enduring witness.

Nietzsche's idealised depiction of the German soul is best captured in his flattering sketch of Goethe, whom he honours as

---

[4] Here Nietzsche appears to channel the wisdom of Zarathustra: 'I say unto you: one must still have chaos in oneself to be able to give birth to a dancing star. I say unto you: you still have chaos in yourselves' (Z P5).

'the last German for whom [he has] any respect' (TI 'Forays' 51). According to Nietzsche, Goethe was

> a sort of self-overcoming on the part of [the eighteenth] century . . . [U]ndaunted, he took as much as was possible upon himself, above himself, within himself. What he wanted was *totality* . . . he disciplined himself into wholeness, he *created* himself . . . Goethe conceived of a human who is strong, highly cultured, skilled in all physical functions, holding himself in check, paying himself respect, who has the prerogative to grant himself the whole range of wealth and naturalness, being strong enough for this freedom. . . (TI 'Forays' 49)

I have cited this passage at length because it faithfully expresses Nietzsche's admiration for Goethe as an exemplar of the (idealised) Germanity he most admires. Because Goethe was able to discipline and master his manifold impulses and talents, Germany was not able to contain him. In the person of Goethe, the German soul exceeded its familiar national boundaries, reaching beyond Germany to influence and inform the culture of Europe itself. Nietzsche thus insists that Goethe was 'not a German event, but a European one' (TI 'Forays' 49).

With this sketch of Goethe in mind, let us return to *BGE*. Nietzsche recalls with obvious delight those

> words of Goethe in which he denounces *as if from abroad*, with impatient hardness, what Germans embrace with pride: the famous German *Gemüt* he once defined as 'indulgence toward the weaknesses of others and oneself.' (BGE 244, emphasis added)

What is important here for our purposes is the customary willingness on the part of Goethe to call his fellow Germans to order, expressing his conviction that the 'weaknesses' in question should *not* be tolerated, much less indulged. Goethe thus rebuked his fellow Germans with the authority of a German, calling them to order and account, while also evincing the clarity of perspective of an under-impressed foreign observer. What Goethe understood, Nietzsche subsequently confides (and affirms), is that

> Germans themselves *are* not, they *become*, they 'develop.' 'Development' is therefore the real German find and coup in the great realm of philosophical formulas... (BGE 244)

When the Germans are at their best, when this process of 'development' leads them upward and onward, they reveal themselves to be responsive to the examples set for them by their leading contributors to a national culture that is simultaneously pan-European in its influences and aspirations. As embodied by Goethe and idealised by Nietzsche, the multiplex German soul achieves its apotheosis in the cosmopolitanism of the 'good European'.[5]

Nietzsche's German contemporaries faithfully exhibit this capacity for internal conflict, but with an important difference: their decadence, diagnosed earlier as a 'disease of the will' (BGE 208), renders them incapable of gathering and containing their manifold impulses within a functioning whole. What was once a productive, excessive riot of internal conflict and self-aversion has degenerated into a destructive, implosive circus of self-contempt. Nietzsche's goal, consequently, is to deliver Germany from its (unacknowledged) self-contempt by placing it in a context – viz., that of a pan-European cosmopolitanism – in which it might learn once again to master its inner contradictions and, so, to derive a productive surge of power from its internal conflicts. The return of Germany and Europe in the best versions available to them will thus require the new 'ruling caste', relying on the advice of counsellor Nietzsche, to reconfigure the geopolitical landscape of contemporary Europe.

In order to do so, the aforementioned 'ruling caste' must reintroduce an effective apparatus of challenges and impediments, against which Germany and Europe might struggle in their efforts to overcome their current limitations. The splintered, empire-crazed nations of Europe must learn to reclaim their central focus

---

[5] In response to 'the old problem: "What is German?"', Nietzsche elsewhere makes the case that the leading figures of German philosophy – Leibniz, Kant, Hegel, Schopenhauer and, implicitly, himself – are in fact 'good Europeans' (GS 357).

and identity, thereby renouncing their dreams of easy riches and imperial plunder, and to assemble their best representatives in a novel arrangement of shared leadership. By restoring a fragmented Europe to wholeness, Nietzsche intends to position Germany to restore itself as well. As it did so splendidly in the case of Goethe, the grander goal of a trans-national, pan-European culture will draw the German soul aloft, beyond its current limits, which have been narrowed considerably by its recent dalliance with fatherlandish nationalism.

Creating a home for European Jewry

Pointing to the recent decline of European arts and letters, with special emphasis on the degeneration of German music, Nietzsche rehearses his claim that the good old days are gone and that a new, as yet undefined, period is dawning (BGE 245–9). His survey of German composers, while illuminating in its own right,[6] is meant to prepare his readers to consider the merits of a very serious indictment: the 'greatest danger' that threatens German music lies in the possibility of 'losing *the voice for the soul of Europe* and sinking to a mere fatherlandishness' (BGE 245). In other words, German music was at its very best when it spoke not only to and for the Germans, but also to and for Europe as a whole. By extension, we apparently are meant to infer that the Germans are at their best when they find and express their national identity within the context of their contributions to a genuinely European (and not merely a German) culture.

In sections 250–1, Nietzsche unveils his most audacious recommendation for achieving the new, reinvigorated European union he envisions: the Jews of Europe must be offered a permanent home and welcomed as equal partners in the new alliance he aims to broker (BGE 251). The motivation for this particular recommendation may be found in his earlier diagnosis of the 'disease of the will [that] is unevenly spread across Europe' (BGE 208).

---

[6] In his letter to Gast on 18 July 1887, Nietzsche claims, citing Widmann, that Brahms, who is not mentioned in *BGE*, 'is most interested in *Jenseits*' (*SB* 8: 112–14/Middleton 1969: 268).

If Europe is 'to *acquire one will* . . . [and thereby] establish goals for millennia' (BGE 208), he advised there, a 'new caste' would need to rule Europe (BGE 208). The primary and immediate objective of this new ruling caste would be to address the 'disease of the will' by rebalancing and reconfiguring the constituent peoples and nations of Europe.

Returning to this proposal in Part Eight of *BGE*, Nietzsche asserts that an untried antidote to this 'disease of the will' is readily available. Having introduced his readers to the 'great play and struggle of forces', which is apparently meant to impress by virtue of its 'extramoral' audacity, he declares that 'A thinker who has the development of Europe on his conscience will, in all his projects for this future, take into account the Jews' (BGE 251). A consideration of the Jews is necessary, he explains, because

> [T]he Jews are without a doubt the strongest, most tenacious, and purest race now living in Europe; they know how to assert themselves even under the worst conditions (better even than under favorable ones), by means of some kinds of virtues that people today would like to label as vices. . . (BGE 251)

As it turns out, in fact, the qualities the Germans currently lack are precisely those possessed in abundance by the Jews. Whereas the Germans are 'still weak and indeterminate', yielding to the prevailing winds of decadence and philistinism, the Jews 'change, *if* they change . . . "as slowly as possible!"' (BGE 251).[7]

Borrowing an epithet from his beloved Horace, Nietzsche describes the Jewish people as '*aere perennius*' – more enduring than bronze (BGE 251). He is 'certain' that 'the Jews, if they wanted – or if they were forced, as the anti-Semites seem to want – even now *could* have the upper hand, indeed quite literally mastery, over Europe' (BGE 251). Aiming to accommodate European Jewry's supposed wish 'to be absorbed and assimilated', he proposes that 'it would perhaps be useful and fair to expel

---

[7] A similarly problematic assessment of European Jewry is found in A 24.

the anti-Semitic screamers from the country [i.e., Germany]' (BGE 251). Presumably, the appeal of doing so is explained by the 'extramoral' calculus that governs 'the great play and struggle of forces': the addition (via enfranchisement) of the Jews and the subtraction (via expulsion) of the anti-Semites would deliver a net gain in the strength, integrity and constancy of will as Europe enters the age of 'grand politics' (BGE 208).[8]

After 'cheerfully' proposing to accomplish this end by matching Prussian officers with Jewish brides, Nietzsche turns to the '*serious*' matter of confronting what he identifies as the 'European problem', the solution to which will involve, as we have seen, 'the cultivation of a new caste that will rule over Europe' (BGE 251).[9] In support of this recommendation, he surveys the comparative strengths and weakness of the peoples and nations he plans to include in this new European ruling caste. According to him, this new ruling caste must be recognisably European in its composition, and it must lay credible claim to the succession of nobility across bygone ages and empires.[10]

Reprising his earlier profiles of the pragmatic English, the cultured French and the militaristic Germans (BGE 208–11), he concludes that their respective advantages and weaknesses confirm the need to assimilate (and subsequently exploit) the strength and spirit of the Jews (BGE 252–5). In order to become a cultural power of truly global dominion, Europe – and the Germans in particular – would need to be prepared to extend the offer of a permanent home to the Jews of Europe. It will not be lost on Nietzsche's intended readers that he has redefined the so-called 'Jewish problem' as what he more accurately identifies as 'the European problem' (BGE 251). His reason for doing so is simple: the Jews are in fact the solution to the 'problem' they are popularly understood to have caused or created.[11]

---

[8] See Lampert 2001: 255–7; and Conway 2014b: 197–202.
[9] On the significance of Nietzsche's fascination with the reinstitution of a caste-based society, see Holub 2016: 195–203; and Drochon 2016: 88–96.
[10] For a discussion of Nietzsche's 'serious' concern with the future of Europe, see Lampert 2001: 255–61.
[11] That the Jews of Europe would not have benefited from the 'homecoming' Nietzsche offers to arrange for them is discussed by Simon 1997: 107; Cancik 1997: 65–9; Emden 2008: 308–23; and Holub 2016: 210–14.

PART EIGHT: PEOPLES AND FATHERLANDS 179

Nietzsche concludes Part Eight by facing up to the political crisis at hand. Confirming that the 'insanity of nationality' is responsible for 'the pathological alienation . . . between the peoples of Europe', he acknowledges that Europe is currently beset by internecine squabbling (BGE 256). At the same time, however, he insists that the current divisions and disputes are in fact recent, artificial, transient and symptomatic of an illness that may yet run its course.[12] Although Europe suffers from an acute 'paralysis of the will' (BGE 208), it may yet return to the robust health for which it is more generally known, admired and feared.[13] The problem for now, he believes, is that the 'insanity' from which Europe suffers is being exploited (and aggravated) by 'politicians of shortsightedness and the hasty hand', who are oblivious to the fact that the 'dissolution politics they practice can of necessity only be entr'acte politics' (BGE 256). As such, these politics are suitable (at best) only for the short term, and only under artificial conditions of distress that these politicians have no incentive to alleviate. Indeed, beneath the superficial flux of division and dissension lies a deeper truth, which Nietzsche now sees fit to disclose: '*Europe wants to become one*' (BGE 256).[14]

This deeper truth is evident to those who are in a position to chart the dominant counter-movement of the nineteenth century in Europe. If we attend closely to the exploits of the 'deeper and more comprehensive human beings of this century', we will detect the 'real overall direction in the mysterious workings of their soul' (BGE 256). *Soul* is numbered here as singular, which suggests that these individuals share in or partake of a single soul, viz. that of Europe, even if each also lays claim to a unique, individuated soul of his own. Apparently, that is, the 'will' of Europe is expressive of a 'soul' that is serially channelled by the exemplars

---

[12] In a related discussion, Nietzsche elsewhere likens the outbreak of European nationalisms to the condition of 'national scabies of the heart and blood poisoning' (GS 377).

[13] In this respect, Europe appears to be in good company, for Nietzsche offers a similar diagnosis of himself in *Ecce Homo*. Although he is a decadent, as he says there, the tenacity of his 'opposition' to decadence confirms that he is fundamentally *healthy* (EH 'Wise' 2).

[14] What Europe now wants, it turns out, is precisely what Napoleon wanted: 'one unified Europe, as is known – as *mistress of the earth* [*Herrin der Erde*] – ' (GS 362). See Shapiro 2016: 88.

whom Nietzsche cites.[15] If we regard these individuals as constituting a continuous spiritual lineage, moreover, we may understand their role in 'prepar[ing] the way for this new *synthesis*' (BGE 256), which, as we have seen, he associates with the post-moral Europe he envisions. Unbeknownst to lesser observers, that is, Europe has consistently expressed its will through its sponsorship of those individuals in whom the possibilities for its future have been tested, assayed and confirmed.

Nietzsche's reference here to a 'new *synthesis*' recalls his more general account of the generation and dissolution of human-sponsored (i.e., intentional, deliberate) forms of social order. According to Nietzsche, viable forms of social order arise only in response to and recognition of the 'wasteful and *indifferent* magnificence' of nature (BGE 188). The project of culture, which Nietzsche hopes to reorient to the period-appropriate values of *life-* and *species-promotion* (BGE 4), thus requires a concerted, coordinated campaign on the part of human beings to impose anthropogenic order and discipline on to nature. As Nietzsche insists in Part Eight of *BGE*, this is true of politics as well. Just as artists must impose order on to the disparate, unfinished media with (and on) which they work, so must political lawgivers impress an enforceable order on to those human beings whom they wish to place in a different or optimised social arrangement.

What Nietzsche means here by a 'synthesis' is the creation of order and meaning through the imposition of form on to an otherwise formless or inert or unrealised substrate (e.g., nature, matter, force, etc.). The imposition of form creates new configurations and endows the resulting whole (or 'synthesis') with meaning, aim, direction and identity. The comparison with artistic creation is apt, Nietzsche believes, inasmuch as an emerging 'synthesis' serves to endow the newly constituted whole with vitality and meaning that were not originally present (or noticed) in the substrate. As such, a 'synthesis' is a whole that exceeds any previously determined sum of its constituent parts. These imposed

---

[15] In his survey of German music, Nietzsche explains that 'with [Schumann] German music was threatened by its greatest danger, that of losing *the voice for the soul of Europe* and sinking to a mere fatherlandishness' (BGE 245).

PART EIGHT: PEOPLES AND FATHERLANDS 181

forms of order will continue to maintain the new 'synthesis' until they wear out, at which point the formerly regnant 'synthesis' will lapse and decay. Deprived of its acquired meaning and vitality, the substrate in question will revert to its previous, unformed condition until another 'synthesis' is achieved by the imposition of another specification of form and order.

As Nietzsche proceeds to explain, the great individuals in question contribute to the eventual realisation of the aforementioned 'synthesis' by 'experimentally [*versuchsweise*] anticipat[ing] the European of the future' (BGE 256). His description here of their envisioned contributions should pique our interest. As we know, *Versucher* is the designation he has proposed in *BGE* for those 'new philosophers' to whom he similarly entrusts the future of Europe (BGE 42–4). Their experiments, like those of the anticipatory heroes under consideration here, will reveal (albeit imperfectly) what Europe may yet become. That Nietzsche's best readers might acknowledge – and, eventually, claim – their rightful place within this lineage of experimenters, as we know, is chief among his objectives in *BGE*.

Unbeknownst to lesser observers, in fact, the new Europe and the new European have already arrived on the scene, albeit in embryonic forms that remain experimental, fragmentary, tentative, unproven and as yet unsustainable. Some of these experiments will fail or already have done so; still others will defy translation (or transplantation) into the new, as-yet-undiscovered landscape of an 'extramoral' Europe that once again has 'become one'.[16] According to Nietzsche, after all, the present never admits of a faithful measure of the future, for the present only ever evinces a limited appreciation of what the future may bear. Still, the present as it is experimentally enacted by these anticipatory heroes is sufficiently bold and intoxicating as to excite in Nietzsche's readers the will to become (or beget) the future Europeans whom he claims to glimpse *in nuce*.

---

[16] As Nietzsche readily concedes, some of the heroes included in this anticipatory lineage may be seen, in 'their foregrounds or in weaker hours, perhaps in old age', to have 'belong[ed] to the "fatherlands" – they were only resting from themselves when they became "patriots"' (BGE 256).

Who are these anticipatory heroes? Nietzsche initially lists Napoleon, Goethe, Beethoven, Stendhal, Heine and Schopenhauer (BGE 256).[17] We apparently are meant to understand that Napoleon established the material and social conditions under which his successors in this lineage have pursued a complementary transformation of European arts and letters. They have done so, as Nietzsche explains, by dint of their experiments at the limits of Europe's current canons of self-understanding, where they have dared to sample the aspirations, virtues, accomplishments and values of the 'European of the future' (BGE 256). Although he does not say so explicitly, Nietzsche apparently understands these anticipatory experiments as either directly or indirectly productive of both the 'European of the future' *and* the Europe of the future. As we shall see, one such experiment, internal to the development of '*French late romanticism*', is especially noteworthy in this respect (BGE 256).

Owing to the results thus far of these experimental anticipations of its future, Europe is now poised on the brink of its next great 'self-overcoming'[18] and its next great incarnation. Hence Nietzsche's point in support of his surprising conclusion: the cumulative achievements of this anticipatory lineage confirm the progression of a subterranean counter-movement that is far grander in scope and formative power than those merely episodic spasms of nationalism and petty politics that appear to rule the day. To view the outbreak of nationalism as indicative of the *real* Europe, or of its authentic will, is to miss the larger trends of European development.[19]

Somewhat surprisingly, Nietzsche also proposes to include Wagner in this esteemed lineage, explaining that we should not hold Wagner's 'misunderstandings' of himself against him (BGE 256). Unbeknownst to Wagner, apparently, his early

---

[17] Nietzsche offers a similar assessment of Schopenhauer, identifying him as a 'good European', in GS 357; see also TI 9: 21.
[18] Nietzsche concludes a similar discussion of the progress of European modernity by declaring that he and his fellow '*good* Europeans' are 'heirs of Europe's longest and most courageous self-overcoming [*Selbstüberwindung*]' (GS 357).
[19] For a persuasive account of Nietzsche's attempt to oppose nationalism with the ideal of 'Europeanism', see Yovel 1998: 132–6.

music authentically expressed the yearning of 'the one Europe, whose soul surges and longs outward and upward from [his][20] multifarious and tempestuous art – where to? to a new light? to a new sun?' (BGE 256). Nietzsche goes so far as to suggest, albeit tentatively and indirectly, that 'Wagnerian music . . . derives from *supra-German* [i.e., authentically European] sources and impulses' – hence the warrant for placing him in this lineage of European (and not merely German) musicians, artists, poets and thinkers (BGE 256).

Although Nietzsche neglects to affix his declarative stamp to this suggestion, he summons the figure of Siegfried, 'that *very free* human being', as evidence of Wagner's supra-German – and, so, supra-nationalistic – aspirations and achievements (BGE 256). In particular, he commends the figure of Siegfried for emitting a pleasing whiff of the 'barbarism' he claims to detect at the molten core of European civilisation. He thus praises Wagner's creation of Siegfried as a potentially salutary corrective to the (otherwise laudable) hyper-refinement of French culture (BGE 256). As we have seen, moreover, Nietzsche may have Siegfried in mind as he trains his best readers to revolt against the morality that has formed (and limited) them. As they rail without measure against the bankrupt regime of Christian morality, thereby attaining their optimal experience of freedom and power, they may put themselves (and others) in mind of the freewheeling, 'barbarian' iconoclasm of Siegfried.

From this high point, of course, Wagner declined precipitously as an artist, as evidenced (in Nietzsche's estimation) by the travesty of *Parsifal*, which he describes as marking Wagner's late-in-life capitulation to Catholicism (BGE 256).[21] If we focus our attention not on the wretched figure of Parsifal, but on the gloriously 'inaccessible' and 'inimitable' figure of Siegfried, we

---

[20] So as to focus on Wagner in particular, I have adjusted Nietzsche's designation from the plural to the singular. In this passage, Nietzsche links Wagner to the leading lights of the '*late French romanticism* of the forties', including Delacroix and Balzac, with whom Wagner belongs 'most closely and intimately' (BGE 256). As Nietzsche explains, 'what is certain is that the same storm and stress tormented them, that they *searched* in the same way, these last great seekers!' (BGE 256)

[21] GM III: 3–4; see also CW 4.

may understand why Nietzsche insists on placing Wagner in the company of those anticipatory heroes who unwittingly express and temporarily serve the will of Europe (BGE 256). We apparently are meant to understand that Wagner's romantic longing, which attained its apotheosis in the 'anti-romantic' figure of Siegfried, both channelled and furthered Europe's will to 'become one'.

Of course, the most important consequence of Wagner's placement in this lineage pertains to the legacy of his greatest disciple: Nietzsche himself.[22] If the Wagner who conjured Siegfried belongs among 'the deeper and more comprehensive human beings of [the nineteenth] century' (BGE 256), then it is hardly a stretch to imagine that Nietzsche, an unabashed champion of *this* Wagner, even to the point of disowning 'the "late Wagner" and his *Parsifal*-music' (BGE 256), *also* belongs in this lineage. Indeed, if we take seriously his 'grateful' reckoning of his many debts to Wagner,[23] we may conclude that his break with the Master played a role in securing his access to the 'signs' he now declares to be 'unequivocal' (BGE 256).

As he jockeys for a position alongside his heroes, Nietzsche intimates that his own placement in this lineage is emblematic of a new, decisive turn in its ongoing elaboration. In his person, the lineage in question embarks upon a distinctly *self-conscious* stage in its service of the subterranean forces pushing Europe towards the unification he foresees.[24] Unlike his predecessors in this lineage, whose influence has been both prodigious and unintended, Nietzsche is determined to seize conscious, voluntary control of the ongoing development of Europe and its emblematic culture. Whereas Goethe, Beethoven, Wagner et al. were seized by transpersonal forces they neither discerned nor understood, Nietzsche aims to advance this lineage in full, conscious appreciation of its

---

[22] Here I follow Lampert 2001: 260–1.
[23] Nietzsche expresses his 'gratitude' for and towards Wagner in CW E.
[24] Nietzsche elsewhere identifies the 'problem' that he and his '*unknown*' friends' now face: 'What meaning [*Sinn*] would *our* entire being [*Sein*] have if not this, that in us the will to truth came to consciousness of itself as a *problem?*' (GM III: 27). He goes on to suggest that their solution to this 'problem' will be integral somehow to the eventual demise of 'morality' (GM III: 27). For an extended discussion of these passages, see Conway 2014b: 209–13.

PART EIGHT: PEOPLES AND FATHERLANDS   185

contributions to the emergence of a 'new European'. He will do so, as we now know, by anticipating the arrival of those 'new' philosophers who will dare to take control of the production of those exotic, norm-shattering exemplars whose exploits serve to motivate a justification of life itself.

How Europe might become one

Nietzsche concludes Part Eight of *BGE* by completing his assessment of the music of Wagner. Crediting Wagner's time in Paris with his creation of Siegfried (BGE 256), Nietzsche suggests that the Germans might derive similar benefits from their prescribed collaborations with the French in the new European ruling caste. He thus ends Part Eight with a final word of caution with respect to the perils of German fatherlandishness.

Pointing once again to the pathetic figure of Parsifal, whom we are meant to receive (and ridicule) as the polar opposite of the heroic type embodied by Siegfried,[25] Nietzsche reminds (or informs) his readers that Wagner's fatherlandishness, expressed so seductively in 'the overture to the *Meistersinger*' (BGE 240), eventually gave way to the 'characteristic religious vehemence' of his late-in-life return to Christianity and his (apparent) fascination with Roman Catholicism: 'For what you hear is *Rome, – without the words, Rome's faith!*' (BGE 256). His point here is that German fatherlandishness is buoyant and seductive in the short term, but debilitating and unsustainable in the long term. Roused but never satisfied, Wagner's audiences eventually must search elsewhere for the cultural elevation his music has moved them to seek. Like the Master, or so Nietzsche openly worries, the Germans may turn to the Church for answers, which, if it were to happen, would seal his diagnosis of German fatherlandishness as little more than a loud and transient expression of nihilism.

Nietzsche's unstated aim in this final section of Part Eight is to demonstrate to his readers that the discipline on offer in *BGE*, which he has made available to them through his programme

---

[25] According to Nietzsche, Wagner's Siegfried attempted to 'abolish the old society . . . by declaring war on "contracts" (on custom, on morality) . . . [E]ven his coming into being is a declaration of war on morality – he is born of adultery and incest' (CW 4).

of education and training, will allow them to become, like him, a particular kind of Wagnerian, a particular kind of German, and a particular kind of European. What his readers are meant to understand, in short, is that they may continue to partake of what is grand and great in German and European culture while immunising themselves against what is not. In doing so, they will reclaim for themselves and, to a lesser extent, for their fellow Germans the 'today' – and its defining 'contradictions' – from which they have been inclined of late to recoil. Or, as he remarks to Carl Fuchs in his letter of 14 December 1887: being a 'Wagnerian' turns out to have been 'an inordinately dangerous experiment; now that I know that it did not *ruin* me, I know also what meaning it has had for me – it was the strongest test of my character. . .'[26] Echoing this sentiment a year later, Nietzsche gratefully acknowledges 'the case of Wagner' as a '*stroke of luck*' for a 'philosopher' like himself (CW E).[27]

The (self-serving) implication here is that the new ruling caste – and, *a fortiori*, the new European order – will not arise on its own, independent of the timely, deliberate, self-conscious intervention staged by Nietzsche in *BGE*. If Europe is to realise its will to '*become one*' (BGE 256), Nietzsche (or someone like him) must intervene *now*,[28] so as to capitalise on the experiments conducted by the anticipatory heroes who have preceded him in the lineage he presumes to join. Indeed, his sense of urgency helps to explain the crucial transition from Part Eight to Part Nine of *BGE*. Having distinguished between 'peoples and fatherlands', and having pronounced the latter option a dead end for Germany and Europe, he takes up the question of 'what is noble?' While his answer to this question is both nuanced and complicated, we are meant to understand that the proposed emigration 'beyond good and evil' will succeed (or fail) on the strength of his efforts to impart to his best readers a new perspective on, and appreciation for, nobility.

---

[26] *SB* 8: 209–11/Middleton 1969: 280–1.
[27] See Harvey and Ridley 2022: 211–28.
[28] I am indebted here to Shapiro's superb discussion of the *kairos* (Shapiro 2016: 102–12).

PART EIGHT: PEOPLES AND FATHERLANDS					187

Review

Having surveyed the virtues on which he and his 'we' might come to rely as they undertake the task reserved for them, Nietzsche turns in Part Eight to a consideration of what Europe may yet become. The guiding assumption here is that the dawning of a new era in European politics, an era of 'large-scale politics', calls for a fresh approach to the question of the future of Europe.

The approach Nietzsche recommends (and models) in Part Eight of *BGE* is bold, 'extramoral', innovative and eminently scientific. Treating the peoples and nations of Europe as disposable configurations of force and vitality, he proposes a geopolitical realignment that will restore unity to Europe and return Europe to its rightful place at the global centre of culture and civilisation. His key contribution to the proposed reconfiguration of European peoples and nations is his recommendation of a new 'ruling caste', which will mobilise the complementary strengths and advantages, respectively, of the Germans, the English and the French. The wisdom of this recommendation will be confirmed, he believes, if (or when) this 'ruling caste' extends to the Jews of Europe a sincere, credible invitation to make Europe their permanent home. With the assistance of the Jews, this new ruling caste will reverse the ill effects of cultural decay and return Europe to a position of global cultural leadership. On the strength of the efforts of Nietzsche and his 'we', Europe once again will become one.

As we shall see, moreover, the auto-immunity regimen he recommends for Germany and Europe, to be achieved through the prescribed 'absorption and assimilation' of the Jews, serves as the model for the auto-immunity regimen he recommends to his best readers. Much as the Germans (and the Europeans more generally) are encouraged to extend a heartfelt offer of homecoming to their supposed nemeses, so Nietzsche urges his best readers to rechristen – and, so, to welcome home – what they have heretofore known (and despised) as their resident evils.

10
Part Nine: What is Noble?

Preview

In taking up the matter of 'what is noble?', Nietzsche returns to a theme he introduced at the close of Part Six of *BGE*. There, we recall, by way of explaining why philosophers tend to be misunderstood and despised, he disclosed their animating 'secret': philosophers challenge the received wisdom of their day, taking particular aim at the defining '*virtues of the age*', not simply to be contrary or 'disagreeable', but to lay claim to 'a *new* greatness of humanity . . . [and] a new untrodden path to making it greater' (BGE 212). Applying this general insight to the particular conditions of late modern European culture, he proceeded to explain that 'belonging to the concept of greatness today are being noble, wanting to be for oneself, being able to be different, standing alone and having to make it on one's own' (BGE 212).

Prior to concluding his exposition in Part Six, Nietzsche flattered his best readers by placing *them* on the 'new untrodden path' that a hypothetical contemporary philosopher would be likely to disclose:

> And the philosopher will reveal something about his own ideal when he posits: 'The greatest should be the one who can be most solitary, most hidden, most deviating, the human who is beyond good and evil, *the master of his virtues*, the one whose will is superabundant; precisely this should be called *greatness*: being able to be just as manifold

as whole, just as broad as full.' And to ask again: today is – greatness *possible*? (BGE 212, emphasis added)

The unnamed philosopher here is almost certainly Nietzsche (or someone under his influence), and the standard of greatness he is presumed to establish conforms to the stated goals of Nietzsche's finishing school for gentlemen. And although Nietzsche consistently identifies himself as only a precursor of those who will install a new, improved ideal of human flourishing, he seemingly cannot resist this opportunity to express *his* ideal for those human (or over-human) beings who will thrive beyond good and evil.

Of particular interest here is the emphasis placed on *selfmastery*, which, as we have seen, is the envisioned outcome of the affective-somatic transformation that his programme of education and training is meant to deliver. As we know, he has urged his best readers to get clearer about who they are and have become, precisely so that they might attempt to make something whole, something disciplined, of the 'manifold' nature they have inherited. To be sure, the self-mastery they will achieve will always be limited, partial and provisional – after all, measure is alien to Nietzsche and his fellow 'semi-barbarians' (BGE 224). Unlike their fashionably enervated contemporaries, however, they will be 'superabundant in will' (BGE 212), which, as we now understand, will enable them to channel their excess vitality towards their pursuit of truth. They will become noble, that is, by disciplining themselves to be zealous, perhaps even fanatical, in their pursuit of truth.

At the time, his best readers might have found it odd that Nietzsche chose to define greatness and nobility in such strongly autarkic, anti-social terms. Before explaining his motivation for doing so, he apparently felt obliged to escort his readers through Parts Seven and Eight of *BGE*, in which, unbeknownst to them at the time, he built the case that would prepare them to consider the new standard of nobility he had introduced, indirectly and ever-so-briefly, at the close of Part Six. Having offered them a historical and political preview of why they must seek greatness in (relative) solitude, contemptuous of the 'virtues of the age' and at arm's length from their underperforming contemporaries, he returns in Part Nine to flesh out this new, period-appropriate standard of nobility.

As he has done throughout *BGE*, Nietzsche once again models to his best readers the outcome he urges them to pursue. The programme of education and training he has conducted will deliver them to an experience of nobility, and he offers his own journey as a template for theirs. Notwithstanding his spurious claim to an ancestry that includes Polish nobility (EH 'Wise' 3), Nietzsche himself stands as an example of someone whose aristocratic soul is neither matched nor confirmed nor reinforced by his social standing. Indeed, his larger critique of his period suggests that nobility of soul is the only worthwhile expression of nobility that late modern European culture is prepared to accommodate. (He regarded the existing European aristocracies of his day as faded, decaying and unable to sustain and reproduce themselves (BGE 258).) So although late modern European culture is in no position to raise and support a traditionally aristocratic class or caste, the decadence of the age affords Nietzsche and his 'we' an unexpected opportunity to aspire to a nobility of soul. Nietzsche thus aims to convince his best readers that he has discovered a previously unknown path to nobility, a path that will lead them into nearly intolerable isolation as they escalate their assault on the virtues and values of the day.

Summary of sections

Part Nine of *BGE* comprises thirty-nine numbered sections (257–96). Nietzsche begins by making a significant down payment on the 'typology of morals' he earlier identified as essential to the establishment of a 'natural history of morality' (BGE 186). In sections 257–60, he discloses the social and political conditions under which the moralities he admires – designated by him as 'master' moralities (BGE 260) – have flourished. These conditions include, most notably, the 'pathos of distance' (BGE 257),[1] which is sustained and nourished by a stable and rigidly designated

---

[1] On the underlying drive structure of the pathos of distance and its relationship to disgust, see Alfano 2019: 208–15.

social hierarchy; and the corresponding pathos of *internal* distance, which arises in the noble soul and accommodates an ever expanding plenitude of diverse affective, psychological and spiritual states (BGE 257). Together, he explains, these conditions make possible the ongoing 'self-overcoming of humanity' (BGE 257), the continuation of which he regards as the single most important aim of any viable civilisation or culture. Indeed, it is the possibility of our continued 'self-overcoming', as confirmed in and by the exploits of the greatest human exemplars, that endows our mortal existence with the secular (or 'this-worldly') justification that human beings naturally seek.

Although the pathos of internal distance is treated only in passing, it plays a crucial role in Nietzsche's account of 'what is noble' in late modernity. The important point to bear in mind here is that the pathos of internal distance typically outlives the demise of the social hierarchy and material conditions that produced and nourished it. (How long it will persist in this case is, of course, difficult to predict or determine. Hence the urgency of Nietzsche's attempt to rally his best readers, in whom he is keen to fan the embers of nobility in late modern European culture.) So although the material and social conditions of nobility no longer obtain in late modernity, the persistence of the pathos of internal distance makes it possible for his readers to cultivate and display the *self-respect* that he later will reveal as emblematic of the noble soul (BGE 287).

A comprehensive study of the 'natural history of morality' reveals that the political and material conditions of nobility are most reliably secured under the impress of the general form of social organisation known as *aristocracy* (BGE 257). The political wisdom encoded in aristocratic societies is evidenced by their signal commitment to the preservation – as opposed, say, to the elimination – of the differences that distinguish the 'higher' types of human beings from the 'lower' and 'lesser' types. This commitment is evidenced most emphatically by the practice, common to all aristocracies, of devoting the greatest share of soul-building resources to the cultivation of the 'higher' types of human beings, even at the expense of starving and/or disenfranchising the 'lower' and 'lesser' (or more common) types.

If the practice of politics aims, as Nietzsche believes it should, at the wilful production and deliberate advancement of culture, legislators must be prepared to consider – and, if necessary, to employ – the most illiberal means and measures at their disposal. Doubling down on his earlier observation that 'slavery . . . is also an indispensable means of spiritual discipline and cultivation' (BGE 188), he explicitly links the enhancement of humanity to the institution (or practice) of slavery:

> Every enhancement so far in the type 'human being' was the work of an aristocratic society – and it will be this way again and again: a society that believes in a long ladder of rank order and value-difference between one person and another in value and in some sense requires slavery. (BGE 257)

Having earlier attributed 'all the enhancements of humans' to 'the discipline of . . . *great* suffering . . .' (BGE 225), Nietzsche apparently means at this point to applaud 'aristocratic societies' for the upbuilding (i.e., 'creaturely') suffering – inflicted, perhaps, via 'slavery' in some form – they tend to legislate. The attraction for Nietzsche of an aristocratic society is that it enables a canny legislator to allocate the diverse resources of a society, including its surplus human resources, to the production of those higher types whose surpassing exploits justify human existence more generally. (According to Nietzsche, as we know, a sustainable will for the future of humankind is dependent upon the regular and timely appearance of these higher types.) He thus attributes his admiration for aristocracy to its intuitive embrace of a simple, basic article of 'belief':

> [S]ociety *cannot* exist for society's sake, but only as the substructure and framework on which a choice kind of being is able to climb up to its higher task and generally to a higher level of *being*. . . (BGE 258)

Harking back to his earlier discussions, Nietzsche describes the thriving aristocracy as 'an incarnate will to power' (BGE 259), which remains viable only if it expresses itself violently, in adventures of 'appropriation' and 'exploitation', against those whom it does not count among its members. Aware that others will be quick to moralise (and, so, condemn) these aristocratic transmissions of will to power, Nietzsche once again insists that moral considerations have no place in our (scientific) considerations of the basic character and processes of life itself. Leaving nothing to the imagination, he asserts that

> [L]ife itself is *essentially* appropriation, injury, overpowering of what is foreign and weaker . . . "Exploitation" does not belong to a spoiled or imperfect and primitive society: it belongs to the *essence* of what lives, as organic basic function, it is a consequence of the actual will to power, which is simply the will of life. – (BGE 259)[2]

Here we recall his earlier indictment of those 'wrongly designated "free spirits"', who, having traced the cause of human misery to the exclusions and hardships mandated by aristocratic societies, offer to promote universal happiness by *levelling* any and all expressions and vestiges of the order of rank (BGE 44). The interpretative error Nietzsche attributed on that occasion to the agents of 'levelling' is similar to the mistake he now traces to those idealists who, yielding to the relentless pressure of the 'democratic' taste, envision a future without exploitation, which he quickly dismisses as no future at all.[3]

Hence his summary indictment of the 'democratic movement' in politics: to be opposed to aristocracy is to be opposed to the ongoing development and enhancement of humankind. If his contemporaries were to succeed in cultivating a practice of politics that does not engage in or tolerate 'exploitation', their success would manifest itself as a collective death wish, as a 'will to *denial* of life,

---

[2] Nietzsche effectively doubles down on this provocative claim in the coda to this section of *BGE*: 'Suppose this is in theory an innovation – as reality it is the *primordial fact* of all history: let us be honest with themselves to this extent! – ' (BGE 259).

[3] For a representative criticism of the political views ostensibly expressed in BGE 259, see Warren 1988: 207–11.

the principle of disintegration and decline' (BGE 259). In sum, as we shall see, any society or polity that attempts to forswear practices and policies tending towards 'exploitation' is certain to become the target and eventual victim of the 'exploitative' sorties of rival societies and polities.

Having reacquainted his readers with the 'extramoral' hypothesis of will to power, Nietzsche delivers a preliminary report of his own efforts to compile a 'typology of morals'. The most basic distinction to be drawn is that between 'master moralities' and 'slave moralities', which corresponds (roughly) to the aforementioned division between the noble (or 'higher') human beings and everyone else (BGE 260). Whereas 'master moralities' are distinguished by the unique set of privileges and responsibilities that accrue to those who are bred for nobility, 'slave moralities' are distinguished by the rationalisations and compensatory fantasies of those who are excluded from lives of noble self-enjoyment. (As we know, the persistence of these rationalisations and fantasies accounts for Nietzsche's determination to develop the anthropological approach that informs his natural history of morality (BGE 186).) Although he does not recommend the 'master' morality of antiquity as a viable option for his best readers – its appearance is Part Nine is primarily meant to demonstrate that human history and pre-history evince a wealth not only of moralities, but also of the noble castes these moralities have served – it is virtually impossible to bracket his obvious preference for this type of morality, especially when compared to any token of the 'slave' type.[4]

Nietzsche develops this influential distinction in his next book, in which he discloses the psychological and affective features that inform the 'modes of evaluation' (or ways of relating to oneself, others and the world) associated, respectively, with the two basic types of morality. The *noble* 'mode of evaluation', of which the master morality is a product, originates in a spontaneous expression of self-affirmation, whereas the 'mode of evaluation' that

---

[4] Partially accounting for his decision to mobilise 'that dangerous slogan worn so well by my last book: "*Beyond Good and Evil*" . . . This at least does *not* mean "Beyond Good and Bad." – ' (GM I: 17).

authorises and sustains the slave morality originates in a reactive condemnation of an oppressor (real or perceived), who is deemed 'evil' (GM I: 10–11).[5] This characterisation is useful for our present purposes, for Nietzsche hopes in Part Nine of *BGE* to articulate a historically specific standard of nobility that is fully consistent with the acculturation (or *breeding*) his best readers have received, involuntarily and to their chagrin, under the sway of various permutations of the slave morality.

Nietzsche's enthusiasm in this section for aristocratic forms of social order is likely to mislead. Even if we agree that 'every enhancement *so far* in the type "human being" was the work of an aristocratic society' (BGE 257, emphasis added), the truth of the matter is that aristocracy as we know it has revealed itself to be a flawed system of social order, for which Nietzsche suggests no credible remedy or alternative. Aristocracies have been unable thus far to compensate adequately for the 'indifference' of nature, and they have failed thus far to contain (or neutralise) the toxic resentment emanating from the lowest orders of a caste-based society. Despite their best efforts, the architects and guardians of aristocracy have failed thus far to deliver the '*as yet undetermined animal*' to the determination that would secure its long-term 'success' and survival (BGE 62). By Nietzsche's own account, in short, aristocracy as we know it has largely exhausted its value as an engine of cultural elevation.[6]

Nietzsche's apparent paean in Part Nine to the wonders of aristocracy in fact conveys an elegy: if humankind is to survive the current, aristocracy-induced crisis, the philosophers of the future will need to design (and implement) a better, more sustainable approach to the task of breeding exemplary human types. Indeed, his main point here is not to extol the virtues of aristocracy, but to isolate that which aristocracies thus far have imperfectly produced and nurtured: *the pathos of distance*, which is emblematic of nobility in all of its most vibrant forms.[7]

---

[5] See Conway 2008: 69–72; and Guay 2022: 35–53.
[6] I am indebted here to Miyasaki 2022b: chs 3–4.
[7] See Alfano 2019: 211–15.

Exploiting a 'turning point in history'

To become noble in the sense that Nietzsche has in mind is to seek and arrange for oneself an optimal relationship to one's unalterable share in the (surprisingly complex) legacy of the slave morality. In the case of his best readers, we know, the limiting conditions of their historical situation include their non-negotiable placement within the endgame sequence of Christian morality. If they wish to contribute meaningfully to the production of a philosophy of the future, they must acknowledge their share in the morality they aim to retire *and* their exclusion from the ranks of those who will emigrate cleanly beyond good and evil.

Yet all is not lost. Indeed, Nietzsche means to persuade his best readers that he and they are poised on the threshold of a 'turning point in history' (BGE 262). Reprising the image of the bow bent nearly to its breaking point (BGE P), he beckons his best readers to envision the ascendant forms of life that will proliferate, or so he promises, once the suffocating authority of the 'old morality' is finally exhausted (BGE 262). It is up to *them*, he thus implies, to preserve the tension stored in the bow, and to do so by steering the decrepit 'old morality' towards its final, self-consuming conclusion. What this means, as we know, is that they must persist in their own feelings of distress while resisting any calls to relieve what others will declare to be a 'state of emergency' (BGE P)

Nietzsche thus invites his best readers to place themselves at (or near) the 'dangerous and uncanny moment' at which 'the greater, more diverse, more comprehensive life *lives over and beyond* the old morality' (BGE 262). To be sure, his characterisation of this conjectured outgrowth is likely to rouse the interest of his best readers. Inasmuch as the transcendent form of life described here is 'greater, more diverse, [and] more comprehensive', it calls to mind the period-appropriate ideal proposed earlier in *BGE* for late modern European culture (BGE 212). Having approached the event horizon of the aforementioned 'turning point in history', he thus implies, his best readers may act to ensure a (relatively) smooth transition from the old to the new. In particular, they may facilitate (and perhaps accelerate) the demise of the 'old' morality, whose faithful agents will preach 'the morality of mediocrity' and thereby attempt to prolong their relevance (BGE 262). Of course, this morality 'must never confess what it is and what it wants' (BGE 262), which renders it ripe for exposure by those who seek *and speak* the truth. Nietzsche thus invites his best readers to play a decisive role in the timely self-overcoming of Christian morality and to accede in the process to the optimal experience of freedom and power that is available to them.

Nietzsche's overtly pejorative reference to the 'old morality' may remind us of his similar attempt, earlier in *BGE*, to discredit the 'old Kant' as a philosophical predator, responsible for bewitching the naïve Tübingen theologians who enthusiastically took up the critical project he inaugurated (BGE 11).[8] Here he means to suggest, along similar lines, that the 'old morality' exerts a similarly retardant pressure on the progress of European civilisation. Just as the 'old Kant' launched the retrograde movement known as German Idealism, so the 'old morality' serves, in its undignified persistence, to postpone the desired emigration beyond good and evil. In both cases, genuine progress requires active measures by those who are prepared to retire what is 'old' against the will of its most determined defenders. In both cases, moreover, what Nietzsche designates as 'old' is not simply decrepit and out of date, but also impedimentary. Indeed, he accuses both the 'old Kant' and the 'old morality' of beggaring the future of European civilisation.

Hence the rhetorical aim of his attention in Part Nine to the process of self-overcoming at various 'turning points in history' (BGE 262). He means to guide his best readers towards an affirmation of the process itself, as opposed to any particular role or place to which they might be assigned within its sweep. If they continue to anticipate an experience of freedom and power that is not available to them, or if they insist on seeing themselves as already residing beyond good and evil, they are unlikely to contribute meaningfully to the campaign to retire the 'old morality'. If they are to be of any use to Nietzsche, they will need to adjust their expectations and accommodate themselves to the larger, impersonal, macrocosmic process he describes.

---

[8] See Conway 2020: 246–56.

What is important here, in short, is the self-overcoming of Christian morality, regardless of one's role in the process that delivers the desired outcome. Indeed, the buoyant *hope* expressed in *BGE*, which Nietzsche invites his best readers to share, is attached not to the success of any merely personal quest or task, but to the success and timely completion of the process of self-overcoming, regardless of one's assigned or likely contribution. Inasmuch as this process is likely to consume the next several centuries, moreover, the hope he invites his best readers to share is attached to a future whose fruition they will not personally witness. Hence the rhetorical challenge he faces in *BGE*: can he persuade the members of his 'we' to contribute to the production of a future whose arrival they will not be in a position to confirm?

The difficulties involved in imparting this particular lesson are on display in sections 263–74. Here Nietzsche attempts to strike an extremely delicate balance. On the one hand, he reveals that 'an *instinct for rank*' can be 'a sign of a *high* rank' (BGE 263). Apparently, that is, someone may be considered noble even if he or she is entirely lacking in the traditional social, political and material indices of nobility. All that is required, apparently, is the aforementioned pathos of internal distance, which engenders a guiding commitment to an (anti-democratic) order of rank, in which nobility is recognised and affirmed. Or, as he explains a few sections later, 'The noble soul . . . *knows itself to be in the heights*' (BGE 265) – *even*, apparently, if the familiar elevating structures of aristocracy are not in evidence.[9] He thus urges his readers to aspire to a nobility of soul *and*, as a result, to guard themselves against those among their associates and contemporaries whom they know to be of a (pity-inducing) lower rank (BGE 269).

On the other hand, Nietzsche is also concerned to persuade his readers that their proper placement *within* the order of rank they are meant to affirm is not likely to coincide with their current (or preferred) understanding of themselves. As we have seen, they must accommodate themselves to a lesser, subordinate role in the

---

[9] In his subsequent account of the noble mode of evaluation, he identifies the pathos of (nobility and) distance as 'the lasting and dominating overall and basic feeling of a higher ruling order in relation to a lower order, to a "below"' (GM I: 2).

self-overcoming of morality. In their case, doing so will be called *noble*, for it will evince their respect for, and affirmation of, an order of rank. While they may take pride in being among the best their twilight period has to offer, they must remain cognisant of their subordinate status and the preparatory role they will play in the production of a philosophy of the future. As we are now in a position to understand, the virtues he recommended to his readers in Part Six – for example, patience, humility and self-restraint – were meant to prepare them to assert their share in the nobility he reveals to them in Part Nine.

Nobility and self-respect

Sections 275–87 deliver a second interlude, replete with pithy epigrams and didactic bits of scripted dialogue. Nietzsche appears to be concerned in these sections to entertain (and pre-emptively deflect) some of the objections that his best readers (or their loved ones) are likely to raise. A theme common to these sections is the extent of the social costs that are likely to be borne by those readers whom Nietzsche successfully recruits into the circle of his 'we'. In particular, those who wish to engage in the 'fore-play' rehearsed in *BGE* should expect to be isolated, alone, misunderstood, nomadic and potentially friendless. Most importantly, perhaps, they should not expect to be acknowledged, much less affirmed, for their contributions to the glorious future he envisions for the 'extramoral' period in the history of European civilisation. These 'good Europeans' are likely to be viewed as bad Europeans, perhaps even as enemies of Europe, by their nationalism-besotted contemporaries.

None of this should matter, however, for, as Nietzsche explains, the noble soul usually requires very little by way of external recognition and validation. In the key insight delivered in Part Nine of *BGE*, he declares that '*the noble soul has respect for itself*' (BGE 287), which means, among other things, that the noble soul may confidently rely on the recognition and affirmation it is prepared to grant itself.[10] Having earlier confirmed that 'the noble human

---

[10] See Thiele 1990: 86–95.

being honors in itself the one who is powerful, also the one who has power over itself (BGE 260), Nietzsche here alerts his best readers to the historically contextualised standard of nobility to which they might aspire. Although they are not likely to put anyone in mind of the nobles of yore, they nevertheless may come to know themselves as possessing (limited) stores of power over themselves and the streams of recognition they receive. In short, the achievement of *self-mastery*, especially as it was lauded in BGE 212, is productive of the desired experience of *self-respect*.[11]

Although he does not say so here, Nietzsche apparently understands the achievement of self-respect as indicative of a just-in-time evolution in the practice (and experience) of *responsibility*. Having initially learned to answer to external others, and subsequently to internalisations of external others, human beings – or, at least, *some* human beings – are finally prepared to answer to themselves. No longer reliant on the recognition of their peers and supposed betters, Nietzsche's best readers will thrive on a steady diet of self-directed recognition, which they hope (but do not necessarily need) to supplement with occasional interactions with like-minded, nomadic others. The key development here involves the transformation of the *conscience* from a judgemental critic, concerned only to harp on lapses, deficiencies, inadequacies and so on, into a wise counsellor, concerned simply to escort the self in question to its next best incarnation (cf. GM II: 2–3).[12]

The implication here is that those who learn to respect themselves are able to weigh the claims of conscience without immediately capitulating to (and collapsing under) the burdens and penalties these claims enjoin. Hence Nietzsche's earlier description of those for whom his best readers are invited to prepare:

> The philosopher, as *we* understand him, we free spirits . . . [is] someone of the most comprehensive responsibility

---

[11] As we have seen, a similar insight informs Nietzsche's appreciative sketch of Goethe, who, he explains, 'conceived of a human [being] who . . . pay[s] himself respect [*vor sich selber ehrfürchtigen Menschen*]' (TI 'Forays' 49).

[12] As he earlier explained, 'When we break in our conscience, it kisses at the same time it bites us' (BGE 98).

who has the conscience for the overall development of humanity . . . (BGE 61)

Once again, we see that *BGE* delivers an outcome contrary to the initial expectations of its most eager readers: rather than liberate his best readers from the moral responsibilities that weigh upon them, Nietzsche rearranges their burdens so that they might become more fully responsible than ever before.

Dionysus revealed

In sections 288–94, Nietzsche acquaints his best readers with the all-but-invisible outward tokens of the 'noble soul' in late modernity: enthusiasm (BGE 288); reclusiveness (BGE 289); a preference for being misunderstood (BGE 290); self-enjoyment (BGE 291); excessive inquisitiveness about oneself (BGE 292); a 'manly' distaste for expressions of pity (BGE 293); laughter and mockery (BGE 294); genius of the heart (BGE 295); and a keen sense of the non-negotiable rhythms of temporality and mortality (BGE 296).

In addition to preparing his best readers for the misunderstandings that await them, Nietzsche also takes care to remind them that they might turn their unfortunate lot to their advantage. (Earlier, as we recall, he encouraged his best readers to adopt as a *nom de guerre*, and exploit to their advantage, the (pejorative) designation – *immoralists* – hurled at them by the 'oafs' among their contemporaries (BGE 226).) In particular, they might safeguard their efforts to retire the 'old morality' by employing misdirection, disguises, pretexts, masks and so on. Thoroughly engrossed in their meaning-conferring efforts to 'translate humanity back into nature' (BGE 230), they will welcome and cheerfully receive the ridicule and invective directed against them. So long as they remain misunderstood by their contemporaries, or so Nietzsche suggests, they may contribute to the production of a philosophy of the future.

In these concluding sections, Nietzsche clearly means to recommend himself as a model for those who wish to partake of the 'superiority of soul' he has described. Absent the familiar touchstones and structures of meaning and value, his best readers would do well to follow his lead, becoming 'hermits' if necessary (BGE 289), turning inward in painful exercises of self-examination and even self-mockery (BGE 290–4), and, finally, attaching themselves to that 'genius of the heart' and 'tempter-god' known as *Dionysus* (BGE 295).[13] Having done so, presumably, they will have taken full advantage of the education and training on offer in the expository body of *BGE*.

This discussion culminates in Nietzsche's paean to the god Dionysus, whom he praises as the 'great hidden one' (BGE 295). His double meaning here is worth noting: Dionysus is 'hidden' not only with respect to his penchant for disguise and imposture, as documented in various mythic accounts, but also with respect to Nietzsche's tactical decision to conceal until now his efforts to enrol his best readers in a Dionysian discipleship. The suggestion here is that his best readers would do well to emulate *this* Dionysus, and especially the 'genius of the heart' that he so artfully displays *and* conceals.

Immediately prior to this section, however, Dionysus receives an ominously indirect introduction. Having alluded to 'a rank order of philosophers according to the rank of their laughter', and having floated the supposition that 'gods, too, philosophize', Nietzsche conjectures that the gods 'laugh in a superhuman [*übermenschliche*] and innovative way – and at the expense of all serious things!' (BGE 294).[14] As we know, Nietzsche has urged his readers on several occasions to subject their most deeply held beliefs and convictions to the kind of scrutiny that might lead them to engage in self-directed mockery and laughter. Throughout *BGE*, in fact, he has modelled to his best readers the cheerfulness and levity that will allow them to subordinate themselves to the larger historical processes they have pledged to further. At one point, we recall, he caps a particularly dire survey of the late modern condition by insisting to his best readers that their *laughter*

---

[13] See Burnham 2007: 218–23.

[14] The convalescent Zarathustra also lends voice to this bit of Dionysian wisdom: 'only this I have learned thus far, that man needs what is most evil in him for what is best in him – that whatever is most evil is his best power and the hardest stone for the highest creator; and that man must become better and more evil' (Z III: 13.2).

may yet have a future, even if nothing else related to them is likely to endure (BGE 223).

Nietzsche's invocation of the god-philosopher Dionysus sets the stage for the final lesson he wishes to impart to his best readers. Here, in the penultimate expository section of the book, he finally offers his best readers 'a bit of a taste' of the Dionysian philosophy he takes himself to espouse. Although Dionysus has only now been named in the text of *BGE*, it should be retrospectively clear that Nietzsche's programme of education and training has been building up to this point, which, as we shall see, introduces cheerful, timely destruction as the *sine qua non* of the Dionysian philosophy he wishes to impart. The big difference here is that Dionysus has finally been identified and named as the patron deity of the discipline Nietzsche has prescribed to his readers. If they agree to sample the appetisers he offers them, they do so fully aware of the provenance of the sustenance they are poised to ingest.

The gist of this philosophy – or, at any rate, of the appetisers served up here – will no doubt unsettle even the most intrepid of Nietzsche's readers. In recounting the (imagined?) conversation in which Dionysus spoke directly to him (cf. BT: AS 6), Nietzsche admits to having been 'startled' by the god's brutal candour (BGE 295), which may be his model for the 'extravagant honesty' (or cruelty) to which he entitles himself and his best readers (BGE 230). According to Nietzsche, Dionysus revealed that he loves humanity, but only conditionally. As such, Dionysus is concerned to 'advance' humanity by making us 'stronger, more evil, and deeper; also more beautiful' than we currently are (BGE 295). Only then, apparently, would we merit the love that the god holds in reserve. We are evidently meant to juxtapose the conditional, merit-dependent love of Dionysus with the unconditional, merit-independent love that is granted to us, supposedly, by the God of Christianity. Nietzsche's point here is that a deity who is satisfied with humanity as it is, expecting nothing more of us than what we already deliver, may not be the patron we need at this particular 'turning point' in our history.

Nietzsche concludes this grim lesson by remarking that we humans, whose cruelty towards one another he has tirelessly chronicled, are in fact 'more humane' than the god Dionysus

(BGE 295). If this gnomic observation is meant to suggest that Dionysus will 'advance' humanity by resorting to methods that are *less* 'humane' than those we have employed in our various efforts to 'advance' (= punish) one another (GM II: 13), we may be justified in receiving this concluding lesson with considerable trepidation. Apparently, that is, those who possess 'the genius of the heart' must be prepared to 'advance' humanity at *any* cost, and with no concern for the feelings or futures of those who are not likely to partake of the advance specified by the god.

If Nietzsche is in fact a disciple of Dionysus, as his reconstructed dialogue is meant to confirm, it may be the case that he, too, is prepared to risk the future of humankind in order to secure its eventual emigration beyond good and evil. (If his laughter is similarly 'superhuman', after all, the mockery it conveys presumably will extend even to the 'serious' issue of the continued existence of the human species in its current state and condition.)[15] In that event, he may mean to caution his best readers to gird themselves for a mission in which *they* might perish – whether literally or figuratively – along with the 'old morality' they have been assigned to retire. Indeed, they will succeed in this mission only if they are properly indifferent to their own wellbeing and survival. Here we detect another echo, now more ominous, from the close of Part One: 'But what do *we* matter!' (BGE 23).

Having revealed himself as a disciple of Dionysus, Nietzsche indirectly invites his readers to revisit his remarks throughout *BGE* about the potential uses and abuses of 'experimentation', 'breeding', 'tyranny' and 'slavery' to secure the serial 'enhancements' of humankind. Already troubling in its own right, with its breezy recourse to social engineering and its brutally simplistic valorisation of technical (i.e., means/ends, cost/benefit) rationality, this way of speaking about the acceleration of human progress becomes even more disturbing in light of Nietzsche's avowed allegiance to Dionysus. After all, if 'the discipline of suffering, of *great* suffering . . . has created all enhancements of humans'

---

[15] As Zarathustra ominously admits to his animal companions, 'My torture was not the knowledge that man is evil – but I cried as no one has yet cried: "Alas, that his greatest evil is so very small! Alas, that his best is so very small!"' (Z III: 1.2).

(BGE 225), and if these enhancements have not yet secured the favour of Dionysus, then it may be the case that the disciples of Dionysus are prepared to inaugurate a campaign of amplified, unprecedented suffering, risking humanity as it is in order to produce humanity (or over-humanity) as it may yet become. So long as the human animal remains '*as yet undetermined*' (BGE 62), apparently, any and all tools of human advancement remain on the table.[16]

Having received Nietzsche's invocation of Dionysus, and his veiled warning that the 'advance' of humankind may require the implementation of 'inhumane' measures, his best readers are finally in a position to weigh the pros and cons of the task to which he has recruited them. If they are concerned for their own safety and reputation, or if they require the kinds of assurances that Dionysus extends to no mortals, they are likely to decline Nietzsche's invitation to join him. If, however, they seek to optimise their experience of freedom and power, even by risking their own self-preservation, they are likely to assent to their membership in the 'we' that *BGE* is intended to consecrate. As involuntary agents of the will to truth, they will satisfy their 'extramoral' aspirations by exposing the truth of the 'old morality' and demolishing the lies and illusions on which it trades. They will not escape the gravitational pull of the morality they have pledged to retire, but they will make it possible for others to do so in the future.

That Nietzsche concludes *BGE* with a course of appetisers may disappoint some readers, especially if they were expecting the full banquet they might have associated with being launched or welcomed beyond good and evil. Here two points are worth noting. First of all, Nietzsche has maintained all along that his best readers will find the sweet spot in their historical setting by tempering their audacity with an appropriate accent of humility. Although they will not venture beyond good and evil in the sense that initially might have piqued their interest, they nevertheless are poised to contribute to the timely retirement of the 'old morality' that currently stands in the way. Having preached

---

[16] See Reginster 2006: 242–51.

the virtue of (context-appropriate) self-restraint, Nietzsche may be seen at this crucial juncture to practise it himself, modelling to his readers the restraint that will serve them in their own pursuit of an optimal experience of freedom and power. He is not Dionysus, and it is not his place to serve the main course of the feast that awaits them in the newly transfigured world he has previewed for their edification.[17] As Lampert notes, moreover, in this section Nietzsche addresses his best readers as his 'friends' (BGE 295), which may suggest that he and they finally stand as equals, shoulder to shoulder, before the revealed tempter-god.[18]

Second, Nietzsche is in a position to offer the appetisers in question because he has cultivated in his best readers a hunger for spiritual nourishment – that is, a stomach and constitution for the new, Dionysian experiences these appetisers promise. That they are welcome to sample the appetisers he serves up thus conveys his confidence that he has succeeded in guiding them towards the affective-somatic transformation he has promised to induce in them. They are prepared, finally, to re-enter the world as Dionysian disciples in their own right, which means that they may find the meaning and justification they seek *in* (and not beyond) their mortal, worldly existence.

In light of what Nietzsche says here about Dionysus, however, we cannot rule out the possibility that his decision to serve up these appetisers also signals his deliberate departure from the 'too humane' treatment that human beings have shown one another, allegedly, in their efforts thus far to promote the general 'advance' of humankind. If the stakes are as high as Nietzsche suggests, and the situation as dire as he insists, he may not particularly care if some of his readers are unable to swallow and/or digest the Dionysian appetisers he serves them. Indeed, if these foretastes of the Dionysian philosophy were meant to perform one final selective function, separating his more promising from his less promising readers, he is not likely to be overly concerned by any collateral damage (or indigestion) he has wrought. As he explains

---

[17] He exercises a similar measure of restraint at the conclusion of the second treatise of *The Genealogy of Morality*, where he defers to '*Zarathustra the godless*' (GM II: 25).
[18] Lampert 2001: 290–1.

elsewhere, 'to be ill can even be an active *stimulant* to life, to more life', but *only* if those who are made sick are revealed to be *'healthy in principle'* (EH 'Wise' 2). Making his readers sick may be his only means of knowing with certainty that they are sufficiently healthy for the Dionysian discipleship in which he has provisionally enrolled them.

Nietzsche closes Part Nine (and the expository body of *BGE*) by acknowledging that some of the thoughts he has expressed in the book have already grown stale and dull. In committing these thoughts to print, he suggests, he has done them an injustice. Much like the philosophers whom he has lampooned throughout the book, he has succumbed to the temptation to 'immortalize' thoughts that are 'tired and worn down' (BGE 296). Displaying the degenerate 'afternoon' colours in which his over-ripe words now present them, his 'old, beloved – *wicked* thoughts' are barely recognisable, or so he fears. His point here is not to disparage the wisdom he has endeavoured to convey to the readers of *BGE*, but to acknowledge the folly involved in any attempt to immortalise what cannot be preserved. Having caught himself in the act, and hoping to limit the damage he has done, he takes his leave. (A similarly valedictory paragraph in *The Gay Science* is identified as an 'epilogue', which faithfully describes Nietzsche's status in *BGE* after having unmasked himself.)

If Nietzsche were solely reliant on his words to convey the '*wicked* thoughts' he wishes to bequeath to his best readers, we might be tempted (and perhaps also obliged) to receive BGE 296 as an admission of his failure to consecrate the 'we' he has presumptively addressed throughout. Fortunately for Nietzsche and his best readers, however, his (admittedly inadequate) words have been conveyed in the context of the programme of education and training that *BGE* was meant to administer. Indeed, we are now in a position to understand that the affective-somatic transformation he has initiated in *BGE* has been meant to translate his (dying) words into the (living) flesh of his readers. Even as his over-ripe words cause his '*wicked* thoughts' to shed their vibrant and exquisite coloration, the discipline he has modelled to his 'we' will retain (and perhaps amplify) their native vitality.

As Nietzsche prepares to bring *BGE* to a timely close, and as his readers prepare to disperse in their respective efforts to complete the 'task' assigned to them, they might very well forget or misplace his formerly vibrant words of wisdom, encouragement and provocation. If he has been successful in building (and consecrating) his 'we', however, his best readers will be far less likely to lapse from the way of life into which he has initiated them. They will be known to kindred noble souls, after all, not by the fidelity of their recitation of Nietzsche's teachings and slogans, but by the self-respect they now display in both word and deed.

One final point bears noting, When Nietzsche confirms in *Twilight of the Idols* that he is the 'last disciple' of Dionysus, he also identifies himself as 'the teacher of the eternal recurrence' (TI 'Ancients' 5). If the pairing of these two forms of identification is understood to suggest their linkage or mutual implication, then it may be the case that *BGE* also conveys the famously elusive teaching of eternal recurrence. In that event, we may be meant to appreciate the discipline embedded in *BGE* as an initiation into a worldview or way of life informed (and perhaps transfigured) by this teaching. As we shall see, this supposition would certainly be consistent with the Alpine imagery and *ethos* – '6000 feet above man and time' – of the 'Aftersong' with which *BGE* concludes. When Nietzsche's readers revisit the 'Aftersong', they will not only reimagine the soaring peaks and rarefied air of the Upper Engadine, but also renew the experience of affective-somatic transformation with which they will forever associate this halcyon setting.

Review

Having delivered a withering critique of late modern European culture, from which his readers might have concluded that all is lost, Nietzsche turns in Part Nine to illuminate a standard of nobility to which his best readers may credibly aspire. Despite partaking of none of the familiar material or social indices of nobility, Nietzsche and his best readers nevertheless may avail themselves of the *nobility of soul* of which self-respect is the hallmark. The self-respect he recommends to his readers in Part Nine is thus presented as the yield of their success in two related ventures: 1) the acquisition of a depth of self-knowledge that is sufficient to liberate them from the prejudiced belief in moral opposites (e.g., 'good' vs. 'evil'); and 2) sufficient progress towards the affective-somatic transformation that will enable them to pursue (and enjoy) the optimal experience of freedom and power that is available to them.

In their capacity as disciples of Dionysus, finally, Nietzsche's best readers are apparently licensed to employ less 'humane' measures in the pursuit of their assigned 'task'. As they endeavour to 'translate humankind back into nature' (BGE 230), they are likely to bust myths, step on toes, shatter norms, bruise feelings, discredit reputations and slay sacred cows. What is not yet clear, perhaps because it has not yet been determined by Nietzsche's individual readers, is how much further they will be willing to go, how much less 'humane' they plan to become. As 'scholars', after all, they are a fairly bookish, buttoned-down bunch. But as warrior-scholars, inspired by the iconoclasm of Siegfried and buoyed by the teachings of Dionysus, who knows what their future might hold?

11
From Lofty Mountains: 'Aftersong'

Preview

Nietzsche closes *BGE* with an 'Aftersong', in which he extends a heartfelt invitation to those unknown 'friends' who, he hopes, might contribute to the production of a philosophy of the future. Those readers who genuinely aspire to the nobility of soul described in Part Nine of *BGE* are now urged to join him in friendship and mutual recognition, but *only* if they reunite with him as equals.

That Nietzsche elects in this final instalment of the book to *sing* to his best readers is certainly noteworthy. Having offloaded his most precious teachings and insights, and having acknowledged the folly of his efforts to 'immortalize whatever cannot live and fly much longer' (BGE 296), he presumably has nothing more to say to say to these readers. This does not mean, however, that he has nothing more to offer them.[1] As we know, he has been concerned throughout *BGE* to preside over a programme of education and training, which is meant to immunise his best readers against the loneliness, ridicule and rejection that he knows (from experience) they will be obliged to endure. Towards this end, he has been careful not simply to make his case discursively and dialogically, but also to initiate his best readers into the affective-somatic modes of existence – for example, habits, customs, practices and routines – that he deems appropriate to the preparatory labours to which he

---

[1] Here I follow Zittel 2014: 214–16.

has recruited them. As we have seen, moreover, the philosophy of the future that he envisions will attain its optimal realisation not as a set of teachings, but as a *way of life* that is closely attuned to the mortal rhythms of an affirmatively worldly existence.

Unlike those philosophers who do not practise what they preach, Nietzsche bids *adieu* to his readers by demonstrating for them the depth and intensity of his own affective-somatic transformation. In doing so, as we shall see, he also models to his readers the extent of the immunity he has acquired with respect to the twin temptations – pity and disgust – that will torment them in their carefully cultivated loneliness and isolation. His 'Aftersong' is thus intended as a final souvenir of their matriculation through his finishing school for gentlemen.

We know that Nietzsche strongly identifies with those Provençal poets, the 'knight-troubadours' of the '*gai saiber*', whom he praises as the progenitors of the European lineage in which he intends to take his rightful place (BGE 260). It thus comes as no surprise that he would conclude his 'prelude to a philosophy of the future' with an 'Aftersong', viz., a poetic farewell in which he bears witness to his own share in the affective-somatic transformation he has promised to induce in his readers. Having offered to equip his best readers with an alternative set of 'value-emotions', which are meant to convey their acquired wish to acknowledge 'untruth as a condition of life' (BGE 4), he closes his lessons to them with a song, whose 'truth value' is likely to be considered beside the point.

What he wishes to convey to them in this 'Aftersong' is therefore of the utmost importance, for it is intended to sustain them as they forge onward (and upward) without him. His 'Aftersong' thus stands as the final (and enduring) lesson imparted to those who have enrolled in (and graduated from) his finishing school for gentlemen.

Summary of stanzas 1–13

The poem 'From Lofty Mountains' comprises fifteen stanzas. The initial thirteen stanzas are repurposed (with minor emendations) from a poem composed by Nietzsche in 1884. The final two stanzas of the 'Aftersong' were added in 1886 and provide a Zarathustra-inspired resolution to the hermit's plight. Presumably, the addition of these final two stanzas qualifies the 'Aftersong' as an appropriately lyrical coda to the expository body of *BGE*.[2]

In its original form, the poem was presented as conveying 'A Hermit's Yearning'. The hermit in question is none other than Nietzsche,[3] and the 'yearning' to which the poem lends its lyric is his desire for worthy companionship. As the poem in its original form makes clear, the hermit Nietzsche has determined that the 'time of day' is ripe for the task that awaits him. Having arrived at 'lifetime's noon', he pauses to gauge the proximity of the 'friends' whose approach he awaits. Whether the task in question *requires* the support of others is not entirely clear. What we know is that the hermit 'yearns' for companionship, provided that the 'friends' who join him will neither limit nor slow his ascent. In its original form, the poem concludes without arriving at a proper resolution. The hermit's yearning has been voiced, his former friends have been sent away, his invitation to worthy companions has been renewed, and the urgency of the 'time of day' has been noted. Whether any potential friends accept this invitation, much less join the hermit on his terms and at this altitude, is not revealed.

As we shall see, the original poem is very much a reflection of Nietzsche's experience in Sils Maria. A 'hermit' there by choice, he was fortified by the crisp, clean mountain air and enthralled by the picturesque Alpine setting of the village. His long, usually solitary walks afforded him the time, cadence and inspiration to work out some of his most influential philosophical insights. His experience in Sils Maria was also important for the clarity with which it prefigured his destiny and the obstacles he would encounter along the way.[4] While his work obliged him to cultivate a hermit's

---

[2] Here he follows the lead of Zarathustra, who similarly concluded his adventure not with another speech, but with a song ('The Yes and Amen Song', in which he professed his love of eternity) (Z III: 16; see Loeb 2010: 190–4). In its original version and edition, *Zarathustra* was published in three parts. The fourth part was added later and printed in a limited edition.

[3] In his letter of 24 September 1886 to Malwida von Meysenbug, Nietzsche refers to himself twice as 'the hermit of Sils Maria' (*SB* 7: 256–8/Middleton 1969: 256). See also Young 2010: 393–4.

[4] When Nietzsche revisits his teaching of the 'death of God', he places himself and his 'we' in the 'mountains', where the 'shadows that must soon envelope Europe really *should* have arrived by now' (GS 343).

solitude, his ensuing loneliness rendered him vulnerable to the temptations of pity and disgust. Those who made the extra effort to visit him in Sils were likely to be overvalued, while those who never bothered were likely to be undervalued. For reasons both personal and philosophical, the themes of isolation and loneliness became ever more central to his philosophy.

Nietzsche presented the original poem to Heinrich von Stein (1857–87) in a letter composed in November of 1884 (*SB* 6: 564–7).[5] Stein had visited Nietzsche in Sils Maria, and Nietzsche evidently saw in him a potential 'friend' who might satisfy a hermit's yearning for companionship.[6] But the envisioned friendship was not to be. Stein replied to Nietzsche's token of intimacy by inviting him to join a group of Wagnerian acolytes who discussed the works and reception of the Master. Having sealed his break with Wagner and Wagnerism in 1878, Nietzsche was appalled at the prospect of a friendship predicated on a common appreciation (or idolatry) of Wagner.[7] Simply put, Nietzsche realised that he had misjudged his young acquaintance, owing perhaps to a wishful naivety born of the hermit's loneliness.[8]

This specific misjudgement bears further attention, for it is an occupational hazard encountered by Nietzsche, Zarathustra and all higher types who are burdened by the loneliness of their respective pursuits of a singular existence. Having spied in Stein the *promise* of a meaningful friendship, Nietzsche determined that an invitation to intimacy might close the gap between promise and fulfilment. In other words, he took pity on Stein and, in doing so, revealed the depth of his yearning for meaningful recognition. Availing ourselves of a distinction drawn by Zarathustra, we may conclude that Nietzsche wishfully mistook a (mere) *neighbour* – to

---

[5] See Zittel 2014: 207–9.
[6] Nietzsche conveyed similarly high praise for Stein in his letter to Overbeck of 14 September 1884 (*SB* 6: 530–2). As Nietzsche became convinced that Stein's allegiance to Wagner was unshakeable, however, he began to communicate his doubts about his young friend. In his letter to Malwida von Meysenbug of 26 March 1885, he lamented that 'poor Stein . . . thinks R. Wagner is a philosopher' (*SB* 7: 29–31).
[7] I am indebted here to Hayman 1980: 276–83; Lampert 2001: 295–9; Young 2010: 392–4; and Acampora and Ansell-Pearson 2011: 212–14.
[8] That Nietzsche pitied Stein – and subsequently overcame his pity – is confirmed in EH 'Wise' 4.

whom one turns when one does not 'love [one]self enough' – for a (genuine) *friend*, 'in whom the world stands completed' (Z I: 16). In any event, as we shall see, the upshot of Zarathustra's speech is echoed in the final lines of the revised version of this poem: one may expect to acquire worthwhile friends only when one has succeeded in befriending oneself (Z I: 14). In its essence, that is, the hermit's yearning lends voice to an as-yet-undiagnosed yearning for *himself*, which, as Nietzsche and Zarathustra eventually come to understand, is in fact an undiagnosed expression of the hermit's lingering self-contempt.

Stanzas 1–3

The first three stanzas of the 'Aftersong' establish a nervously celebratory tone. Having arrived at 'lifetime's noon', Nietzsche pauses as he waits for his 'friends' to catch up to him before continuing. Indeed, the 'noon of life' is presented here as a signal achievement on his part, a milestone he has earned by merit of his diligence in attending to his labours of self-overcoming. As he explains elsewhere, the 'great noon' marks the season or time of day 'when the most select dedicate themselves to the greatest of all tasks' (EH: bt 4).[9] The hermit Nietzsche has paused, presumably, to welcome those with whom he will undertake the 'task' he has revealed to them in *BGE*, that of 'translating humankind back into nature' (BGE 230).

That Nietzsche finds himself waiting, impatiently, is our first sign of the hermit's distress. If he has arrived at his 'lifetime's noon', why does he not continue to press forward (and upward) on his own? While it certainly would be enjoyable to do so with like-minded companions, why would he allow a single precious moment to pass? As we shall see more clearly as we progress, Nietzsche's pause in the first stanza is indicative of his tendency to *pity* the poky friends whom he awaits. As we also shall see, his pity for them is indicative in turn of his failure as yet to attain the self-respect that he has identified as the hallmark of the 'noble soul' (BGE 287). He pauses, in other words, not so much to hail

---

[9] The metaphor and image of 'noontide' is productively explored in Hough 1997: ch. 3.

his prospective friends one more time – this is but a pretext – but to grant himself a temporary reprieve from his difficult, lonely labours of self-overcoming.[10] Rather than address his besetting self-contempt, of which his 'yearning' is symptomatic, the hermit prefers to blame those nameless others who, he pretends, cause him to delay his ascent.

In the second and third stanzas of the poem, Nietzsche continues to favour an apostrophic mode of address, speaking to those who are not (yet) within earshot. Confirming that the glacial summit where he now stands is the ideal place for them to begin their work together, he sweetens his pitch to the companions whose arrival he awaits. Describing the breathtaking Alpine scene as if it were set *for them*, as yearning, much as he does, for their approach, he wonders aloud where the recipients of his 'honey' might be.[11] Suggesting that the education and support he has lent thus far ought to have sufficed, he lays the foundation for his subsequent claim that he is not at fault for the failure of the anticipated rendezvous.

Nietzsche mobilises a similar image in the opening scene of *Zarathustra*, Part IV, where we find the central character sequestered in his mountaintop retreat. Rather than descend once again, Zarathustra has resolved to reserve himself for those who make their way to the mouth of his cave. Convinced that this new strategy will insulate him from the pity and disgust that wrecked his initial efforts to recruit worthy disciples, Zarathustra awaits the arrival of those who, enticed by nothing more than the 'honey' of the 'wisdom' he exudes, are willing to risk themselves to enjoy his company (Z IV: 1).[12] As we shall see, this strategy is preferred by those who have not yet fully befriended themselves, that is, those who remain as yet dangerously reliant on the companionship, recognition and affirmation of unripe, unworthy others.

---

[10] As Nietzsche astutely observes, 'Whoever despises himself still respects himself as a despiser' (BGE 78).
[11] The opening speech of *Zarathustra*, Part IV, is called 'The Honey Sacrifice' [*Das Honig-Opfer*]. See Zittel 2014: 219–21.
[12] Here I follow Lampert 1986: 292; Gooding-Williams 2001: 269–76; and Loeb 2010: 95–101.

Stanzas 4–8

In the fourth stanza of the poem, Nietzsche's mood turns dark and dismissive. His friends have arrived, but his reunion with them is not the joyful, galvanising event he had anticipated. Detecting in them an apprehension that he probably should own for himself, he claims to sense their dissatisfaction, as if they, too, had been looking forward to a more joyful reunion. Rather than voice his own disappointments with respect to them, however, he dwells on what he conjectures to be their disappointments with him.

What he senses in his recently arrived companions, from whom we hear neither confirmation nor dissent, is that he has changed. The Nietzsche whom they had expected and hoped to meet, presumably on the strength of their earlier interactions with him, is not the Nietzsche who welcomes them to this Alpine summit. That he has 'changed' in their eyes is no doubt true in several respects. First, his continued labours of self-overcoming have delivered him to an elevated state of soul. Having struck out on his own, '[He] stayed alive / Where no one lives, polar wastes that bears survive, / Lost to man and God and curse and prayer. . .' What they see before them, or so he conjectures on their behalf, is a Nietzsche who has learned to live (and thrive) at a height that may not suit them. Second, he apparently will do nothing to ease their acclimatisation to his company in this new setting. Having shed the teacherly pose, tone and countenance through which they originally came to know him, he is now disinclined to cheer or spur their progress. Third, he is apparently prepared to evaluate their friendship not on the basis of their potential progress, which might tempt him to pity them, but on the basis of their actual progress, which, he insists without evidence, is underwhelming. Despite the risks they have endured and the stamina they have displayed, they apparently have misplaced his main lesson for them. Claiming to detect in them the 'shock . . . of love and fear', he resolves to send them away.

Nietzsche's reception of his late-arriving friends thus betrays a significant measure of narcissism on his part. Is it not possible to interpret their ascent as a sign of *their* growth and outgrowth? Perhaps they too have arrived on this glacier at their own 'lifetime's noon'? If he would invite (or allow) them to speak, he might learn of *their* trials and adventures, of *their* growth and advance in excess of his prescriptions for them. That they are in fact (and wish to remain) his disciples, as he suggests is the case, may not be true at all. If anyone remains invested in maintaining an unbalanced friendship, is it not he, the hermit who yearns, it would seem, simply for the sake of yearning?

And even if his conjectures about these late-arriving friends are correct: so what?[13] Why must he tarry with them, even if for their own good, and delay his own progress? As we know from *BGE*, expressions of pity for others are often outward expressions of one's own self-contempt. One discovers or invents flaws in others in order to remain attached to them and, thereby, to distract oneself from the (admittedly difficult) task of addressing one's own failings (BGE 273). Indeed, the Nietzsche who appears in the opening stanzas of the 'Aftersong' is a Nietzsche who as yet lacks the courage to move forward on his own, a Nietzsche who has failed as yet to befriend himself. His soul is not yet noble, for it lacks the telltale virtue of self-respect (BGE 287).

In Stanza 8, Nietzsche's disappointment in his late-arriving friends gives way to outright hostility. Here it becomes clear that he cannot abide their gaze, in the glare of which he is revealed to them (and us) as needy, vulnerable, lonely and dependent on them for recognition. Having acquired the 'strength' of a '*wicked hunter*', he warns these former friends not to test his skill with the bow.[14] They must leave, he insists, 'for [their] own good'. No longer merely dismissive of them, he now presents himself as a potential menace to their wellbeing.

Stanzas 9–12

Having urged his (former) friends to turn back, Nietzsche now addresses his heart, which is understandably shaken by the collapse

---

[13] The Nietzsche described in this stanza has apparently misplaced the occasion-appropriate wisdom of Zarathustra: 'Whoever climbs the highest mountains laughs at all tragic plays and tragic seriousness' (Z I: 7).

[14] For an account of Nietzsche as a Philoctetes figure (and Stein as a Neoptolemus figure), as proposed by Nietzsche in his letter to Stein of 14 September 1884 (*SB* 6: 533), see Lampert 2001: 296–9.

of the anticipated rendezvous. He advises his heart to 'open [its] doors', for '*new* friends [may] come along'. He similarly cautions his heart to relax its ties to those former friends who have failed to measure up. Although his heart may feel 'old' as a result of this most recent disappointment, he urges it to become 'young' once more, perhaps as a result of this particular misadventure.

Here we may be put in mind of the unripe Zarathustra, who, throughout his Prologue, spoke regularly to his heart, occasionally urging it, much as Nietzsche does in this stanza, to remain open despite multiple setbacks. The case of Zarathustra is also relevant here inasmuch as he dared to open his heart to unknown others, but not, at least initially, to *himself*.[15] As we shall see, this self-imposed limitation is a recipe for persistent disappointment and the 'yearning' to which it gives rise. Indeed, the Nietzsche whom we encounter in the initial thirteen stanzas of the 'Aftersong' is a Nietzsche who has not yet opened his heart to himself, which is why he conjectures *ad nauseam* about those friends who have disappointed him. Until he is able to befriend himself, the status of other, potential friends – including those whom he is so keen to banish – will remain indeterminate.[16]

Although he initially claimed to have disowned these erstwhile friends for their own good, as if he were concerned to spare them his wrath, he finally concedes in stanza 12 that they are *not* the friends of which he had 'dreamed'. Simply put, he has outgrown them, or so he now insists. Despite their success in joining him in the rarefied air of this Alpine setting, they are not prepared to renounce their subordinate status. As he explains to no one in particular, only 'He who transforms stays to [him] related', implying

---

[15] That Zarathustra is obliged to endure a painful journey of self-discovery and self-integration is now widely understood as central to Nietzsche's rhetorical and philosophical aims in the book. See, for example, Bennholdt-Thomsen 1974: 19–50; Lampert 1986: 13–82; Higgins 1987: 119–58; Rosen 1995: 23–53; Hough 1997: 85–118; Gooding-Williams 2001: 45–100; and Loeb 2010: 85–118.

[16] If we take to heart the example of the convalescence of 'friend Zarathustra', Nietzsche will finally befriend himself only when he is able to *sing* to his soul (Z III: 14–16), which, in the context of *BGE*, would mean that he finally acknowledges his own company, counsel and recognition as sufficient. Presumably, that is, 'friend Zarathustra' persuaded Nietzsche of the healing properties of the dithyramb. In short, the capacity to sing to oneself (and, of course, to draw strength and meaning from the song) is indicative of a noble soul (BGE 287). See Loeb 2010: 198–206.

without evidence that his newly arrived (and hastily departed) friends were either unwilling or unable to keep up with him.

Again, how he knows this is not at all clear. His minimal and distanced contact with his former friends suggests that his concerns about their persistent inadequacy may be suggestive of a self-fulfilling prophecy. So long as the friends of which he had 'dreamed' do not arrive, after all, he may rationalise the pause he seems determined to prolong, thereby deferring indefinitely his remaining labours of self-overcoming. In that event, he would have been correct when he wondered, in stanza 5 if, as a function of his ongoing self-estrangement, he was 'wounded and blocked by his own victory'. As we shall see, he is unable as yet to enjoy his 'victory' because he remains dependent on the recognition and affirmation of worthy others, none of whom are available to praise his achievement. Despite his very real 'victory', as confirmed by the advent of his 'noon of life', he persists in a condition of ongoing self-estrangement. As yet unable to 'rechristen' what is 'evil' in him as what is 'best' in him (BGE 116), he continues to deny himself the recognition and affirmation for which he yearns. If he is to continue his ascent, he will need to heal this wound and become to himself the worthy friend he seeks in unworthy others.

Stanza 13

Finally returning the focus of his address to his 'lifetime's noon', Nietzsche claims to be refreshed and renewed. Rather than settle for companions who would require his ongoing patronage, he looks forward to the arrival of *real* 'friends' – namely, those who will ascend to his height on the strength of their own volition, initiative and resolve. These new friends will join him, he believes, not because they need him to ease their burden, but because they enjoy his company and admire in him the nobility they have cultivated in themselves. Such 'friends', we apparently are meant to believe, will approach Nietzsche neither as needy supplicants nor as greedy subordinates, but as full partners in the great 'task' they will tackle together.

The problem with this seemingly self-reviving resolution is that any 'new' friends who happen along are likely to elicit and receive the same treatment as the 'old' friends whom he has most recently banished. Until Nietzsche addresses his own self-contempt—that is, his failure thus far to befriend himself—he will remain locked in a tiresome cycle of repetition. Any 'new' friends who might appear are likely very soon to become 'old' friends. Not unlike the great Groucho Marx, the hermit Nietzsche presents himself as reluctant to join any club that would welcome him as a member (cf. BGE 102).

Summary of stanzas 14–15

Thus concludes a slightly altered version of the original poem. As it turns out, Nietzsche was wrong about Stein, mainly because he was wrong about himself. Rather than simply replicate the poem in its original form, he crafts the 'Aftersong' on the strength of three notable upgrades.

First, he has grafted the original poem on to the expository body of *BGE*, which may prompt us to interpret the poem as addressed no longer to its original recipient (Stein), but to the members of the 'we' he has endeavoured throughout *BGE* to consecrate. In its new setting, the poem thus confirms that 'it is time' ['s *ist Zeit!*'] to retire the 'old' morality.

Second, he adds two new stanzas to the original poem, which, in altering its context and presentation, warrants the (new) title he affixes to the repurposed poem. As we shall see, these additional stanzas update the original poem by exposing the overwrought 'yearnings' of the hermit as symptomatic of his failure to achieve the self-integration that would occasion in him the self-respect that is characteristic of a noble soul (BGE 287).

Third, he explicitly identifies his repurposed poem not only as a *song*, but also as a particular type or genre of song, viz. an *aftersong*, which, as some scholars have suggested, may be modelled on the Greek epode.[17] Inasmuch as the song in question appears

---

[17] See Lampert 2001: 295–7; Burnham 2007: 229; and Acampora and Ansell-Pearson 2011: 212–13. While the 'Aftersong' plays a conclusive role, like the epode, it is not immediately obvious what triadic structure or composition it is meant to conclude. I am intrigued by Zittel's suggestion that '*From Lofty Mountains* is a mini-drama, a spectacle' (Zittel 2014: 230).

'after' the expository body of *BGE*, it serves as a valedictory coda to the programme of education and training in which Nietzsche has enrolled his readers. If we bear in mind that Nietzsche reveals himself in Part Nine as 'the last disciple and initiate of the god Dionysus' (BGE 295), we may receive his 'Aftersong' as an attempt to compose a late modern dithyramb.[18]

At the same time, however, the song in question is also meant to serve a memorial or commemorative function. It is to be sung, eventually, in remembrance of one who has departed. Taken together, these two meanings of 'Aftersong' suggest a mixed or hybrid musical genre: Nietzsche sings his farewell to his readers, thereby completing their education and training, and he does so by modelling to them the therapeutic art of composing *in advance of one's death* the requiem one hopes will be sung in one's memory.[19] The process of composing such a song, which, as we shall see, obliges one to summon the friends one needs and deserves, is thus recommended by Nietzsche as an effective hedge against the twin temptations – pity and disgust – that his best readers are likely to face as they become mountain-dwelling hermits in their own right.

Stanza 14

It is worth noting here that Nietzsche does not attempt to finesse or disguise the discontinuity between the original poem and the final two stanzas that complete the 'Aftersong'.[20] The discontinuity stands forth like a scar, which he displays to his best readers as an enduring sign of his growth and self-overcoming. Much as

---

[18] According to Nietzsche, *he* 'is the inventor of the dithyramb', which, he explains, is the language an evolved 'spirit speak[s] when speaking with himself alone' (EH: tsz 7).

[19] In his letter to Carl Fuchs on 14 December 1887, Nietzsche explains that 'The *Hymn* [*to Life*] . . . is of course really intended to be sung one day "in my memory": it is meant to be something of mine that will survive, assuming that I myself *survive*' (*SB* 8: 209–11/ Middleton 1969: 280–1).

[20] As Nietzsche has cautioned his readers, 'In the writings of a hermit we can always hear something of the echo of the wasteland, something of whispered tones and the furtive looking around of solitude; even from his strongest words, from his very shouts there is the sound of a new and more dangerous kind of silence, of keeping silent' (BGE 289).

the duelling scar on the bridge of his nose bears public witness to the youthful folly of his days as a university student, so the nested presence of his original poem adverts to the maturation to which the 'Aftersong' attests.

Rather than rubbish the original poem or disown his efforts to befriend Stein, Nietzsche presents these missteps as productive of his current incarnation. Apparently, that is, the properly noble soul regrets nothing.[21] Even an ill-considered gift to an overvalued recipient may be rehabilitated and repurposed for a new occasion. In short, the likelihood (or necessity) of *failure* is built into the poem and affirmed as such: for all who aspire to climb ever higher, there will be hardships, setbacks, challenges, temptations and crises of courage along the way. These are presented in the 'Aftersong' as conducive to the growth his best readers will undergo as they trace their own paths through the lofty mountains. In short, if one wishes to grow and ascend, one must seek out sources and structures of resistance that credibly bespeak the possibility of failure.[22]

Nietzsche's affirmative response to his misjudgement of Stein thus accounts for his decision to add the final two stanzas of the 'Aftersong'. Rather than renew indefinitely an invitation that was prematurely extended, he tacks in a very different direction, as evidenced by his confirmation (in stanza 14) that the hermit's lament has come to an end. The yearning to which the hermit lent his plaintive voice is now attached to (and satisfied by) a 'friend' who is worthy of his companionship.

Before revealing the identity of this 'friend of noon', Nietzsche acknowledges the mediating efforts of an unlikely benefactor, whose timely intervention prompted the hermit to cease his baleful yearning.[23] This unlikely benefactor, whom Nietzsche identifies as a 'wizard' [*Zaubrer*], is not the long-awaited 'friend of noon', but he qualifies as a friend nonetheless, for he arrived at

---

[21] I am indebted here to the general interpretation advanced by Nehamas 1985: ch. 6.
[22] I am indebted here to Reginster 2006: 248–51.
[23] For an interpretation of *Mittags* as a time or season ripe for self-overcoming, see Hough 1997: 106–18; Gooding-Williams 2001: 249–50; Loeb 2010: 133–8; and Zittel 2014: 216–18.

'just the right time' [*zur rechten Stunde*] to disrupt a self-limiting cycle of repetition. As a result, the hermit's yearning finally 'flew / Before [he] could speak', as he turned his attention from the alleged deficiencies of his friends to the very real self-estrangement from which he continued to suffer. The intervention of this benefactor was neither pleasant nor kind, but it compelled Nietzsche to identify the genuine cause or source of his lament, which lay, as we have seen, in his as-yet-unacknowledged reserves of self-contempt.

If we may generalise from the experiences related by Nietzsche and Zarathustra, we may conclude that one's 'just-in-time friends'[24] are those who cruelly disabuse one of an enabling fantasy, while one's 'friends of noon' are those who, gently but firmly, guide one towards the best version of oneself, viz., the version of oneself that merits a commemorative requiem. The case of Zarathustra is exemplary in this respect. In the wake of his long-deferred confrontation with his 'abysmal thought', which was stirred in him by his 'just-in-time friend' – viz. the soothsayer (Z II: 19) – Zarathustra relies on his companion animals to succour him throughout his period of convalescence. Rather than allow him to wallow in self-pity, the animals pointedly remind him of who he is and must become, going so far as to preview for him what are likely to be his final (and triumphant) words before 'going under' (Z III: 13.2).[25] As we learn in stanza 15, a similar assistance is afforded Nietzsche by 'friend *Zarathustra*', who accompanied Nietzsche as he pursued a similar goal of self-integration. Owing to the encouragement of such a friend, Nietzsche avows, 'One turned into Two', which is his way of saying that the succour afforded him by 'friend *Zarathustra*' enabled him, finally, to befriend (and recognise) himself.

The trope of 'One turning into Two' recurs occasionally in Nietzsche's poetic oeuvre.[26] In the 'Aftersong', he employs this trope to convey the salutary outcome of an achievement of self-integration. A previously derelict 'One' – viz. the yearning

---

[24] So as to capture the intended distinction between two kinds of 'friend', I have replaced Del Caro's 'friend when times were bleak' (in stanza 14) with 'just-in-time friend'.
[25] Here I follow the interpretation advanced by Loeb 2010: 198–204.
[26] See Grundlehner 1986: 252–8; and Zittel 2014: 211–12.

hermit – becomes 'Two' by adopting a newly welcoming and newly inclusive relationship (or cluster of relationships) to himself. Rather than continue to accept (or insist on) an opposition between what is said to be *good* (or 'light') and *evil* (or 'darkness') within himself, the hermit in question eliminates (or at least relaxes) these oppositions. Upon reclaiming the passions, affects, needs and vulnerabilities he had been taught to disown, the hermit ceases his yearning and becomes – perhaps for the first time – *productively* diverse and manifold (BGE 212). In achieving (something like) the affective-somatic transformation on offer in *BGE*, the formerly derelict 'One' becomes 'Two' in the sense of finally befriending himself. In this newly achieved posture of self-respect, the 'One' in question has become more fully immunised against the twin threats of pity and disgust. Having become a friend to himself, the no-longer-yearning hermit may survive indefinitely on a steady diet of his own company, his own counsel and his own recognition.[27] If (or when) he falters along the way, he may summon his 'friends of noon', who will remind him once again of who he is and must yet become.

For those who endeavour to climb ever higher, as Nietzsche hopes is true of the readers to whom he sings at the close of *BGE*, both types of friend will be needed. As his best readers become Alpine 'hermits' in their own right, they are likely to require the services of the first type of friend, the 'just-in-time friend', especially if, in their loneliness, they are tempted to tarry with unworthy acolytes and flatterers. As they are made aware of their residual self-contempt, which they will understand to account for their willingness to delay their prescribed ascent, they will have need of the second type of friend, the 'friend of noon', who will guide them through their convalescence and escort them to their desired achievement of self-respect and self-integration.

In stanza 14, Nietzsche describes his unnamed benefactor, that is, his 'just-in-time friend', as a 'wizard' [*Zauberer*]. This is almost certainly an allusion to Richard Wagner, whom Nietzsche occasionally described in similar terms, especially when documenting

---

[27] Hence his account of 'the language of the *dithyramb*' as the 'language . . . a[n evolved] spirit speak[s] when speaking with himself alone' (EH: tsz 7).

the deleterious spell cast by Wagner on the besotted youth of Germany (CW P; TI 'Germans' 2).[28] Of course, Nietzsche may also mean on this occasion to acknowledge Wagner's (unwitting) benefaction on a more personal level. Nietzsche was understandably smitten when, after making Wagner's acquaintance in Leipzig, he embarked upon a friendship with the already famous composer.[29] After an initial period of infatuation, however, Nietzsche came to realise that their friendship was permanently and unacceptably unbalanced. He had grown dangerously dependent on Wagner's recognition, which he would continue to receive, he eventually understood, only if he agreed to remain frozen in the subordinate position of an errand boy or junior partner. Most notably, his friendship with Wagner would oblige him to consign his own musical aspirations to a state of permanent eclipse. No other place or position was available to him if he wished to remain in Wagner's circle. Owing to his friendship with Wagner, that is, Nietzsche became painfully aware of a weakness within himself – namely, a need for recognition verging upon servility – which he would need to address if he were ever to become the philosopher and person he wished to be.

Wagner became Nietzsche's benefactor, his 'just-in-time friend', by delivering a painful lesson pertaining to the perils of unbalanced, non-reciprocal friendships. As Nietzsche took this lesson to heart, moreover, he gained insight into the dynamics of unbalanced relationships more generally, for example, those between Zarathustra and the 'higher men', and those between himself and the readers of *BGE*. For that bounty of insight, he assures us, he is 'grateful' to Wagner (CW E), whom he hails as 'the greatest benefactor of [his] life' (EH 'Clever' 6). According to Nietzsche, moreover, he repays Wagner for his benefaction by preserving his living legacy, as expressed in his creation of Siegfried, while denouncing his degenerate legacy, as exemplified by Parsifal. On the strength of this odd currency of repayment, Nietzsche boldly nominates *himself* as Wagner's proper heir and foremost appreciator (CW E).

---

[28] See, for example, the (first) Postscript to *The Case of Wagner*, where he refers to Wagner as 'this old wizard [*Zauberer*]! This Klingsor of all Klingsors!' (CW P).
[29] See Hayman 1980: 96–100; Young 2010: 74–8; and Harvey and Ridley 2022: 135–42.

Stanza 15

As we learn in the final stanza of the 'Aftersong', Nietzsche's 'friend of noon' is none other than Zarathustra. The hermit of Sils Maria has satisfied his yearning, in other words, not by wasting his time on yet another promising (but callow) protégé, but by reserving himself for those 'friends of noon', *even if invented and/or imaginary*, who are supportive of his pursuit of self-integration.[30] The takeaway here is that invented (but worthy) friends are preferable to real (but unworthy) friends. Indeed, here we encounter a practical sense in which 'untruth' may be regarded as a 'condition of life' (BGE 4): if one's flesh-and-blood companions are impediments to one's ongoing labours of self-overcoming, fabricated (or virtual) companions may (and perhaps must) be recruited instead. Not unlike the worthy pessimist who is said to have summoned the divine spectator whose attention he believes he deserves (BGE 56), the hermit Nietzsche is seen to have conjured the 'friend of noon' whose recognition he sought. And if he has produced thereby a *circulus vitiosus amicus*, so be it. What matters here is his return to health, the restoration of his will for the future of humanity, and the cessation of his self-destructive yearning.

Much as Nietzsche earlier 'invented' the 'free spirits' who would keep him company throughout his protracted period of 'convalescence' (HAH I, P), so he summoned another imaginary friend, Zarathustra, who was tasked with escorting him to the desired achievement of self-integration. Although the 'Aftersong' does not specify the benefits provided by 'friend *Zarathustra*', we are warranted in assuming that he assisted Nietzsche much as his own 'friends of noon' – viz. his gregarious animal companions – had served him in a similar period of convalescence. Just as Zarathustra's animals exhorted him towards the very best version of himself, reminding him of his vocation[31] while anticipating

---

[30] I am indebted here to Hough 1997: 91–100, 116–18; Gooding-Williams 2001: 291–302; and Loeb 2010: 66–84.

[31] Zarathustra's companion animals remind him that his 'destiny' lies in being and becoming 'the teacher of eternal recurrence' (Z III: 13.2). And although Zarathustra does not explicitly assent to this destiny – he has barely begun his period of 'convalescence', after all – Nietzsche himself concludes the expository body of *Twilight of the Idols* by unambiguously claiming this destiny for himself (TI 'Ancients' 5).

his final words (Z III: 13.2),[32] so 'friend Zarathustra' urged (and enabled) Nietzsche to become what he was. Hence the wedding announcement that appears in the final line of the 'Aftersong', which heralds in Nietzsche the long-awaited merger of the 'light' and 'darkness' he carries within himself.

Review

The hermit of Sils Maria yearns no more. And although Nietzsche idealises his readers in order to immunise himself against pity and disgust, his idealisation of the 'we' also serves to remind his real readers – much as Zarathustra reminded Nietzsche, and Zarathustra's animals reminded Zarathustra – of who they are and must yet become. If Nietzsche's readers can manage to glimpse themselves in the 'we' he has consecrated in *BGE*, they may be able to sustain their will for the future as they perform their lonely labours of self-overcoming.

When tempted in their loneliness by either pity or disgust, Nietzsche's best readers need simply recall his teachings and renew the companionship these teachings presuppose. Although he will not accompany them in person along the Alpine paths they will tread, his teachings (and the wisdom these teachings contain) will be with them, potentially, for the rest of their lives. As they recall their experiences with Nietzsche and Zarathustra, they too may know the joy and self-sufficiency of the 'One turned to Two'. This is the case, he apparently means to suggest, because his best readers will be those who have not only heard and considered his teachings, but also made these teachings their own, thereby incorporating his wisdom into the newly configured habits and practices they have come to enact. In short, he will succeed in producing the 'philosophy of the future' precisely to the extent that he is able to replicate himself in his best readers, thereby turning 'One into Two' as a hedge against the missteps that a hermit's loneliness is likely to induce.

---

[32] See Loeb 2010: 74–81.

As we assess the poetic conclusion of *BGE*, we are in a good position to consider – and, perhaps, to appreciate – why Nietzsche insisted all along on producing in his best readers an affective-somatic transformation.[33] As they gather for the 'task' reserved just for them, it will not suffice for them to see and understand the world differently. If Nietzsche is to succeed in consecrating the 'we' he has provisionally directed, his readers also must come to experience the world differently, such that they acquire a novel set of relationships to themselves and their contemporaries. Only in that event might they express their will for the (indeterminate, open) future of humanity.

This transformation is furthermore intended to be either permanent or readily amenable to renewal. Membership in Nietzsche's 'we' is meant to immunise his best readers against the loneliness they are bound to experience and the temptations that are reserved for them. As members of this select, battle-tested 'we', Nietzsche's best readers may avail themselves when necessary of the 'One becomes Two' companionship to which he alludes in his 'After-song'. If their education and training have progressed and taken shape as planned, he (and Zarathustra) will always be with them, replicated in them through the affective-somatic training they have undergone.

---

[33] It seems to me that some such transformation would be consistent with, and perhaps ingredient to, what Strong calls 'the politics of transfiguration' (1975: ix–xi, 12–19).

Glossary of Key Terms

The **natural history of morality** envisioned (and partially developed) by Nietzsche in *BGE* is meant to equip his readers with an alternative to the flawed approaches to the history of morality that were current and influential at the time. In an effort to distinguish himself from those historians of morality who seek (and regularly claim to find) the 'foundation' of morality (BGE 186), Nietzsche recommends a more broadly descriptive (i.e., anthropological) approach that accounts for the material and social conditions under which particular moralities have risen and flourished (or not). The natural history of morality described in *BGE* is intended, on the one hand, to discourage its practitioners from projecting their own beliefs and values on to the history of morality, and, on the other, to document those unanticipated eruptions of active forces (e.g., will to power) that Nietzsche's timid rivals have neglected (or refused?) thus far to acknowledge. His signal contributions towards this end in *BGE* include his recognition of the will to power as 'the *primordial fact of all history*' (BGE 259) and his influential distinction between two basic types of morality: the *master morality* and the *slave morality* (BGE 260).

Nihilism is the general condition of decline in which human beings find themselves unable to muster a credible, sustainable will for the long-term future of humanity. No longer inclined towards the kinds of goals and tasks whose committed pursuit would justify the suffering that attends their mortal, worldly existence, human beings increasingly devote themselves to causes and pursuits that promise momentary, transient or short-term satisfactions.[1] At the endpoint of this dreary arc of devolution stands the blissed-out 'last man', who, according to Zarathustra, looks forward to 'an agreeable death' as his reward for perfecting the virtues of selflessness (Z P5). As the haunting spectre of the 'last man' is meant to convey, the advent of nihilism signals the rise of the 'will to nothingness', which is the will never to will again (GM III: 1, 28).

The **overman** [*Übermensch*] is the signature teaching of Zarathustra and, to a significantly lesser extent, of Nietzsche himself. In *Thus Spoke Zarathustra* (1883–85), the central character presents his teaching of the 'overman' as both an alternative and an antidote to the moral and religious ideals that have prevailed over the development of European civilisation. Whereas these ideals have collectively demeaned humankind, teaching human beings to despise their finitude and frailty, the overman is a celebration of humankind as it is and may yet become. Zarathustra's teaching of the overman thus promotes a life of self-possession, self-mastery and self-sufficiency, wherein human beings lay unmitigated claim to their passions, creativity, and the full range of their modes of embodiment. In other words, Zarathustra presents the rise of the overman as emblematic of the next great stage in the development of humanity.

Although the teaching of the overman does not appear in *BGE*, Nietzsche's readers are apparently meant to understand that the willed production of the overman—that is, the next iteration in the ongoing evolution of humanity—will be the crowning achievement of the 'extramoral' period, over which the 'new' philosophers will preside as 'commander and legislators' (BGE 211). The teaching of the overman is also previewed in Nietzsche's breathtaking sketch of the alternative 'ideal' – that of 'the most exuberant, lively and world-affirming human being' (BGE 56) – that may yet arise in the aftermath of the death of God. That the human being in question – viz. the worthy pessimist – responds to the death of God by 'insatiably shouting *da capo*' (BGE 56), thereby expressing his unqualified affirmation

---

[1] See Reginster 2006: 21–5.

of his post-theistic existence, furthermore suggests that the alternative 'ideal' glimpsed here is related to Nietzsche's teaching of eternal recurrence.

The **pathos of distance** is the defining feature of the experience, shared by all individuals of noble breeding and station, of a rank ordering of human types and of the lives to which these types are best suited (GM I: 2). Those who are noble not only know and feel themselves to be better, stronger and more deserving than ordinary (= lesser, lower) human beings, but also understand that they are (rightfully) held to higher standards of virtue, beauty, comportment and responsibility. Although the superior prowess of the nobles is regularly demonstrated in their interactions with one another (and in their limited, fleeting encounters with lower human types), their orienting pathos of distance requires no external justification or empirical confirmation. Those who are noble rely exclusively on the recognition and validation of those whom they know to be like them. What this means, according to Nietzsche, is that the pathos of distance is likely to survive the destruction of the most conspicuous of the material and social indices of a formerly thriving aristocracy. This is the case, apparently, with his target readers in *BGE*, whom he urges to cultivate and enact the 'self-respect' that he reveals as the hallmark of a noble soul (BGE 287).

The **religious neurosis** is Nietzsche's preferred diagnosis of those troubled souls who, under the disciplinary auspices of European Christianity, have turned against themselves in order to secure a prohibitively costly experience of themselves as self-policing sinners. A notable product of Christianity's defining emphasis on self-denial and self-sacrifice, the religious neurosis bears witness to the success of a directed campaign to rid the soul of anything that might render it interesting, threatening, enticing or distinctive. Deemed 'good' (and redemption-bound) by his fellow sufferers, the religious neurotic anaesthetises himself by directing against himself the full fury of his righteous, sin-seeking will (GM II: 22). Duly narcotised by the *'emotional excess'* he has orchestrated within his otherwise vacant soul (GM III: 20), the religious neurotic may appear to unsuspecting witnesses to have attained a desirable state of tranquillity and composure. In truth, however, the religious neurotic gains only a temporary respite from his spiritual suffering. He does so, moreover, by compounding his despair with the physiological distress associated with extreme self-denial.

Owing to the normalisation of Christian morality across the peoples and nations of late modern Europe, the religious neurosis has attained the status and proportions of an uncontained epidemic. What this means, according to Nietzsche, is that European Christianity is no longer willing – much less able – to serve as an effective instrument of political discipline and social control.

Self-overcoming [*Selbstüberwindung*] is Nietzsche's preferred term for the process of immanent self-transformation in which all living creatures (without exception) participate (cf. Z II: 12). Living beings 'overcome' themselves by dint of their native dynamism, which compels them to evolve novel incarnations as they amass and discharge their accumulated stores of strength. At the conclusion of its unrelenting struggles with external forces and alien entities, an organism 'overcomes' itself by unintentionally giving rise to its *other*, which it has inadvertently fortified and empowered. Indeed, the emergent product of any instance of 'self-overcoming' is simultaneously like and unlike the 'self' that has been 'overcome' in the process.

In addition to directing the life processes of individual organisms, the 'law' of self-overcoming (cf. GM III: 27) also governs those anthropogenic regimes and institutions that are responsible for imparting to individuals, tribes, peoples and nations the values and ideals that guide their most vital endeavours. In urging his readers to join him in hosting the 'self-overcoming of morality' (BGE 230), for example, Nietzsche authorises them to declare morality itself to be immoral, thereby turning the residual authority of morality against its generative source. Having inadvertently empowered Nietzsche and his kindred 'immoralists', morality will overcome itself in and through their efforts to expose the immoral truth of Christian morality.

The **slave revolt in morality** is the (conjectured) event that Nietzsche deems responsible for promoting the emergence of a type of morality (viz. the *slave* morality) in which suffering is honoured as the primary index of one's supposed 'goodness'.

He elsewhere confirms that the founding event in question is none other than 'the birth of Christianity out of the spirit of *ressentiment*' (EH: gm; cf. GM I: 10).

As he explains in *On the Genealogy of Morality*, the '*slave* morality' arose only in reaction to a historically prior morality that favoured 'noble' (or 'masterly') types. The 'noble' morality was predicated on the virtues of spontaneous self-assertion, uncompromising self-possession and martial physicality. Noble and masterly types naturally and instinctively celebrate themselves (and everything pertaining or belonging to them) as 'good' [*gut*], while regarding everything and everyone else as 'bad' [*schlecht*]. By way of contrast, slavish types always initiate their evaluations by denouncing the 'hostile external world' against which they must struggle. The slaves pronounce their masters 'evil' [*böse*], and only as an afterthought proclaim themselves 'good' on the basis of the suffering they endure (GM I: 7–10).

In essence, the 'slave revolt in morality' transpired when the 'slaves' claimed to choose and prefer the suffering inflicted on them by their 'noble' tormentors and captors. In addition to providing the 'slaves' with a psychological defence against the suffering they would endure in any event, the 'slave revolt' also had the unintended effect of disarming the nobles, who gradually lost interest in causing suffering that was desired, even craved, by the 'slaves'. By dint of their revolt against the nobles, the slaves were able not only to transform their unhappy, unchosen destiny into their crowning virtue, but also to derive enormous power from their powerlessness.

According to Nietzsche, the **will to power** is the fundamental (or 'cardinal') drive of all living beings. (He thus claims, for example that 'life simply *is* will to power' (BGE 259).) In response to those rival theorists who identify *self-preservation* as the most basic instinct, Nietzsche contends that species and organisms in fact aim at the amoral imposition of power over lesser and weaker life forms. While it is true that diseased and distressed organisms seek to husband their strength in an instinctive effort to preserve themselves in their diminished vitality, healthy organisms instinctively seek to amass and expend their native stores of strength – *even if doing so places them at mortal risk* – in order to secure for themselves the enhanced 'feeling of power' that warrants their ongoing existence (GM III: 7). Nietzsche is sufficiently confident in his understanding and account of will to power that he 'conceives' of the (soon-to-be restored) science of psychology as 'morphology and *doctrine of the development of the will to power*' (BGE 23).

The **will to truth** is the impulse to create meaning for one's mortal, worldly existence by seeking – and, ideally, possessing – the truth, which is deemed (but not demonstrated) to be inestimably valuable for creatures such as ourselves. So long as we seek the truth and maintain our belief in its redemptive properties, we may expect to secure for ourselves the conditions of a meaningful existence, notwithstanding the suffering, disappointments and slights we inevitably will endure.

In a culture or civilisation animated and shaped by the will to truth, for example, European civilisation, individuals seek the truth *not* on the basis of a careful, reasoned determination of its actual value for them, but on the strength of their unexamined conviction that '*Nothing* is needed more than truth' (GS 344). Truth is believed to be necessary, Nietzsche surmises, because the world of flux and appearance, viz., the physical world in which human beings transact their precarious finite existence, has been determined by priests and sages to stand in need of the metaphysical (or otherworldly) redemption that truth alone is believed to provide. Having exposed the will to truth as trading on an unacknowledged *faith* in the redemptive properties of truth, Nietzsche aims in *BGE* to prepare his readers to acknowledge *untruth* as a complementary 'condition of life' (BGE 4).

Guide to Further Reading on *Beyond Good and Evil*

In English

Christa Davis Acampora and Keith Ansell-Pearson, *Nietzsche's Beyond Good and Evil: A Reader's Guide*, Continuum, 2011.

Douglas Burnham, *Reading Nietzsche: An Analysis of Beyond Good and Evil*, McGill-Queen's University Press, 2007.

Maudemarie Clark and David Dudrick, *The Soul of Nietzsche's Beyond Good and Evil*, Cambridge University Press, 2012.

Laurence Lampert, *Nietzsche's Task: An Interpretation of Beyond Good and Evil*, Yale University Press, 2001.

Brian Leiter, *Nietzsche on Morality*, Routledge, 2002.

Vanessa Lemm, *Homo Natura: Nietzsche, Philosophical Anthropology and Biopolitics*, Edinburgh University Press, 2020.

Simon May, *Nietzsche's Ethics and his War on 'Morality'*, Oxford University Press, 1999.

Alexander Nehamas, 'Who are "The Philosophers of the Future"? A Reading of *Beyond Good and Evil*', in *Reading Nietzsche*, ed. Robert C. Solomon and Kathleen Marie Higgins, Oxford University Press, 1988, 46–67

Leo Strauss, 'Note on the Plan of Nietzsche's *Beyond Good and Evil*', in *Nietzsche: Critical Assessments of Leading Philosophers*, ed. Daniel Conway, vol. IV, Routledge, 1998, 174–91.

Alan White, 'The Youngest Virtue', in *Nietzsche's Postmoralism: Essays on Nietzsche's Prelude to Philosophy's Future*, ed. Richard Schacht, Cambridge University Press, 2001, 63–78.

Julian Young, *Friedrich Nietzsche: A Philosophical Biography*, Cambridge University Press, 2010.

In German

Marcus Andreas Born and Axel Pichler (eds), *Texturen des Denkens: Nietzsches Inszenierung der Philosophie in 'Jenseits von Gut und Böse'*, Walter de Gruyter, 2013.

Marcus Andreas Born (ed.), *Friedrich Nietzsche: Jenseits von Gut und Böse*, Walter de Gruyter, 2014.

Andreas Urs Sommer, *Kommentar zu Nietzsches Jenseits von Gut und Böse*, Walter de Gruyter, 2016.

Bibliography

Abbey, Ruth. 2020. *Nietzsche's Human, All Too Human: A Critical Introduction and Guide*. Edinburgh: Edinburgh University Press.
Acampora, Christa Davis. 2013. *Contesting Nietzsche*. Chicago: University of Chicago Press.
Acampora, Christa Davis, and Keith Ansell-Pearson. 2011. *Nietzsche's Beyond Good and Evil: A Reader's Guide*. London: Continuum.
Alfano, Mark. 2019. *Nietzsche's Moral Psychology*. Cambridge: Cambridge University Press.
Ansell-Pearson, Keith. 2018. *Nietzsche's Search for Philosophy: On the Middle Writings*. London: Bloomsbury.
Ansell-Pearson, Keith, and Rebecca Bamford. 2020. *Nietzsche's Dawn: Philosophy, Ethics, and the Passion of Knowledge*. Chichester: Wiley-Blackwell.
Babich, Babette. 1994. *Nietzsche's Philosophy of Science: Reflecting Science on the Ground of Art and Life*. Albany: State University of New York Press.
Bennholdt-Thomsen, Anke. 1974. *Nietzsches Also Sprach Zarathustra als literarisches Phänomen*. Frankfurt am Main: Athenäum.
Bishop, Paul. 2022. *Nietzsche's The Anti-Christ: A Critical Introduction and Guide*. Edinburgh: Edinburgh University Press.
Born, Marcus Andreas. 2015. 'Perspectives on a Philosophy of the Future in Nietzsche's *Beyond Good and Evil*', in *Nietzsche's Free Spirit Philosophy*, ed. Rebecca Bamford. London: Rowman and Littlefield, 157–68.
Brobjer, Thomas. 2010. *Nietzsche's Philosophical Context: An Intellectual Biography*. Champaign: Illinois University Press.

Brusotti, Marco. 2013. '"der schreckliche Grundtext homo natura"'. Texturen des Natürlichen im Aphorism 230 von *Jenseits von Gut und Böse*', in *Texturen des Denkens*. *Nietzsches Inszenierung der Philosophie in 'Jenseits von Gut und Böse'*, ed. Marcus Andreas Born and Axel Pichler. Berlin: Walter de Gruyter, 259–78.

Burnham, Douglas. 2007. *Reading Nietzsche: An Analysis of Beyond Good and Evil*. Montreal: McGill-Queen's University Press.

— 2014. 'The Suicide and Rebirth of Religion. The third part: "das religiöse Wesen"', in *Friedrich Nietzsche: Jenseits von Gut und Böse*, ed. Marcus Andreas Born. Berlin: Walter de Gruyter, 69–89.

Cancik, Hubert. 1997. '"Mongols, Semites and the Pure-Bred Greeks": Nietzsche's Handling of the Racial Doctrines of his Time', in *Nietzsche and Jewish Culture*, ed. Jacob Golomb. London: Routledge, 55–75.

Church, Jeffrey. 2019. *Nietzsche's Unfashionable Observations: A Critical Introduction and Guide*. Edinburgh: Edinburgh University Press.

Clark, Maudemarie. 1990. *Nietzsche on Truth and Philosophy*. Cambridge: Cambridge University Press.

Clark, Maudemarie, and David Dudrick. 2012. *The Soul of Nietzsche's Beyond Good and Evil*. Cambridge: Cambridge University Press.

Cohen, Jonathan R. 2010. *Science, Culture, and Free Spirits: A Study of Nietzsche's Human, All-Too-Human*. Amherst, NY: Humanity Books.

— 2014. 'Nietzsche's Second Turning', *Pli: The Warwick Journal of Philosophy*, 25: 35–54.

Conway, Daniel. 2008. *Nietzsche's On the Genealogy of Morals: A Critical Guide*. London: Continuum.

— 2010. 'Life After the Death of God: Thus Spoke Nietzsche', in *The History of Continental Philosophy*, Volume II, ed. Alan D. Schrift and Daniel Conway. London: Acumen, 103–38.

— 2014a. 'We Who Are Different, We Immoralists', in *Nietzsche's Political Theory*, ed. Manuel Knoll and Barry Stocker. Berlin: Walter de Gruyter, 287–311.

— 2014b. 'Nietzsche's Immoralism and the Advent of "Great Politics"', in *Nietzsche and Political Thought*, ed. Keith Ansell-Pearson. London: Bloomsbury Academic, 197–217.

— 2020 '"The Honeymoon of German Philosophy": Nietzsche and the Tradition of German Idealism', in *The Palgrave Handbook of German Idealism and Existentialism*, ed. Jon Stewart. Basingstoke: Palgrave Macmillan, 241–66.

Dellinger, Jakob. 2013. 'Vorspiel, Subversion, und Schleife: Nietzsches Inszenierung des "Wille der Macht" in *Jenseits von Gut und Böse*', in *Texturen des Denkens. Nietzsches Inszenierung der Philosophie in 'Jenseits von Gut und Böse'*, ed. Marcus Andreas Born and Axel Pichler. Berlin: Walter de Gruyter, 165–87.

Drochon, Hugo. 2016. *Nietzsche's Great Politics*. Princeton: Princeton University Press.

Emden, Christian J. 2008. *Friedrich Nietzsche and the Politics of History*. Cambridge: Cambridge University Press.

— 2014. *Nietzsche's Naturalism: Philosophy and the Life Sciences in the 19th Century*. Cambridge: Cambridge University Press.

Franco, Paul. 2011. *Nietzsche's Enlightenment: The Free-Spirit Trilogy of the Middle Period*. Chicago: University of Chicago Press.

Gooding-Williams, Robert. 2001. *Zarathustra's Dionysian Modernism*. Stanford: Stanford University Press.

Grundlehner, Philip. 1986. *The Poetry of Friedrich Nietzsche*. Oxford: Oxford University Press.

Guay, Robert. 2022. *Nietzsche's On the Genealogy of Morality: A Critical Introduction and Guide*. Edinburgh: Edinburgh University Press.

Harvey, Ryan and Aaron Ridley. 2022. *Nietzsche's The Case of Wagner and Nietzsche Contra Wagner: A Critical Introduction and Guide*. Edinburgh: Edinburgh University Press.

Hatab, Lawrence J. 2008. *Nietzsche's Genealogy of Morality: An Introduction*. Cambridge: Cambridge University Press.

Havas, Randall. 1995. *Nietzsche's Genealogy: Nihilism and the Will to Knowledge*. Ithaca, NY: Cornell University Press.

Hayman, Ronald. 1980. *Nietzsche: A Critical Life*. London: Penguin.

Higgins, Kathleen Marie. 1987. *Nietzsche's Zarathustra*. Philadelphia: Temple University Press.

Holub, Robert C. 2016. *Nietzsche's Jewish Problem: Between Anti-Semitism and Anti-Judaism*. Princeton: Princeton University Press.

Hough, Sheridan. 1997. *Nietzsche's Noontide Friend: The Self as Metaphoric Double*. University Park, PA: Penn State University Press.

Hui, Andrew. 2019. *A Theory of the Aphorism: From Confucius to Twitter*. Princeton: Princeton University Press.
Huxley, Aldous. 1928. *Proper Studies*. Garden City, NY: Doubleday, Doran.
Janaway, Christopher. 2007. *Beyond Selflessness: Reading Nietzsche's Genealogy*. Oxford: Oxford University Press.
Katsafanas, Paul. 2016. *The Nietzschean Self: Moral Psychology, Agency, and the Unconscious*. Oxford: Oxford University Press.
Lampert, Laurence. 1986. *Nietzsche's Teaching: An Interpretation of Thus Spoke Zarathustra*. New Haven: Yale University Press.
— 2001. *Nietzsche's Task: An Interpretation of Beyond Good and Evil*. New Haven: Yale University Press.
Leiter, Brian. 2002. *Nietzsche on Morality*. London: Routledge.
— 2019. *Moral Psychology with Nietzsche*. Oxford: Oxford University Press.
Lemm, Vanessa. 2020. *Homo Natura: Nietzsche, Philosophical Anthropology and Biopolitics*. Edinburgh: Edinburgh University Press.
Loeb, Paul S. 2010. *The Death of Nietzsche's Zarathustra*. Cambridge: Cambridge University Press.
May, Simon. 1999. *Nietzsche's Ethics and his War on 'Morality'*. Oxford: Oxford University Press.
Middleton, Christopher (ed. and trans.). 1969. *Selected Letters of Friedrich Nietzsche*. Chicago: University of Chicago Press.
Miner, Robert. 2022. *Nietzsche's Gay Science: A Critical Introduction and Guide*. Edinburgh: Edinburgh University Press.
Miyasaki, Donovan. 2016. 'Feeling, not Freedom: Nietzsche Against Agency', *Journal of Nietzsche Studies*, 47.2: 256–74.
— 2022a. *Nietzsche's Immoralism: Politics as First Philosophy*. New York: Palgrave Macmillan.
— 2022b. *Politics After Morality: Toward a Nietzschean Left*. New York: Palgrave Macmillan.
Nehamas, Alexander. 1985. *Nietzsche: Life as Literature*. Cambridge, MA: Harvard University Press.
Nietzsche, Friedrich. 1886. 'Attempt at a Self-Criticism' [retrospective Preface added to the 1886 edition of *The Birth of Tragedy*]
— 1967. *The Birth of Tragedy* (with *The Case of Wagner*), trans. Walter Kaufmann. New York: Viking Penguin.

— 1974. *The Gay Science*, trans. W. Kaufmann, New York: Random House.
— 1980. *Sämtliche Werke: Kritische Studienausgabe in 15 Bänden*, ed. G. Colli and M. Montinari. Berlin: Deutscher Taschenbuch Verlag/de Gruyter.
— 1982. *Thus Spoke Zarathustra*, in *The Portable Nietzsche*, ed. and trans. W. Kaufmann, New York: Viking Penguin.
— 1986a. *Human, All Too Human: A Book for Free Spirits*, trans. R. J. Hollingdale. Cambridge: Cambridge University Press.
— 1986b. *Sämtliche Briefe: Kritische Studienausgabe in 8 Bänden*, ed. G. Colli and M. Montinari. Berlin: Deutscher Taschenbuch Verlag/de Gruyter.
— 1995. *Unfashionable Observations*, trans. Richard T. Gray, in *The Complete Works of Friedrich Nietzsche*, volume 3. Stanford: Stanford University Press.
— 2007. *Ecce Homo: How to Become What You Are*, trans. Duncan Large. Oxford: Oxford University Press.
— 2014a. *Dawn: Thoughts on the Presumptions of Morality*, trans. Brittain Smith, in *The Complete Works of Friedrich Nietzsche*, volume 5. Stanford: Stanford University Press.
— 2014b. *Beyond Good and Evil: Prelude to a Philosophy of the Future and On the Genealogy of Morality*, trans. Adrian Del Caro, in *The Complete Works of Friedrich Nietzsche*, volume 8. Stanford: Stanford University Press.
— 2021. *The Case of Wagner, Twilight of the Idols, The Antichrist, Ecce Homo, Dionysus Dithyrambs*, and *Nietzsche Contra Wagner*, trans. (in various configurations) Adrian Del Caro, Carol Diethe, Duncan Large, George H. Leiner, Paul S. Loeb, Alan D. Schrift, David F. Tinsley and Mirko Wittwar, in *The Complete Works of Friedrich Nietzsche*, volume 9. Stanford: Stanford University Press.
Owen, David. 1995. *Nietzsche, Politics & Modernity*. London: Polity.
— 2007. *Nietzsche's Genealogy*. Stocksfield: Acumen.
Parkes, Graham. 1994. *Composing the Soul: Reaches of Nietzsche's Psychology*. Chicago: University of Chicago Press.
Pippin, Robert. 2010. *Nietzsche, Psychology, and First Philosophy*. Chicago: University of Chicago Press.

—— 2019a. 'Nietzsche's Masks: Philosophy and Religion in *Beyond Good and Evil*', in *Nietzsche's Metaphilosophy: The Nature, Method, and Aims of Philosophy*, ed. Paul Loeb and Matthew Meyer. Cambridge: Cambridge University Press, 106–23.

—— 2019b. 'Figurative Philosophy in Nietzsche's *Beyond Good and Evil*', in *The New Cambridge Companion to Nietzsche*, ed. Tom Stern. Cambridge: Cambridge University Press, 195–221.

Plato. 2002. *Five Dialogues: Euthyphro, Apology, Crito, Meno, Phaedo*, 2nd edn, trans. G. M. A. Grube, rev. John M. Cooper. Indianapolis: Hackett Publishing.

Reginster, Bernard. 2006. *The Affirmation of Life: Nietzsche on Overcoming Nihilism*. Cambridge, MA: Harvard University Press.

Richardson, John. 1996. *Nietzsche's System*. Oxford: Oxford University Press.

—— 2008. *Nietzsche's New Darwinism*. Oxford: Oxford University Press.

—— 2020. *Nietzsche's Values*. Oxford: Oxford University Press.

Ridley, Aaron. 1998. *Nietzsche's Conscience: Six Character Studies from the Genealogy*. Ithaca, NY: Cornell University Press.

Rosen, Stanley. 1995. *The Mask of Enlightenment: Nietzsche's Zarathustra*. Cambridge: Cambridge University Press.

Shapiro, Gary. 2016. *Nietzsche's Earth: Great Events, Great Politics*. Chicago: University of Chicago Press.

Simon, Josef. 1997. 'Nietzsche on Judaism and Europe', in *Nietzsche and Jewish Culture*, ed. Jacob Golomb. London: Routledge, 101–16.

Solomon, Robert C. 2003. *Living with Nietzsche: What the Great 'Immoralist' Has to Teach Us*. Oxford: Oxford University Press.

Sommer, Andreas Urs. 2014. 'Philosophen und philosophiches Arbeiter. Das sechste Hauptstück: "wir Gelehrten"', in *Friedrich Nietzsche: Jenseits von Gut und Böse*, ed. Marcus Andreas Born. Berlin: Walter de Gruyter, 131–45.

—— 2016. *Nietzsche-Kommentar: Jenseits von Gut und Böse*. Berlin: Walter de Gruyter.

Strauss, Leo. 1998. 'Note on the Plan of Nietzsche's *Beyond Good and Evil*', in *Nietzsche: Critical Assessments of Leading Philosophers*, volume 4, ed. Daniel Conway. London: Routledge, 174–91.

Strong, Tracy B. 1975. *Friedrich Nietzsche and the Politics of Transfiguration*. Berkeley: University of California Press.

—— 2003. 'Where Are We When We Are Beyond Good and Evil?', *Cardozo Law Review*, 24.2: 535–62.

Thiele, Leslie Paul. 1990. *Friedrich Nietzsche and the Politics of the Soul: A Study of Heroic Individualism*. Princeton: Princeton University Press.

Van Tongeren, Paul. 2014. 'Nietzsches "Redlichkeit". Das siebte Hauptstück: "unsere Tugenden"', in *Friedrich Nietzsche: Jenseits von Gut und Böse*, ed. Marcus Andreas Born. Berlin: Walter de Gruyter, 147–65.

Warren, Mark. 1988. *Nietzsche and Political Thought*. Cambridge, MA: MIT Press.

White, Alan. 2001. 'The Youngest Virtue', in *Nietzsche's Postmoralism: Essays on Nietzsche's Prelude to Philosophy's Future*, ed. Richard Schacht. Cambridge: Cambridge University Press, 63–78.

Young, Julian. 2010. *Friedrich Nietzsche: A Philosophical Biography*. Cambridge: Cambridge University Press.

Yovel, Yirmayahu. 1998. *Dark Riddle: Hegel, Nietzsche, and the Jews*. University Park, PA: Penn State University Press.

Zittel, Claus. 2014. '"In öden Eisbär- Zonen": Die Schlussverse "Aus hohen Bergen. Nachgesang"', in *Friedrich Nietzsche: Jenseits von Gut und Böse*, ed. Marcus Andreas Born. Berlin: Walter de Gruyter, 207–36.

Index

Abbey, Ruth, 55, 237
Acampora, Christa Davis, 82, 88, 147, 152, 160, 213, 220, 235, 237
Alfano, Mark, 47, 153, 190, 195, 237
Ansell-Pearson, Keith, 34, 55, 82, 88, 148, 152, 160, 213, 220, 235, 237–8
anthropological approach, 75–6, 82–3, 109–11, 113, 115, 194, 229
aristocracy, 9, 121, 190–5, 231
astrology, 25–6

Babich, Babette, 9, 17, 237
Bamford, Rebecca, 34, 237
Bishop, Paul, 60, 77, 237
Brobjer, Thomas, 100–1, 237
Brusotti, Marco, 159, 238
Burckhardt, Jacob, 8, 14
Burnham, Douglas, 50, 67, 82, 88, 90, 93, 119, 121, 139, 159, 164, 202, 220, 235, 238

Christianity, 17, 35, 42, 72–80, 82, 84–5, 92–5, 103, 107, 156, 203, 231–3
Christian morality / morality of good and evil, 9, 17, 25, 27, 29, 65, 77, 80, 94, 105, 107, 122, 144, 146, 150, 155–60, 165–8, 183, 196–8, 232–3
Christian truthfulness, 9, 35, 65, 103, 158–9, 161, 165
Church, Jeffrey, 57, 238
Clark, Maudemarie, 17, 27, 29, 41, 47–8, 50, 67, 128, 162, 235, 238
Conscience, 62–3, 66–7, 75–6, 91, 102, 115, 133, 140, 164–5, 177, 200–1

Dawn, 33–4, 55–6
Del Caro, Adrian, 6, 33, 73, 223, 241
Dellinger, Jakob, 3, 239
democracy / democratic movement, 12, 30, 48, 109, 119, 125, 128, 130, 141, 154, 170–3, 193

INDEX

Dionysus, 31, 52, 69, 88–9, 98, 128, 164, 201–9, 221
dogmatism, 19–36, 53, 69, 72
Drochon, Hugo, 169, 176, 239
Dudrick, David, 17, 27, 29, 41, 48, 50, 67, 128, 162, 235, 238

Ecce Homo, 5, 9, 11, 46, 162, 179
Emden, Christian, 17, 48, 75, 111, 142, 178, 239
eternal recurrence, 88–90, 208

Franco, Paul, 34, 55, 159, 239
free spirits, 31, 56–8, 60–1, 64–6, 69, 71–2, 95, 105, 120, 125, 143, 167, 193, 200, 226
Fuchs, Carl, 88, 156, 186, 221

Gast, Peter, 11, 176
good Europeans, 29, 31–2, 145, 172, 175, 181–2, 187, 199
Gooding-Williams, Robert, 2, 10, 215, 218, 222, 226, 239
grand politics, 131, 169, 178, 182
Guay, Robert, 195, 239

Harvey, Ryan, 186, 225, 239
Hatab, Lawrence, 144, 239
Havas, Randall, 39, 41, 162, 239
Hayman, Ronald, 213, 225, 239
Hebrew Bible, 77, 82, 84
Holub, Robert, 178, 239
homines religiosi, 76, 82–3, 150
homo natura, 62, 160–2, 165, 168
Hough, Sheridan, 214, 218, 222, 226, 239
Human, All Too Human, 55, 241
Huxley, Aldous, 40, 240

immoralism, 63–4, 71, 92, 104, 155–60, 201, 232

Janaway, Christopher, 8, 64, 104, 147, 153, 166, 240
Jesus, 11, 60, 107

Kant, Immanuel, 15, 85–6, 132, 175, 197
Katsafanas, Paul, 47–8, 153, 240

Lampert, Laurence, 1, 27, 29, 50, 56, 67–8, 73, 75, 82, 88, 91, 93–4, 119, 140, 144, 150, 152, 156, 159, 164, 166, 178, 184, 206, 213, 215, 217–18, 220, 235, 240
Large, Duncan, 9, 241
Leiter, Brian, 2, 47–8, 104, 111, 147, 160, 235
Lemm, Vanessa, 64, 76, 144, 159, 161, 165–7, 235, 240
Loeb, Paul, 64, 89, 147, 212, 215, 218, 222–3, 226–7

martyrs, 58–60, 80, 90, 105
May, Simon, 64, 104, 144, 235, 240
Middleton, Christopher, 8, 12, 14, 30, 88, 154, 156, 176, 186, 212, 221, 240
Miner, Robert, 39, 240
Miyasaki, Donovan, 2, 6, 195, 240

natural history of morality, 109–10, 114–17, 119–23, 190–1, 229
nihilism, 9, 16–17, 57, 77, 85–7, 90, 130, 185, 229–30

nobility, 7, 46, 55, 59, 82, 85, 89–91, 93, 100, 114, 141, 156, 164, 178, 186, 188–91, 194–201, 208, 210, 215, 217–20, 222, 231, 233

On the Genealogy of Morality, 8, 36, 57, 61, 69, 77, 80, 130, 206, 233
Overbeck, Franz, 30, 154, 213
Owen, David, 64, 144, 147, 166, 241

Parkes, Graham, 47, 151, 241
Parsifal, 183–5, 225
Pascal, Blaise, 14, 76, 94, 100
philosophers of the future, 4, 7, 29, 41, 56, 66, 69–71, 96, 120–3, 137–8, 141, 158, 162, 167, 195
Pippin, Robert, 3–4, 37, 67, 73, 86, 90, 100–1, 241–2
Plato, 22, 27–8, 59, 72
Platonism, 17, 28, 35, 42, 73
psychology, 11, 47–51, 62, 65, 67, 70, 73–4, 80, 82, 100–3, 110, 115–16, 125, 129–30, 150, 164, 191, 194, 233–4

Redlichkeit, 63, 143, 165
Reginster, Bernard, 87, 205, 222, 230, 242
Richardson, John, 39, 48, 144, 166, 242
Ridley, Aaron, 64, 144, 162, 186, 225, 239, 242

sacrifice, 14, 39, 57–60, 72, 76–8, 85–90, 120, 139, 215, 231

Schopenhauer, Arthur, 79, 100, 175, 182
science, 3–5, 9, 12–13, 15–18, 25, 35, 38–40, 42, 45, 48–50, 56–8, 73, 75, 80, 85–7, 90, 101, 111–15, 122, 124–5, 128, 130–1, 139–40, 144–6, 155, 157, 159–62, 168, 234
self-contempt, 17, 81, 87, 104, 126, 139, 148, 150, 155, 162, 175, 214–17, 220, 223–4
selflessness, 15, 56, 79, 113, 129, 134, 139, 150, 154, 230
self-overcoming, 29, 32, 36, 45–6, 48, 61, 64–5, 83–4, 113, 154, 167, 174, 182, 191, 197–9, 214–16, 219, 221–2, 226–7, 232
Shapiro, Gary, 32, 179, 186, 242
Siegfried, 9, 155, 166–8, 183–5, 209, 225
Socrates, 59–60, 101, 114, 133
Solomon, Robert, 147, 158, 165, 235, 242
Sommer, Andreas Urs, 76, 88, 127, 144, 236, 242
Strauss, David, 57–8, 70
Strauss, Leo, 73, 75, 164, 235, 242
Strong, Tracy B., 4, 66, 169, 228, 243

Taine, Hippolyte, 8
The Gay Science, 38, 162, 207
Thus Spoke Zarathustra, 5, 6, 8, 10, 11, 45, 161, 173, 202, 212, 215, 230

van Tongeren, Paul, 64, 165, 243
Versuch / Versucher, 66, 68, 120, 127, 181
von Goethe, Johann Wolfgang, 100, 173–6, 182, 184, 200
von Meysenbug, Malwida, 12, 212–13
von Seydlitz, Irene, 2
von Seydlitz, Robert, 8
von Stein, Heinrich, 213, 217, 220, 222

Wagner, Richard, 9, 79, 155, 166–8, 171–2, 182–6, 213, 224–5
White, Alan, 159, 235, 243
will to nothingness, 41, 85–90, 130, 230
will to power, 38, 44–53, 62, 65–8, 80–2, 111–12, 123, 161, 167, 170, 192–4, 229, 233–4
will to truth, 17, 27, 33, 35–43, 46, 51–6, 64, 70, 103, 128, 162–3, 184, 205, 234

Young, Julian, 14, 48, 94, 212–13, 225, 235, 243

Zarathustra, 5, 6, 10, 20, 30, 37–8, 40, 45–7, 100, 202, 204, 206, 211–15, 217–18, 223, 225–8, 230
Zittel, Claus, 210, 213, 215, 220, 222–3, 243

EU representative:
Easy Access System Europe
Mustamäe tee 50, 10621 Tallinn, Estonia
Gpsr.requests@easproject.com

www.ingramcontent.com/pod-product-compliance
Lightning Source LLC
Chambersburg PA
CBHW070323240426
43671CB00013BA/2345